GENDER, MODERNITY AND LIBERTY

GW00703406

GENDER, ଛ MODERNITY AND ଔ LIBERTY

MIDDLE EASTERN AND WESTERN WOMEN'S WRITINGS: A CRITICAL SOURCEBOOK

EDITED BY
REINA LEWIS AND NANCY MICKLEWRIGHT

I.B. TAURIS

LONDON · NEW YORK

Published in 2006 by I.B.Tauris & Co Ltd
6 Salem Road, London W2 4BU
175 Fifth Avenue, New York NY 10010
www.ibtauris.com

In the United States of America and Canada
distributed by Palgrave Macmillan a division of St Martin's Press
175 Fifth Avenue, New York NY 10010

Copyright © Reina Lewis and Nancy Micklewright, 2006

The right of Reina Lewis and Nancy Micklewright to be identified as the authors
of this work has been asserted by the author in accordance with the Copyright,
Designs and Patent Act 1988.

All rights reserved. Except for brief quotations in a review, this book, or any part
thereof, may not be reproduced, stored in or introduced into a retrieval system, or
transmitted, in any form or by any means, electronic, mechanical, photocopying,
recording or otherwise, without the prior written permission of the publisher.

Hbk ISBN-10 1 86064 956 4
    ISBN-13 978 1 86064 956 1

Pbk ISBN-10 1 86064 957 2
    ISBN-13 978 1 86064 957 8

A full CIP record for this book is available from the British Library
A full CIP record is available from the Library of Congress

Library of Congress Catalog Card Number: available

Typeset in Times by JCS Publishing Services
Printed and bound in Great Britain by TJ International Ltd, Padstow, Cornwall

❧ CONTENTS ❧

❧ LIST OF ILLUSTRATIONS ❧

ഔ Acknowledgements ര

This project has benefited from the help of a number of people, and we would like to take this opportunity to thank them: Teresa Heffernan for responding to several queries; Steve and Josh Berer for providing technical assistance with computer matters; Susan Lawson for working so hard on the copyright clearances; Elizabeth Frierson for sharing information on several points; Margot Badran and Ayfer Neyzi for generously sharing research material and forgoing copyright fees; the librarians of the University of East London, and the staff of the Special Collections Reading Room at the Getty Research Institute; Frances Terpak, Senior Collections Curator for Photography at the Getty Research Institute; and staff at the British Library, especially for help in tracking down obscure sources.

In addition, Reina Lewis wishes to acknowledge the invaluable support of a Research Fellowship from the Leverhulme Trust, and the School of Social Sciences, Media, and Cultural Studies at the University of East London, who have supported this project with sabbatical leave, and with a contribution from the publication fund.

We are grateful to the following for permission to reproduce from the following sources: Extract from Leyla Saz Hanımefendi, *The Imperial Harem of the Sultans*, reprinted with kind permission of Ayfer Neyzi; extract from Huda Shaarawi, *Harem Years*, reprinted with kind permission of Margot Badran; extract from Halide Adıvar Edib, *Memoirs of Halidé Edib*, reprinted with permission of John Murray (Publishers) Ltd; extract from Ruth Frances Woodsmall, *Moslem Women Enter a New World*, printed by permission of HarperCollins Publishers Ltd; extract from Musbah Haidar, *Arabesque* published by Hutchinson, used by permission of The Random House Group Limited; extract from Emine Foat Tugay, *Three Centuries: Family Chronicles of Turkey and Egypt*, reprinted by permission of Oxford University Press. Every effort has been made to trace the copyright holders of the illustrations and text reprinted in this book. The publishers would be glad to hear from any copyright holders they have not been able to contact and to print due acknowledgement in the next edition.

ഇ NOTE ON LANGUAGE ക

All the sources extracted in this collection (with the exception of two, see the Introduction) were written and published in English. But they do use many Ottoman and Arabic terms, names and place names. Transliteration conventions were not standardised in this period, and we have reproduced the extracts without alteration, so the reader will find some words rendered into English in a variety of ways. In addition, the Ottoman and Turkish sources come from a period that saw a major intervention into written language. Before 1928 people in the Ottoman Empire and the early Turkish Republic wrote down the Ottoman language in the Arabic script. In 1928 this Ottoman, or Osmanlı, form was replaced by modern Turkish, written in the Roman alphabet and purged of many of the Arabic and Persian features that had characterised Ottoman. For writers living through this change, conventions of transliteration were still unstable, and this is another reason why words and names appear in diverse forms. One feature of the transition to modern Turkish was a change in the use of several letters, so that, for example, b became p, d became t.

We have left the primary sources unchanged and in our editorial commentaries we have used modern transliteration conventions and the contemporary Turkish form of current or Ottoman terms. Personal names appear throughout as used by their authors (e.g. Zeyneb not Zeynep, Edib not Edip) except for major historical figures, such as sultans, who appear in the modern spelling. The same applies to place names.

Ottoman naming conventions also changed during this period. Traditionally Ottomans did not use surnames; people of middle to upper rank were distinguished by an honorific and those of lower status were often identified by function. The respectful way to address a woman of some status was to follow her personal name with hanım (meaning lady, or woman). Men of status could be known as bey, paşa, efendi (in ascending order of importance). Surnames in Turkey were introduced in the 1930s, when Mustafa Kemal took on Atatürk as a second name (and validation of his role as father of the nation).

We have used the honorific hanım (previously transliterated variously as hanoum, knanum, hanum) for the Ottoman women featured here (except for Halide Edib who had acquired a second name by the time she wrote her memoirs). However, instead of applying the modern spelling to all authors, we have, for ease of reference, retained the transliteration with which a particular author was associated (e.g. Zeyneb Hanoum, Melek Hanum).

Where Ottoman terms appear in their modern usage, using Turkish diacritics, most letters are pronounced the same as in English, with a few exceptions:

c   j

ç	ch
ı	like the io in lotion
ş	sh, as in yaşmak, yashmak
ğ	silent, lengthens preceding vowel

✐ WRITING CHANGE: ✑

MIDDLE EASTERN AND WESTERN WOMEN
IN DIALOGUE

Gender, Modernity and Liberty presents a dialogue between Western and Middle Eastern women that is often presumed never to have happened. Not only were women from the Middle East imagined to be shut up in a harem all day without access to education, ideas or the outside world, but the extent to which Western women travellers were able to engage with women in the regions they visited has until recently been overlooked.

Covering a hundred years from 1837, this collection focuses on writings by women from and about Istanbul (formerly Constantinople) and Cairo, key locations for the flowering of Middle Eastern feminism. It was in these closely connected metropolises that the articulation of women's views was particularly advanced in the last century of the Ottoman Empire. The development of Arab nationalism leading to the eventual independence of Egypt (an already semi-autonomous Ottoman dominion) was mirrored by the rise of Turkish nationalism, with the modern-day Turkish Republic emerging as another successor state of the Ottoman Empire at the end of the First World War. In both countries and by all sides of the political spectrum, the role of woman as either guardian of tradition or at the vanguard of change was hotly contested. The writers in this sourcebook chronicle the gendered aspects of different versions of modernity. This was the period that saw the emergence of organised feminism in both East and West, alongside the advent of industrialised modernity in the West, and the accelerated participation of Egypt and Turkey in world markets. As part of these regional modernities a critical dialogue – intellectual, political and personal – between women in the Middle East and with those in the West was integral to the development of autonomous women's emancipatory campaigns and to their contributions to nationalist activism and national reforms (see Badran and Cooke 1990, and Meriwether and Tucker 1999).

The sources extracted here – all but two of them originally written in English[1] – are available now because there was at the time a market for women's accounts of harem life. Western interest, though often prurient, placed a high premium on renditions of the segregated world to which Western men were not permitted entry. For Western women travellers, writing about the lives of Middle Eastern women enticed their publishers and readers and helped them establish reputations as writers able to earn, in some cases essential, income. For educated, elite Middle Eastern women, the opportunity to publish accounts of their lives provided a chance to correct the Western stereotypes that not only blighted their individual dealings with Westerners but also, as they and their male counterparts were acutely aware, informed Western foreign and imperial policy. Middle Eastern women writing in English knew that they had a dual audience: the Western reader who was curious about foreign lands and also the reader at home who was interested in local debates about the changing role of women in society. In Egypt and in the Ottoman cultural centres from the mid-nineteenth century, progressive men saw female advancement as integral to general social and political emancipation. Though men were more often questing for educated, cultured consorts than aspiring to autonomy for women (Fleischmann 1999), the male support available to women in the Middle East was a source of wonder and envy to their beleaguered Western sisters. The limitations and potential of this male support for female emancipation and its wider implications for women, citizenship, and society, were keenly observed by the Western women whose reports figure here. Like the Middle Eastern authors, their contemporaneous accounts are at times prescient, at others they reveal a hope for equality that was not to be realised. In Egypt, the feminist contribution to the anti-British nationalist struggle was betrayed by a nationalist model of modernity that did not feature gender equality. In Republican Turkey, on the other hand, the eventual advent of a state sponsored feminism that suppressed autonomous women's organisation (Arat 1994), did provide Turkish women with enfranchisement and social rights in advance of women living in parts of Europe and under Western mandates in the Middle East.

The sources in this collection are united in their concern with the condition of women: although authors take different positions on questions of female suffrage, women's work, education, and religion, all of them establish connections between the lives of women in the East and in the West. For some the comparison is direct, and the West does not always come out on top. For others it is implicit. As Billie Melman (1992) has demonstrated, Western women evaluated the harem in relation to historical changes in their own situation, from the eighteenth-century interest in women's sexual freedom to the nineteenth-century approval of the constraints on husbands' conjugal and social rights (as discussed by Julia Pardoe). The same is true of Middle Eastern women's writing about Western society and values. In each case, the ways in which Western and Middle Eastern women observed and commented on each other's lives is informed by the concerns of their own society at that moment in time and by their desire to intervene in the gender relations of that society. The excerpts in this book demonstrate the cultural and political agency of women in the Middle East and the West at a time when women in both areas were beginning to emerge into the public roles and rights that we recognise today.

The sixteen extracts in the book are organised chronologically to illustrate the sequence of social and political change, demonstrating how the significance of certain issues – and the ways in which they were discussed – altered in relation to local and international developments. Women's writing was structured not just by their own changing concerns, but by the shifting terms of contemporary discourses, such as nationalism. Accordingly, this book can also be read thematically, dipping into different extracts with the assistance of the extract introductions that, as well as providing biographical information, identify each author's relationship to a series of overlapping themes. These, which are outlined in more detail in the rest of this introduction, include topics such as sexual politics (centred on the harem, the family and polygyny); education; nationalism; religion and faith; feminism; slavery and race; and the body, dress and self-presentation.

EXOTICA AND AUTHENTICITY: THE MARKET FOR WOMEN'S ACCOUNTS

For the West, the territories of what we now know as the modern Middle East (itself a controversial category), were generally conceptualised within the vague but evocative term of the 'Orient'. As Edward Said (1978) demonstrated, the geography of this Oriental realm was largely imaginary and into this conceptual division of the world fell the territories of what remained in the early nineteenth century of the once vast Ottoman Empire. This division of space was not neutral: the Orient came to stand as the opposite to the (equally imaginary) realm of the West. In making this division, Said argued, the West through a series of mechanisms inevitably positioned itself in a 'relational superiority' to the East. The implications of this for our project relate not just to the conceptualisation of geographical space but to the very business of making representations of territories and their inhabitants. Opinion is divided on the directness of the relationship between Orientalist cultural production and Western colonialism (MacKenzie 1995), but it can be argued persuasively that the knowledges created by Western Orientalist scholars and artists often contributed implicitly or explicitly to the formation of colonial and imperial ideologies by depicting the East – even when the difference was registered as exciting or valuable – as ultimately inferior to the West (Mills 1991, Suleri 1992).

Whether they saw themselves as augmenting or challenging existing Orientalist knowledges, women writers understood that their representations of the Orient never stood alone: Orientalism was a citational discourse, the authority of which rested on the circulation and repetition of Western knowledges about the Orient. Travel writing, including travel writing by women, was a very popular literary genre in the nineteenth century (Birkett 1989, Mabro 1991), with harem literature operating as a related field that gave particular priority to women's publications. Recognising this, Sophia Poole in 1842 prefaced *The English-woman in Egypt* by telling the reader that she was requested to write by her brother, the famous Orientalist and Egyptologist Edward W. Lane, because she could supply information 'available only to a lady'. Nearly a century later Grace Ellison confirmed that 'a chapter, at least, on harem life will always add to the value of the book' (Ellison 1915: 15). The extent to which Western women challenged Orientalist knowledges (Lowe 1991, Lewis 1996, Cherry 2000) or supported them by always taking them as the base-line of discussion (Yeğenoğlu 1998) is a matter of debate. But women who wrote about the harem knew full well that their work was read, commissioned and distributed as specifically female-produced work, for which there was a sizeable market.

Brought out by respectable publishing houses, women's books often went into second and third editions: Lady Brassey's travel accounts, for example, were bestsellers in their time, running to several editions and translated into French and German. Many women's sources were published in both Britain and the United States, whilst some Middle Eastern women's accounts written in English also appeared in other European languages. Several sources were also printed in India, thereby reaching the British and indigenous readers in Britain's colonies. The amount of critical attention these titles received varied, but most garnered some press in both the West and the Middle East (where women's publications were reviewed in the Ottoman and Arabic general and women's press and also in the foreign-language press that served the region's foreign communities). Sometimes books were covered in response to the prominence of the author's life, such as the reviews of Melek Hanoum's notorious escape to France, or Halide Edib's public status as a writer and nationalist. The interconnections between East and West also produced audiences in the Middle East for Western women's accounts. Some of Ellison's reports for the *Daily Telegraph* appeared in the Ottoman constitutionalist paper *Tanin* and she, Brassey and Demetra Vaka Brown recount that their work was read by Middle Eastern women. Thus the dialogue between Western and Middle Eastern writers took place also through the exchange of their work and their often shared agenda of feminist and social activism.

Although Western women in the nineteenth century emphasised the being-there-ness of their personal harem accounts, they were careful not to be over-taken by their evocative location: they did not want to become part of the Oriental spectacle that they depicted. They knew that their work was read with presumptions about the gender-appropriate behaviours expected of Western women, as well as with Orientalist assumptions about the Eastern harem. So, though they peppered their books with references to their harem visits, often using titles that emphasised their presence in harems (such as Lott's *The English Governess in Egypt: Harem Life in Egypt and Constantinople*) and illustrations that anchored them to Eastern locations (for example, Plate 6) they also took care to remind the reader of their distance from the objects of their scrutiny. No matter how positive their view of Middle Eastern women, somewhere the line was drawn. For example, Pardoe in the early nineteenth century and Elizabeth Cooper in the early twentieth century dismiss as garish the local aesthetic sensibility that informs Egyptian women's selection of Western consumer goods. By the twentieth century, changes in the literary market were moving harem accounts away from the personal memoir style to the more 'objective' social science model of the ethnographic-style survey, favoured by Cooper, writing in

1914, and Ruth Frances Woodsmall, in 1936. As recent critical appraisals have shown (Geertz 1984), these different models were rarely absolutely divided, with the imagined objectivity of ethnography being itself subjective and gendered. Ellison, writing in 1915, demonstrates the unevenness of this transition, continuing and adapting previous models in her combination of personal narrative and political commentary.

Middle Eastern women were even less able to avoid being identified with the content of their books and generally presented their work specifically in the form of personal narrative. Where they do offer social commentary coded in political and ethnographic terms (also something that occurred more in the twentieth century), it is often anchored in the personal experience that validated their accounts, as seen in Edib's later books on Turkish international relations (Adak 2004). Another way in which Middle Eastern women substantiated their accounts and raised them above the merely anecdotal was through the citation of other sources: Emine Foat Tugay and Musbah Haidar both verify their versions of public events involving members of their prominent families by quoting from 'authoritative' Western publications, Eastern publications and private Western and Eastern correspondence and memoirs. This intertextuality immerses their books in an international political and social literary exchange.

When they wrote in English, these women knew they would also reach a readership at home, where English and French were the languages of elite literary status. Elite and middle-class women were sometimes literate only in foreign languages: religious education often taught girls only to read rather than to write in Arabic, or Ottoman; the foreign-run missionary and independent schools, which provided much of the middle-class female education in the region throughout the nineteenth century, gave instruction in English or French; whilst the foreign governesses who educated the majority of elite women were rarely literate in Arabic or Ottoman (Baron 1994, see also Haidar). In this way, the decision to write in English, rather than French or German, also reveals the material effects of the different spheres of imperial and cultural influence of the Western nations (for example, the significance of the American College for Girls in Istanbul, attended by Halide Edib, or the francophone missionary schools that educated many Syrian-Egyptian feminist pioneers, Hatem 1992). Nonetheless, the ability to read and discuss in English and French created an interpretive community for contemporary readers that connected Middle Eastern subjects to each other and to Western correspondents and contacts.

Familiarity with European literature attested not only to one's elite status but was also formative of intellectual opinion, constitutive of a new sensibility and new cultural forms among Middle Eastern subjects that had particular significance for women (see Brassey). Imported French and English literature was combined with existing literary traditions to produce the newly emergent novel in Arabic and Turkish (Paker 1991) where not only was the status of women used as a vehicle for discussion about reform, but also women writers themselves appeared in greater numbers as authors. Alongside the novel, autobiography also developed in a new form. In distinction to previous conventions of Arabic and Ottoman life, writing that had largely excluded women (Badran and Cooke 1990), the new autobiography was taken up from the start as a genre that facilitated the expression of women's life stories, often merging with the biographies of Middle Eastern and Western women (past and present) that formed a staple of the burgeoning women's press (Baron 1994, Booth 2001). Operating from the 1890s mainly in Istanbul and Cairo (see Baron 1994, Frierson 1995, Nelson 1996), the new women's periodicals, written primarily in Ottoman and Arabic, but also in French and English, offered a space for women writers to critique local gender norms and to engage with Western attitudes and events. In Egypt, the flourishing Arabic women's press created new professional opportunities for middle-class women as editors and writers (Baron 1994), as had been the case in Europe and America.

If Western women were wary of being over-identified with their harem location, for Middle Eastern women, who were both the author and the subject of harem accounts, the ramifications were even more problematic as they struggled to tell their stories and sell their books without being overtaken by the worst of harem stereotypes. They all regarded their writing and publication as an intervention into the formation of public opinion at home and abroad: Zeyneb Hanoum's claim that all books on the harem were lies and should be burned not only expressed rage at the misrepresentations with which she found herself contending, but also served to authenticate her account as valuable insider knowledge. Where her complaint was posed generically, other women made counter-claims against specific writers. Edib, who urged Ellison to help the British rename harems as 'homes', was scathing about Vaka Brown's first book (*Haremlik*), and used her personal experience to discredit the latter's version. Although it was their main selling point, Middle Eastern women did not find that their authenticity was taken without question: reviews of Zeyneb Hanoum used her European bloodline as grounds to challenge her authenticity.

The nature of this challenge reveals the premium that was placed on authenticity and how tenuous it could be to establish. The ability to spot a fake was a valuable way to establish one's credibility. When an unknown source ('Adalet') appeared as a 'Voice from a Harem' in the British journal *The Nineteenth Century* in 1890, the British writer Lucy Garnett was quick to proclaim it a fake (Garnett 1890–1: 471). Pointing out the inconsistencies in the account that meant that it could not be by a Muslim woman, Garnett, the respected author of several volumes of ethnography on Turkey, sought to enhance her status in the field by recognising and dismissing phoney contenders.

FEMINISM IN EAST AND WEST

For the West, the mid to late nineteenth century was the period in which bourgeois feminism emerged as a powerful force. In these decades middle-class women began to develop the philanthropic activities in welfare provision that were eventually to result in professional opportunities; women writers began to be published in ever-greater numbers; women artists successfully agitated for access to professional training. Working-class women, often in non-unionised and casual employment, had begun to make their voices heard, showing increased participation in trade unions from the 1880s. By the early twentieth century, union activism was providing a route to professional and social advancement for some working-class women comparable to the benefits of philanthropy for middle-class women (Anderson and Zinsser 1988). The campaign for the vote, a mainly middle-class concern in Britain and America in the mid-nineteenth century, had gained working-class women's support by the turn of the century. Widespread campaigning was split in Britain between the largely law-abiding National Union of Women's Suffrage Organisation (under Millicent Garrett Fawcett) and the militant Women's Social and Political Union (led by Emmeline Pankhurst), meeting with brutal government suppression (to the horror of Ottoman observers like Zeyneb Hanoum). With the outbreak of the First World War both wings suspended campaigns for the patriotic duties that were in the end to sway public and political opinion in favour of the franchise (awarded to women over twenty-eight in 1918 and over eighteen in 1928). In America women (except for those from Native American communities) were enfranchised in 1920. Throughout all this, various strains of 'feminist Orientalism' (Zonana 1993) evaluated the situation of women in the East as a measure of Western women's conditions.

The conditions and campaigns of Western women were also followed keenly by women in the Middle East. Though Middle Eastern feminists often sought solidarity and assistance (in education, training, political lobbying) from the West, they also found themselves simultaneously having to challenge Western imperialist assumptions. Arguing that Middle Eastern women should not simply mimic the West, they proffered a cogent critique of the limitations of Western so-called liberation and asserted their rights to adopt Western feminist ideals selectively.

With male reformers and conservatives writing about female emancipation from the mid-nineteenth century, literate elite women entered the fray – challenging the conventional prohibition on women speaking outside the home. In Istanbul, Fatma Aliye Hanoum, daughter of a leading Tanzimat reformer, responded to clerical anti-feminism with articles in the Ottoman press and a publication in French on women's rights (Frierson 1995). In Egypt, Hanna 'Kawrani and Zaynab Fawwaz debated the way forward on women's rights in the press in 1892 (Badran 1996). In welfare provision, too, women began to assert a direct public presence. Having previously operated behind the scenes through conventions of benevolence, social activism for elite women became increasingly possible in the early years of the twentieth century, often positioning lower-class women as recipients of public social welfare activities rather than as colleagues. For most women, these gender campaigns were seen as part of a project of national social rejuvenation – whether it was to reform the Ottoman Empire or to break away from Ottoman and British control. In Istanbul, Edib was involved in the establishment of the Women's Red Crescent and Teali-i Nisvan Cemiyati (Society for the Elevation of Women), set up during the Balkan War (1912–13) to provide nursing and to offer vocational training for women.

In Egypt, women's charitable organisations began in the first decade of the twentieth century with a range of welfare organisations established by minority populations (frequently also demarcated on religious lines, e.g. Maronite, Coptic, Greek Orthodox), as well as prominent Muslim charities that often ran with the support of royal women, like the dispensary for poor women and children established in 1909. Literary self-improvement groups that developed at the same time involved middle-class as well as upper-class women (Baron 1994). The start of the First World War gave Egyptian women's organisations, like many others in the region, a specifically nationalist focus, and in 1918 an alliance was formed with the nationalist anti-British Wafd ('Delegation'), creating the Wafd Women's Central Committee (WWCC) in 1920, with Hoda Shaarawi as president. By the 1920s international suffrage campaigns were well organised and Middle Eastern feminists participated, with varying degrees of state support. In 1923 Shaarawi was invited to take an Egyptian delegation to the International Woman Suffrage Organisation in Rome, leading to the formation of the Egyptian Feminist Union (EFU). Ottoman, and later Turkish, feminists were similarly involved in international feminist campaigns, often having to challenge the Eurocentric bias of Western feminists, even when the specific concerns of Eastern women were on the agenda. This collaboration with international Western suffrage organisations was an extension of a long-standing regional perspective in which women from the elite understood themselves to be bound together by a commonality of interests that transcended differences of religion, ethnicity, language and region (Fleischmann 1999). The emergence of the modern nation-state meant that the potential inclusiveness of earlier identifications as Ottoman now gave way to more localised affiliations. But alliances between women from across the Middle East continued into the twentieth century, increasingly based on anti-imperialist politics, especially in the context of the Western mandates after the First World War. At the start of our period, in the nineteenth century, the broader regional differences within the Ottoman empire meant that factors that affected social change – the impact of the central bureaucracy, the role of the local religious hierarchy, the nature and impact of the European presence – were played out differently in the various cities and hinterlands of the empire. In contrast, the major urban centres of Istanbul and Cairo, where there were the greatest numbers of literate women, were connected through a variety of political and social ties, and exposed to a similar level of European presence (Davis 1986).

Travel:
REGIONAL AND INTERNATIONAL CONNECTIONS

Our period marks the start of a significant growth in the number of European visitors to Istanbul and Cairo, made easier by the increased availability of regular
steamship travel. It is at this conjuncture that our earliest writer, Julia Pardoe,
arrived in Constantinople in 1837, just before the advent of the Tanzimat reforms
that heralded major social and political changes in the Ottoman Empire. She thus
provides a view of Ottoman women's lives in the last years of the old order and
illuminates the nature of Western travellers' experience just before the advent of
organised tourism. Similarly, Sophia Poole and Emmeline Lott were in Egypt
just before Cooke's tours started to arrive in 1869. Their books describe an experience of the Middle East that was still available to only very few Western
women. The vast increase in Western women's travel and its immense impact on
the interaction between Western and Middle Eastern women can be seen in
Annie Jane Harvey's writing when, in 1871, just four decades after Pardoe, she
complained that it was almost impossible to get into the best harems, so demand-
ing were the now-numerous Western lady travellers. As Western women from
the middle and upper middle classes began to be able to travel, not just those
from the aristocracy and upper class, they started to visit harems other than those
of the royal families and the Ottoman upper elite. With contacts fostered by their
men's business connections, Western women began to produce accounts of more
middle-income Middle Eastern homes (Yeazell 2000).

Developments in travel extended the number and type of situations in which
Western and Middle Eastern women could meet. In our period, elite women from
the Middle East met Western women working as governesses; through connections forged by male relatives, who made up the growing number of commercial
and diplomatic male personnel working in the Middle East; as missionaries; and
through friends. Introductions through personal contacts gained access to harems
for Western tourists, some of whom went on to forge friendships with the women
they met. Lady Brassey, for example, met the Egyptian princess Nazli Hanoum
on several occasions, renewing their friendship whenever their shared social circle brought them together in Cairo or Istanbul. Though Ottoman women often
welcomed the chance to meet Western visitors, the increased numbers of tourists
and what was written about them, meant that Ottoman women were also often
unwilling to present themselves as tourist spectacle: Haidar, for one, complained
about the ignorance of American visitors. Women also met each other through
their shared reading of each other's publications and subsequent invitations to
visit and correspond. In the later years of the Ottoman Empire when more emancipated men took their educated wives to official functions, women met each
other in mixed company as well, when previously most contact, certainly with
Muslim women, had taken place in single-sex environments. In addition to elite
women's habits of local travel throughout the Ottoman dominions (often making
long visits to members of the extended family), the turn of the century saw small

numbers of Turkish and Egyptian women (Muslim and non-Muslim) travelling to Europe and North America, to accompany male relatives, fleeing political persecution, or for pleasure and education.

EMPIRES:
LOCAL AND INTERNATIONAL RELATIONS OF POWER

The period covered by this book begins during the rule of Muhammad Ali (1769–1849) in Egypt, and just prior to the far-reaching government reforms of the Tanzimat (1839–76) in the Ottoman Empire. These reforms were initiated by the Ottoman sultans who hoped to use Western ideas and education to form a centralised bureaucracy and military loyal to the palace, in order to diminish the increasingly threatening power of the existing ruling class. Though the Tanzimat reforms were undertaken to protect the multi-ethnic, supra-national ideal that was the Ottoman Empire, they did in the end produce the independent intelligentsia and bourgeoisie that were to be central to the eventual formation of the modern nation-states that succeeded the empire. An era of rapid modernisation, the years covered by our sources are marked by shifting attitudes to the West in which Western technologies were often admired whilst Western social mores and associated morals were as often disparaged as they were emulated. In all this, the debate about women's conditions in relation to nation and religion took on a heightened significance. As well as the desire of the Ottoman state and individuals to revitalise society, the Tanzimat measures were also influenced by Western imperial policy in the region, notably the British, who, for a number of reasons, wanted the empire to remain intact but to see it operate on a more centralised model. Opinion is divided about the extent to which Western powers determined the course of Ottoman domestic policy, but it was a major factor. It was also a variable factor, as the policies of the different Western powers shifted in response to their internal concerns and their rivalries with each other. The threats to the Ottoman Empire raised by the insurrection of subject dominions varied depending on the attitude of the Western powers.

One such example is the fluctuating status of Egypt, which, though nominally an Ottoman dominion since the sixteenth century, was frequently only tenuously within Ottoman control. By the mid-seventeenth century, Egypt was dominated by the local Mamluks (descendants of the Muslim military dynasties that ruled Egypt from 1250 to 1517), and between 1798 and 1801 was briefly occupied by Napoleon Bonaparte, until an Anglo-Ottoman alliance repelled the French. The ensuing struggle between the Ottomans and the Mamluks was resolved in 1805 when the Ottoman general Muhammad Ali (born in Macedonia of Albanian extraction) took power with local support. Made governor by the Ottomans, Muhammad Ali initiated a comprehensive programme of economic reform that saw Egypt develop as one of the main suppliers of cotton to the textile trade of Britain's industrial revolution. He was intent on strengthening his domain, and to this end brought in technical and military trainers from Europe and began a series of expansionist campaigns to protect Egyptian trade routes.

Muhammad Ali's military prowess again came to the aid of Sultan Mahmut II in 1824 when he was called in to help defend Ottoman sovereignty in Greece. By the early nineteenth century the Ottomanist ideal was starting to disintegrate as local nationalisms, based on the Western romantic nationalist ideal, began to take hold and subject populations tried to break from Ottoman control. Although Muhammad Ali's campaign in Greece was initially successful, Britain, Russia and France intervened, making the Greeks the first Ottoman population to achieve independence in 1829. The Greek revolt was followed by a series of revolts among the Serbs, Albanians, Armenians and Bulgars, none of which led yet to independence but which, with the fluctuating and self-interested support of the European powers, were to punctuate the region until the loss of European territories in the Balkan Wars of 1912–13 and the decisive results of the 1914–18 First World War. But whilst Egypt had come to the Ottomans' rescue in Greece, the invasion of Syria, by Muhammad Ali and his son Ibrahim in 1831–3, brought them into direct conflict with the Ottoman army, eventually threatening the imperial stronghold of Istanbul itself. In this instance the Great Powers intervened to support the Ottomans, forcing Muhammad Ali to withdraw, though he temporarily retained Syria and Crete. In 1839 another successful Egyptian revolt was suppressed by the Ottomans with the aid of the British under Palmerston, who at that time wished to preserve the Ottoman Empire to keep the balance of power in the region against Russia and to protect the overland trade route to India. Muhammad Ali was contained in Egypt but given the right to hereditary rule. As viceroy, or khedive (prince), he presided over a magnificent court where the incorporation of European commodities provided an opportunity to display his vision of a moderated Westernisation to his subjects and to Western visitors – such as Poole, who attended his daughter's wedding in 1845. On Muhammad Ali's death in 1849, the throne passed to his sons, including the Khedive Ismail who continued his father's modernisation programme. One sign within his own household of Ismail's embrace of the well-established links to Europe, especially Britain, was the appointment of Emmeline Lott as governess to his son Ibrahim in 1865. But the modernisation plans were, like the Suez Canal, often reliant on foreign funding. When continued fiscal imprudence led to bankruptcy, foreign banks gained extensive control of the Egyptian economy – as was also to be the case in the Ottoman Empire. In 1879 the Ottoman sultan deposed Ismail in favour of his son Tawfik Paşa. Faced with the 'Urabi revolution (initially supported by Shaarawi's father, Sultan Paşa), when Egyptian army officers challenged the power of the Turko-Circassian elite, Tawfik invited the British to help restore order, prompting in 1882 an occupation that would continue until Egyptian independence in 1954.

Elsewhere in the Ottoman dominions, secular-influenced training establishments were set up to produce the vocational, military and civilian (male) personnel necessary to implement the Tanzimat plans. Started by Sultan Mahmut

II (1808–39), educational initiatives from the Tanzimat years continued under Sultan Abdülhamit II (1876–1909), who moved away from his predecessors' thoroughgoing adoption of Western models to a policy that was more critical and adaptive. In Egypt, from the 1880s the British occupation meant that state education was more directly influenced by foreign colonial interests, but here too the integration of secular education always involved a relationship to Islam (Fortna 2002).

At the same time, the development of the economy following Western industrial models helped to foster a nascent merchant middle class that was drawn largely, though not entirely, from the minority populations, notably Greeks, Jews and various other Eastern Orthodox and Christian communities (Quataert 1994). The non-Muslim populations of the Ottoman Empire, who had traditionally enjoyed relative levels of autonomy at the same time as they were taxed differently and excluded from some official offices, were often the preferred partners of the foreign companies that had long been given preferential trade terms under the capitulations (Göçek 1996). In addition, the minority populations were themselves a source of Orientalist fascination to Western visitors, many of whom (such as Pardoe) provided detailed descriptions of their distinctive social customs and were alert to their role as style leaders in the incorporation of Western goods. As the Westernising sensibilities of the Tanzimat stimulated the demand for foreign goods among the wider population, the increase in foreign trade further enhanced the power of a now largely independent merchant class that was significantly non-Muslim (a situation that continued into the twentieth century). Added to this, the Ottoman state was hugely reliant on European loans, the interest payments for which took up more than half of the state's total revenues by the last years of the Tanzimat. These loans were overseen from 1881 by the powerful and largely foreign- and minority-run Public Debt Administration. Though never as established as in the far more industrialised West, the Ottoman middle class and the bureaucrats formed a new power bloc that was replacing the older ruling class as the hegemonic class. Later, these Westernised intellectuals and bureaucrats were to be the driving force behind the development of the Young Ottomans who formed the late Tanzimat opposition (concerned at the abuse of power possible within the vast Tanzimat machine). It was these groups and their heirs who came to prominence again in the next wave of reform under the Young Turks in the early twentieth century.

Another facet of opposition that was to have an ongoing influence through the last decades of the Ottoman Empire was organised in defence of Islamic principles and came from the artisans and lower ranked clerics and civil servants who had tended to lose power and influence under the Tanzimat reforms (Kandiyoti 1991). Sultan Abdülhamit, who revoked the Tanzimat constitution in 1876, took a pan-Islamist position, emphasising his role as caliph (spiritual leader of the world's Muslims). In trying to strengthen the political unity of the *umma*, the pan-national community of believers, he hoped to extend his authority over Muslim territories beyond the Ottoman Empire and thus to improve his leverage with the Western powers. In contrast, pan-Ottomanism held to the ideal of the multi-ethnic Ottoman Empire and aimed to preserve this in the face of what were seen as divisive movements for local autonomy. This was by and large the position of the Young Turks during their period of organising in exile at the turn of the twentieth century, when their number included Muslims as well as representatives of minority populations. Though Young Turk alliances were often racked by intense differences of opinion, it was not always competing (proto)national ambitions that were the primary cause of ideological dispute.

The Young Turk group that were to lead the revolution in 1908 were the Committee of Union and Progress (CUP) with whom Edib was to be associated. Though Abdülhamit features in several of our accounts as a repressive tyrant, the Young Turks initially intended only to limit his power through the reactivation of the Tanzimat constitution. It was only after the counter-revolution in 1909 – which Emine Foat Tugay's father was involved in quelling – that Abdülhamit was replaced by his brother Mehmet Reşat V, who reigned until 1918.

The Young Turk revolution of 1908 ushered in the Second Constitutional Period that lasted until Turkey's defeat in the First World War in 1918. The Ottomans entered the First World War on the side of the Germans, marking a shift away from the links to Britain of previous cabinets, notably that headed by Kâmil Paşa, the father of Ellison's friend Makboulé (given the alias of Fâtma or Fâtima in her books). Tugay's father, who in 1913 was the Ottoman ambassador to Berlin, advocated neutrality but was overruled. With promises of support against the much feared threat of an (Allied-sponsored) Russian incursion, the Ottomans fought on the losing side.

The Allies occupied Istanbul in 1918, an event that for Muslim Turks was an affront beyond compare. For some in the minority populations, however, the arrival of Western personnel was welcome, leading to further splits within Ottoman society. The British-backed Greek invasion at Izmir in 1919 further weakened the integrity of what was left of the empire in Anatolia. The fault-lines of class and ethnicity within Ottoman society that had been established during the Tanzimat now came to play a major role as Turkish nationalism emerged as a focal point for resistance to the foreign occupation. Although the Young Turks had promised inclusion for minority populations, many in the minority populations wanted greater devolution than the Young Turks had envisaged.

With Sultan Mehmet VI (Vahideddin) in Istanbul under the control of the occupying Allies, the focus of resistance switched to Ankara, where the nationalists under Mustafa Kemal (later Atatürk) had set up headquarters. From here he directed a 'war of liberation' (1918–22) against the occupying powers and the collaborating government. The nationalists were joined by Edib and her second husband Adnan Adıvar. They had fled Istanbul when her prominence, having delivered a dramatic speech against the Greek invasion during the public rally in Sultanahmet Square, put her in too much danger of arrest. Though many peasant women were involved in the armed insurrection (as was the case in Egypt), few elite women took a combat role, tending towards political campaigning and administrative functions. Edib, however, did see active service as a translator with the nationalists. When the Istanbul government accepted the terms of the Treaty of Sèvres (10 August 1920), under which Turkey lost all her European and Arab territories, the nationalists declared them to be traitors and pressed forward with the war. In September 1922, the nationalists won, eventually declaring the Turkish Republic on 29 October 1923, with Kemal as its first president. For the early republicans, the status of the Turkish woman and her image at home and abroad was to become a central preoccupation of their modernising mission. At home, the old style of harem femininity so intriguing to our earlier writers was increasingly regarded as a sign of a decadent ancien régime. In contrast, the new republic sought to model female citizens who could contribute to the welfare of the new nation and whose image would replace that of the languid harem lady in the eyes of the world. In the bid to present feminism as a wing of state benevolence, the autonomous women's organisations that had worked with the nationalists were initially refused official recognition, until being reformed into the state-sanctioned Turkish Women's League in 1924. After bestowing the vote on women in 1934, Mustafa Kemal dismantled the League in 1935 when the Turkish delegation to the twelfth International Woman Suffrage Alliance, held in Istanbul, took a pacifist position at odds with government policy.

In Egypt, the First World War saw the end of the link to the Ottoman Empire but a new phase in imperial control when the British made Egypt a Protectorate in 1914. Already by the end of the nineteenth century, the British occupation had become a focus for developing Egyptian nationalism, and this entered a new stage in 1914 when the hopes of Egyptian nationalists, like the other Arab nationalists encouraged to revolt against the Ottomans by the Allies during the First World War, were raised by promises of autonomy after the war. (Some factions in Egypt had, however, until the dissolution of the empire, seen the Ottomans as potential supporters in the struggle against the British, Baron 1994.) Having spent the war years planning for independence, the nationalist Wafd organised a violent revolt in 1918 when Britain sought to retain control of the country. With Wafd leaders exiled, the organisation's vice president, Shaarawi's husband Ali Shaarawi, played a major role, as did Hoda. The revolt saw Hoda Shaarawi and other upper-class women, alongside less secluded non-elite women, emerge dramatically onto the streets in both specially organised women's public demonstrations and mixed marches against the British (Fleischmann 1999). The campaign against British occupation lasted until 1922 when the British declared Egypt a monarchy, under their chosen ruler Fuad I, still limiting the king's executive powers. But when the Wafd were able to form a government in 1924, women, who had been included in the draft constitution of the resistance years, were excluded from the franchise and Shaarawi and the Wafd Women's Central Committee split from the Wafd, undertaking nationalist campaigns independently and through the Egyptian Feminist Union (EFU). The EFU campaigned for the franchise as part of a nationalist project for equal citizenship, linking women's improved social role to the right to participate in nation building. Like their Turkish counterparts, Egyptian feminists, especially the EFU, played a prominent role in international suffrage organisations, using these to harness international support, especially once Turkish women were enfranchised in 1934. Joining with the Wafd and male nationalists during the nationalist crises that punctuated the 1930s and 1940s, Egyptian feminists met with continued opposition to the vote from male nationalists, even though women were achieving advances in education and employment. When the British were finally ousted by a military coup in 1954 the newly established Egyptian republic awarded women the vote in 1956.

SOCIAL STATUS AND SLAVERY

The Middle Eastern women writers in our selection were all elite – since poorer women were rarely literate and did not in this period leave written first-person accounts of their lives (see Tucker 1985). Within their shared social strata, the women in our sample came from a variety of backgrounds. Some were born into the highest levels of elite status: like Haidar, whose father, as one of the serifs of Mecca, was of royal status; and Tugay who was the granddaughter of the Khedive Ismail; whilst Zeyneb Hanoum, Leyla Saz Hanımefendi and Edib had fathers who were part of the upper palace bureaucracy. Other women married into the elite, such as Melek Hanoum, whose family background (Greek mother, Armenian father) was not so elevated. In the upper levels of the elite, such marriages from outside the empire and outside the Muslim community were a common feature and formed a significant part of the elite's international dimension. That Haidar had a British mother and Zeyneb Hanoum a French grandfather was not untypical. This aspect of Ottoman society was often noted in the nineteenth century by outside observers but had in fact been a characteristic of the Ottoman elite for centuries.

Another way in which women from outside the immediate community entered the families of the Ottoman and Egyptian elite was through concubinage, as had initially been the case with Tugay's Circassian grandmother. Drawing especially on women from the central Asian regions of Circassia and Georgia, concubinage was a form of slavery that occupied a particular and elevated status within the socially stratified structure of Ottoman and Egyptian slavery (Peirce 1993). Slavery, a subject that nearly all commentators felt obliged to cover, was very different in the Ottoman Muslim system to the plantation slave systems of the Christian West (Toledano 1982). The Muslim system did not regard slavery as a permanent identity. Manumission was encouraged (often given after several years' service, at the time of marriage or on the birth of children). To be the child of a slave, as was the case for many in the elite – especially the sultans – was not a matter of shame. Though slavery was to decline over the course of the nineteenth century, the imperial and elite households of Istanbul and Cairo were for much of our period staffed by enslaved women. Light and heavy household work was carried out by slaves (who were often, but not exclusively, black Africans, see Leyla Saz Hanımefendi, Tucker 1985), whilst household management fell to other slaves who were able to assume positions of considerable power and influence. With elite women often taking young girls into their homes for training, those who showed appropriate potential (beauty, accomplishments, intelligence) were able to make good marriages to rich men or be placed in wealthy homes as concubines (Davis 1986). The concubine classification was quite outside the Western concept of slavery: concubines were in effect consorts and Western observers, many of whom were preoccupied with ending the Ottoman slave trade, were at a loss to know how to deal with the 'unfree' status of these socially elevated educated women who did not fit their narrow definition of slavery. Western observers did often note that domestic slaves were treated as, and understood themselves to be, part of the family. In light of this, also, they were struck by the democratic nature of Middle Eastern social relations (see Ellison), where the doors of the household were always open to needy relatives and the poor of the city were never turned away (a point reiterated by Middle Eastern writers, see especially Tugay).

The different forms of social stratification within Middle Eastern society were registered by some Western observers (such as Cooper), but Middle Eastern women were clearly vexed that their place within a finely delineated local hierarchy was often misread by Western contacts. When Middle Eastern women travelled to the West their perceived social status was sometimes worryingly repositioned. Zeyneb Hanoum found her Ottoman elite status was undermined by the transition to Europe, and in this context experienced the insurrectionary street activities of the British suffragists as alarmingly de-gentrifying. This was a concern for British feminists too, who, in the pre-war period, often took great care to control the perception of their public demonstrations (Tickner 1987). But other more elite Middle Eastern women evidence no such concern about loss of status: Tugay reports as a matter of course that her father took the family to the fashionable cities and resorts of Europe for long periods at precisely the same time. Women from royal families in particular were part of an international web of extended family and political relations. This involved travel and communication that connected them across and beyond the Ottoman territories and gave them personal access to the key players in regional and world events (see caption to Plate 11).

THE HAREM AND POLYGYNY

For women in the Middle East and those that observed them the subject that none could avoid was the harem. Each knew that the image of the secluded women of the polygnous harem was central to the fantasy logic of Western Orientalism. The harem was part of a system of segregation that within Islamic conceptualisations of space and society protected the status of the holy (*haram*). Originally applying to the person of the sultan as caliph, and by extension to his household, the harem was a system that provided a cordon between the divine representative and the rest of the world and could, for example, be made portable by means of an honour guard to protect the sultan as he journeyed through his realm (Peirce 1993). As a concept the harem came to be applied to women and was accompanied by conventions in dress that, for example through veiling, similarly enclosed the harem's inhabitants in its protection, thus allowing them to pass through spaces outside its physical confines. As it emerged as a domestic system, segregated living served to separate women from men who were not closely related to them by demarcating the separate spaces of the *selamlik* (men's quarters open to male visitors to the house) and the harem (the space only available to women and children and to familial men). Within Islamic thinking this segregation served to protect the *umma* from the chaos of *fitna*, the uncontrolled force that would be released by the unmonitored association of non-familial men and women. This was based on an understanding of female sexuality as active and potentially unstoppable (Mernissi 1985), which was a stark contrast to the tendency within Christian Western thought to regard female sexuality as passive – a formulation that was beginning to emerge particularly powerfully in the nineteenth century.

In contrast to the affective ideal of monogamous Christian marriage that was to take such hold as part of the West's transition to industrialised modernity, stood the evocative idea of the harem. This, for the West, was inevitably understood as polygynous, existing in Western stereotype as an eroticised space in which a single man (generally elevated to the level of sultan) had unfettered access to endless numbers of women, whose lives he controlled with despotic ruthlessness. The harem in Western Orientalist writing and art was generally depicted as a space in which listless uneducated women sat passively awaiting their chance to meet their master's sexual needs, punctuated only by murderous rivalries between themselves or by untold female perversions.

Islamic law did permit a man to marry up to four wives, though this was regulated by the stipulation that each wife should be treated equally – emotionally and materially. In addition, men were permitted unlimited numbers of concubines. But few men could afford to do either of these things and polygyny and concubinage were predominantly the practices of the elite rather than the mass of the population. Certainly, Western women travellers were keen to visit polygynous households, though these were rare by the mid-nineteenth century and almost disappearing by the twentieth (Harvey, Ellison). This fascination with and overestimation of the frequency of polygyny was shared by the Ottomans themselves who, as Duben and Behar (1991) explain in relation to Istanbul, imagined polygyny to be far more frequent than it in fact was.

Alongside the theological formulations that structured the harem system were a series of social conventions that ordered how women might inhabit spaces inside and outside the home. This social element is central to the understanding of the harem system, polygyny and the veil: whatever their apparent divine origination, all were practised and experienced as social habits that variously affected the lives of different social groups. But, more than this, and important for the dialogue that this book studies, segregated living was part of a spatial system that impacted on everyone who passed through the Middle Eastern regions where it applied. If we think of spatial relations as socialising relations (Lefebvre 1991, Massey 1994), we can begin to see how those who fell within and outside segregating communities found that the harem system regulated where they could go and what they could see or how they could be seen.

The architectural character of Istanbul and Cairo changed dramatically during the period covered by this book as the Egyptian khedives (notably Ismail) and the Ottoman sultans rebuilt parts of their capitals on Western lines, often merging Western designs in public buildings (such as schools) with Islamic divisions of internal space (Çelik 1986, Fortna 2002). Nonetheless, by the last decades of the nineteenth century many private homes were being set up in buildings that fostered new types of living arrangements. In Istanbul, fashionable new apartment blocks accommodating nuclear rather than extended families were first inhabited by minority population families and a few from the Muslim elite (like Edib), before being taken up by a wider middle-class Muslim population in the First World War period. In Cairo in the 1870s and 1880s, Khedive Ismail created a modernist enclave of Western-style villas designed without the lattice windows of harem gender seclusion, that also aimed to avoid the ethnic and religious segregation of the old city's divided quarters by encouraging a mixed population (Badran 1996). In the modernising centres of Istanbul and Cairo the spaces occupied by women underwent profound changes as part of this process of selective adaptation of Western good and behaviours (Frierson 2000a). As was typical of debates in and about the Middle East, women's presence and dress in the changing cityscape was regarded, and often erroneously misinterpreted by the Western observer, as a general indicator of standards of 'civilisation'.

WOMEN'S PUBLIC PRESENCE

The 'veil' – the term the West commonly used for the variety of dress forms by which women concealed parts of their face, head, and body when outside the home – was also a social practice that impacted mainly on elite and urban female populations. Although many identify veiling as a religious requirement of Islam, veiling is pre-Islamic in origin and was practised at various times by diverse ethnic populations of the Middle East, including Christian, Coptic and Jewish women (Keddie and Baron 1991). Though Coptic Egyptian women still veiled into the twentieth century (Baron 1994), veiling had by the nineteenth century become a largely, though not exclusively, Muslim practice, and was regarded as Muslim by most outside observers.

The types of garments that formed Middle Eastern women's outerwear changed over time and varied across region and social group and were policed with varying degrees of intensity and success by state, religious and family forces. But, for the West, the veil was often understood in largely symbolic ways outside its historically specific type and application. The veiled woman was an object of mystery who stood in for all the (beguiling and dangerous) imagined mysteries of the East. For Western men the desire to see behind the veil was typically driven by sexual desire to access what they presumed to be the hidden beauties so jealously guarded by the sultan and his eunuchs. In more general terms this desire to penetrate behind the veil can be seen as part of a colonial desire to penetrate land and conquer territories, even when the desire to encourage Middle Eastern women to unveil could also be coded as a philanthropic desire to liberate them from the 'backwardness' of indigenous patriarchal oppression. In this, the unveiled body was equated to progressive modernity and rationality (as was later also to be the case in Turkish Republican modernising rhetoric).

The veil was not always regarded by Western women as an oppressive practice. From Lady Mary Wortley Montagu in 1763 to Pardoe in 1837, the ability of veiled women to move unchallenged through the streets was a matter of envy to Western women who, if they came from the middle and upper classes, found their public movements monitored and curtailed. By the time Ellison was in Istanbul in the early twentieth century, middle-class women had more freedom of movement in the West and the *yaşmak* was to be desired simply because 'no more becoming a headdress has ever been invented for women' (Ellison 1928: 33).

For Middle Eastern and Muslim women the veil was perceived in relation to different concepts of public and private. The division of space under the harem system is often interpreted to mean that women who were secluded had no role in public life. But this would be to misunderstand the nature of public and private in segregated societies. In the West, the feudal model of production and the aristocratic structure of household space had been by the nineteenth century largely replaced by a bourgeois conceptualisation of work as an activity that took place away from the home. The much discussed Victorian ideology of the separate spheres of public and private, in which bourgeois women were depicted as rooted in the home safely removed from the world of work and politics, is now apprehended to have been an idealisation of spatial relations that were in fact more porous than was sometimes imagined at the time or in twentieth-century histories (Davidoff and Hall 1987, Gleadle 2001). But the notion of a division between public and private did (and does) have a strong currency in the minds of the West, who therefore saw (and often continue to see) the secluded woman as existing entirely outside the realm of influence, ideas and public life.

In the Middle East context the notion of public was different. First, far from being an isolated sexual prison, the harem was a space in which women and families lived, worked and entertained. Women who lived in elite harems regularly visited each other and were served by women merchants who visited them at home. Secondly, among men from the upper bureaucracy and the military, the household (as in the imperial household) was the space in which politics and business took place. Thus, just as royal women in the imperial harem were able to exercise great influence, so too could the wives, daughters, and concubines of elite men. For these and other reasons the harem was, thirdly, its own form of public, based on an audience of women who communicated information between themselves and to their men. Melek Hanoum, writing in 1872 about her elite harem of the previous three decades, prides herself on the number of appointments she influenced whilst her husband was governor of Jerusalem. Although Melek Hanoum may in fact have abused her political power in her attempt to amass wealth (Schick 2005), the exercise of some degree of political power by the women of the elite was a well-known and widely accepted aspect of the political system. Similarly, Ellison describes how in the household of Kâmil Paşa, then Grand Vezir, the *selamlik* was full of male visitors, whilst his daughter received requests for favours in the harem. This fusion of household and state advantaged elite women, whose opportunities to exercise political and economic power diminished with the Tanzimat's centralisation of state bureaucratic functions (Meriwether and Tucker 1999). At the same time in Egypt, lower-class urban women found that the centralising integration of the Egyptian economy into European markets weakened the local and informal networks (often fostered in women's spaces such as the public baths) that had previously supported their economic agency (Tucker 1985). Fourthly, women's presence in the domain outside the home had for a long time been achieved by other means: charitable donations, often to found *medresses* (religious schools) or build fountains that bore their name was another method by which women's identities entered the public domain. Just as women in the West were to move from charitable welfare work to professional training in nursing and teaching, so too did this existing tradition of female philanthropy pave the way for women's entry into professional public work in the Middle East (see Shaarawi, Edib, Tugay). The social practices of religious observance also brought women into contact with each other and provided a mechanism for creating and fostering personal and political alliances, such as the provision of feasts during Ramadan described by Leyla Saz Hanımefendi. In these and other ways, women exercised political and social agency within a segregated realm that was related to the whole of society.

Clothes:
MODERNITY AND CONSUMPTION

As in the West, debates about modernity often centred on women's appearance in public and on the family behaviours they oversaw at home. In the context of debates about modernisation and Westernisation, dress and the domestic use of Western goods were key indicators by which Middle Eastern society evaluated political positions and attitudes to modernisation. Sometimes the use of Western commodities indicated a definite sense of political allegiance, sometimes merely a vague sense of progressiveness (Duben and Behar 1991), but much of it took place in the harem quarters and was undertaken by women. Women's consumption of goods, both from within the Ottoman Empire and from the West, had long been a significant arena for the display of female influence and power (Micklewright 2000). But, as the numbers of Western items (from furniture and china to clothes and accessories) increased dramatically during the course of the nineteenth century, these consumer activities became available to a wider section of the female population and were to have a vast impact on the nature of family life. By the 1860s most elite women in Istanbul and Cairo could have had gowns in the latest Paris fashions, either imported directly or made for them by foreign seamstresses who visited the harem. Since Western women's magazines were available in the Middle East and the growing number of local women's magazines had regular fashion features, elite women were well aware of the latest Western trends. By late in the century women were increasingly shopping outside the harem, visiting merchants in the bazaar or in the European quarters, and, subsequently, patronising the new-style department stores (Leyla Saz Hanımefendi, Shaarawi). Not only did women purchase entire Western ensembles, but they also adapted traditional Ottoman clothing to accommodate Western interventions. The significance of the adoption of Western fashion, including corsets, cannot be overstated. As well as creating a different silhouette for the female body, corsets required different bodily behaviours – to loll on low divans was no longer comfortable (see Vaka Brown). Far more suitable for this attire were the newly acquired Western chairs that gradually altered traditional floor-level living and brought about changes in social habits that, like the differentiated take-up of Westernised clothing, were initially more widespread among the elite than among the middle and lower classes (Cooper, Woodsmall). But, whatever their particular relationship to Western styles of dress, when Middle Eastern women went out of the house – still protected by the modest nature of Middle Eastern outerwear – little of this was visible to the Western observer (Brassey). And when Western women visited Middle Eastern homes, the women of the house tended to wear their finest 'Oriental' ensembles, knowing full well what their guests wanted. So visitors rarely saw the Paris fashions, though those that did commented on them. What many did not comment on were the ways in which conventional garments had been adapted to accommodate Western aesthetics and body shapes, because they did not know enough about Middle Eastern fashion to recognise such alterations (Micklewright 1986).

Not surprisingly, given that the veil served to protect female modesty and family honour, Middle Eastern society reserved its greatest regulatory interest for women's outerwear. In Istanbul and Cairo over the decades covered by this volume, a number of different garments were in use and were subject to legislation. These ranged from the transparent gauze *yaşmak*, that revealed the eyes and loosely veiled the face, to the voluminous black *çarşaf*, a loose cloak gathered at the waist, that, like the Egyptian *hijab*, was sometimes worn with a thick black face veil, the *peçe* in Turkey or the *burqa* in Egypt. The historical record as to how these styles emerged, changed, and were implemented is contradictory, but it would be wrong to imagine that women had no autonomy in the manner of their outer dress (see Leyla Saz Hanımefendi). Forms of outerwear in both cities came in and out of fashion, underwent myriad transformations that kept them in line with Western and local indoor clothing trends, and were worn selectively by women in different parts of the cities to signify class and religious allegiances (Lewis 2004). In all its forms women's clothing can be seen as a series of strategic dress acts (Kondo 1997) which were variously legible to their different audiences. Though it preserved modesty, the veil did not make women invisible. Getting it wrong could be dangerous since this marker of social status could leave one uncomfortably visible compared to the rest of the local female population (Edib 1928).

The prospect of women unveiling was not just important to the West. Some Middle Eastern women were also much concerned with how the veil symbolised their exclusion from circles of power within local patriarchies. They, and the rest of the progressives in Middle Eastern society, were also acutely aware of how much the veil, and the harem it represented, coloured the way their societies were seen by the West. There was, consequently, in the early years of the twentieth century a move among some Middle Eastern feminists to remove the veil, at those moments when it was considered politically useful to stage insurrection in this way. Both Shaarawi and Edib were involved in strategic public unveilings – each of which were subject to wide and sometimes inaccurate reporting. As with the difficulty of recognising changes in clothing, the varieties and different significance of head covering were often hard for the West to evaluate. Edib's apparent unveiling involved the removal of only the face veil. Baring her face was a dress act that made sense within a Middle East dress economy in which retaining the head covering preserved conventions of female modesty. Similarly, Shaarawi removed her face veil in 1923 (a practice already increasingly common among women in her milieu, though Shaarawi had previously retained hers), and then subsequently covered and uncovered her head in different circumstances, and for different photographs. Other Egyptian feminists sought an Islamic route to emancipation and, like the middle-class Malak Hifni Nasif, retained the veil to differentiate themselves from the elite cadre of Westernised feminists like Shaarawi, as well as to preserve their modesty (El Guindi 1999). In Turkey, Edib's use of a headscarf whilst in military service helped to preserve her status as respectable married woman and was important in allowing her to mix with male politicians and soldiers during the conflict. Early Turkish Republican policy after 1923 was characterised by this continuation of traditional models of female modesty within the context of radical social reform (Durakbaşa 1993). Whereas Mustafa Kemal worked hard to remove the veil through social pressure (considering it unwise to try to legislate against it), in Egypt in the early 1920s, as Badran (1996) points out, the removal or defence of the veil did not become a mainstay of anti-colonial rhetoric as it did in other locations, such as Algeria, partly because upper-class Egyptian women often paraded their preference for things French (fashion and language) as a way of slighting the British colonisers. Women throughout the region were aware of the power of politicised consumption choices: in Istanbul, campaigns from the 1880s to buy Ottoman rather than imported textiles were transformed during the Balkan Wars into a determination to buy Turkish (rather than support minority population traders, Frierson 2000b); in Egypt, the WWCC's boycott of British goods and banks in the 1920s spread throughout the country to great effect.

THE BODY AND BEAUTY

Writers in this collection frequently offer commentary on female appearance. This discourse on beauty and dress was a vital component of women's ethnographic and auto-ethnographic reportage. The historical span of our authors reveals the shift in ideals of female beauty, from the sophisticated harem odalisque to the utilitarian woman comrade of the early years of the Turkish Republic. As observers like Woodsmall note, the young women of this latter generation, encouraged to take up new educational opportunities, were well aware that their achievements stood for more than themselves. The consciousness of this responsibility on the part of students and teachers extended to their appearance and comportment, often with strict regulations, such as the requirement to cut long braids into the short bob that signified hygienic modernity (Arat 1999). Where earlier writers had challenged Western presumptions that all Middle Eastern women were oppressed harem slaves by demonstrating the elegance, philanthropy and culture of the elite harem woman, the Turkish Republic now sponsored an alternative nationalist vision of femininity on the world stage with the much lauded participation of an unveiled Turkish woman in an international beauty contest in the 1930s (see Plate 16). That the new female body should be physically fit and active was a plank of feminist and nationalist ideology in Turkey and in Egypt, where, sometimes accompanied by a Quranic justification, the EFU promoted physical exercise for girls and their mothers in the 1930s and 1940s.

EDUCATION

Throughout the period covered by this book, family and social status were key determinants of women's access to education. In the nineteenth century, as in earlier periods, it was only the elite of society who were literate and who received anything but the most rudimentary of education, with even smaller proportions of girls undertaking sustained study. For girls from the minority populations, education was generally arranged under the community *millet* schools and under the foreign-run missionary schools that, appearing in greater numbers from the mid-nineteenth century, acted as a spur to increase state provision for Muslim students. In Istanbul, schools opened for girls during the Tanzimat were extended in the 1870s under Abdülhamit, with a further push for female education in the Second Constitutional Period (1908–18). In Egypt, women's formal education was spearheaded by Muhammad Ali with the establishment of a school for women midwives in 1832 outside Cairo. Foreign and missionary schools, serving mainly Coptic Egyptians, set up in the 1830s were augmented by state-sponsored female education under the Khedive Ismail from the 1870s (Tucker 1985). The option of state education was terminated during the British occupation, rendering middle-class women even more reliant on foreign-run schools. In both countries elite women gained education in greater numbers from the middle decades of the nineteenth century, but, in Cairo as in Istanbul, most wealthy families educated their daughters at home with foreign governesses. Often of questionable pedagogic quality, the advent of the foreign governess provided one of the main circumstances in which elite Muslim women came into contact with Western women and with Western literature and ideas.

The foreign governess was also able to provide the West with glimpses of life in the harem, though she was not always believed: several sources point out the dubious reputation of many governesses. One of the earlier accounts featured here is that of Lott, governess to the son of the Khedive Ismail. The extract from her writings not only details the nature of Egyptian royal domestic life, but dwells on the difficulties faced by the female governess. Like the governess in England, whose awkward position above the servants but below the family was the subject of much concerned debate, the foreign governess in the Middle East factored nationality, religion and ethnicity into the travails of asserting what she perceived to be her correct rank within the household. The sources covered here offer glimpses into both sides of this relationship: if some Middle Eastern women were angered by governesses' negligence as educators (Zeyneb Hanoum), some Western women, whilst not unaware of the governesses' educational and/or moral failings, saw them (the English ones, at least, as far as Ellison was concerned) as important ambassadresses. But in all cases it is agreed that the governess was an important conduit for the transmission of foreign ideas (Woodsmall).

For the Middle Eastern women another deciding factor in their access to education was the presence of a progressive parent, generally their father. For Edib (who as well as having governesses was unusual in attending the foreign-run American College for Girls) and Zeyneb Hanoum, their fathers were the guiding force behind their progressive and Western-style schooling, sometimes in the absence or even against the wishes of their mothers. For the generation of women who came to adulthood at the turn of the century the gulf between them and their mothers could be vast. This change was to become even more marked as the Turkish Republic was established and family pride came often to rest on the visible progress of the educated daughters (Durakbaşa 1993, Arat 1994). In Egypt, the generation who came to prominence in the revolutionary years after the First World War also tended to disassociate themselves from the habits and aspirations of their mothers and grandmothers and from uneducated rural populations, making cross-generational and cross-class alliances more difficult (Hatem 1992). The campaigns by the EFU in the 1920s and 1930s for female state education were part of a nationalist mission to provide Egyptian, rather than colonial, education for male and female citizens. The first secondary state school opened in 1925 in Cairo, strongly supported by Shaarawi and the EFU leadership, with more opening across the country in the decade that followed. These were attended mainly by middle-class girls, but many in the middle class and the elite still preferred to send their daughters to foreign-run schools. Aware that this was unlikely to produce integrated citizens (not least since it discouraged literacy in Arabic), several initiatives developed to persuade these families to support Egyptian-run education, including the private schools run by the campaigning educationalist Nabawiyah Musa, notable for their emphasis on academic achievement (Badran 1996).

Conclusion:
SELLING THE SELF

In the ways that they structured and narrated their accounts, all the women in this book demonstrate a self-consciousness about the project in which they were engaged. Their books did not come into being without the exercise of substantial determination, and they knew they were creating a marketable product. They also knew that they could not determine the reception of their work, and that they might come in for criticism on the grounds of authority, authenticity, and the sheer nerve displayed in writing for publication. Middle Eastern women's first-person narratives were inevitably read as representative of the generality of regional female experience. This was not just a misunderstanding: the writers themselves often specifically positioned their own stories as emblematic as they translated their societies for a foreign readership. This does not mean that their 'autoethnographic' accounts were inauthentic expressions of self or of culture made for export (Pratt 1992). Rather, the intrinsically interventionist nature of writing for the West could call forth the expression of self in ways that were both constraining and liberating. Bound by the flexible conventions of harem literature, the various and new discursive forms that emerged during the timeframe of our study (from the development of Western ethnographic conventions to the advent of modern Arabic life writing) posed different challenges for the generations of women in this collection.

For Middle Eastern writers, the individuated subject that authorises the narrative in the codes of Western autobiography was not necessarily present prior to the writing, nor was it straightforwardly brought into being by the adaptation of this generic form: often something new emerged, specific to the historical moment, to the local and international cultural competencies of the writer, and to the destination of the book. Seen this way, the bewildering combination of

demurral and self-aggrandisement and appeals to external validation that charac-
terise Middle Eastern women's self-presentation are not so much stylistic faults,
as they are essential clues about the complex ways in which gendered and
regional identities are produced. Similarly, the mix of self-depreciation and con-
descension in the writing of Western women reveals the different and related
power structures that framed their lives and their writing. The quest to gain
authority as a traveller/explorer or as an ethnographic observer whilst still maintaining a sufficiently appropriate gender identification was especially acute for
women who aligned themselves with the harem, that most over-determined of
gendered spaces.

The stereotypes and power relations that challenged and lent urgency to the
dialogue between the women in our sample continue to structure the experience
of women today. In the West and in the East we are heirs to the same stereotypes,
amended and revitalised by changing needs and situations. In magazines, films,
fiction and travel writing the image of the Middle Eastern woman – often still
signalled by the endlessly evocative veil – remains a matter of fascination. For
women from the Middle East, in the region and in the diaspora, the struggle to
intervene in political and cultural discourse structured by neo-Orientalism persists. For researchers of Western or Middle Eastern heritage dialogue continues
to be a priority, a pleasure and a challenge. For all these reasons, and others too
numerous to mention, the study of the dialogue carried out across the pages of
this book speaks to us, includes us and enjoins us to think.

NOTE

1   The diaries of Leyla Saz Hanımefendi were written in French and published in the
    Turkish press in the 1920s before being translated and reissued in English. Similarly
    the diaries of Hoda Shaarawi were written in Arabic but were not published in her
    lifetime, appearing in Arabic in 1981 and translated into English by Margot Badran in
    1986.

WORKS CITED

'Adalet' (1890a). 'A Voice from a Harem', *The Nineteenth Century*, vol. 28, August, pp.
    186–90.
—— (1890b). 'Life in the Harem', *The Nineteenth Century*, vol. 28, December, pp. 959–
    66.
Adak, Hülya (2004). 'An Epic for Peace', introduction to Edib, Halide. *Memoirs of Halidé
    Edib* (1926) (Piscataway, NJ, Gorgias Press).
Anderson, Bonnie S. and Zinsser, Judith P. (1988). *A History of Their Own: Women in
    Europe from Prehistory to the Present, vol. 2* (Harmondsworth, Penguin).

Arat, Zehra F. (1994). 'Turkish Women and the Republican Reconstruction of Tradition', in Göçek, Fatma Müge and Balaghi, Shiva (eds). *Reconstructing Gender in the Middle East: Tradition, Identity, and Power* (New York, Columbia University Press).

—— (1999). 'Educating the Daughters of the Republic', in Arat, Zehra F. (ed). *Deconstructing Images of 'The Turkish Woman'* (New York, Palgrave).

Badran, Margot (1996). *Feminists, Islam, and Nation* (Cairo, American University in Cairo Press).

—— and Cooke, Miriam (eds) (1990). *Opening the Gates. A Century of Arab Feminist Writing* (London, Virago).

Baron, Beth (1994). *The Women's Awakening in Egypt: Culture, Society and the Press* (New Haven, CT, Yale University Press).

Birkett, Dea (1989). *Spinsters Abroad: Victorian Lady Explorers* (Oxford, Blackwell).

Booth, Marilyn (2001). *May her Likes be Multiplied: Biography and Gender Politics in Egypt* (Berkeley, University of California Press).

Çelik, Zeyneb (1986). *The Remaking of Istanbul: Portrait of an Ottoman City in the Nineteenth Century* (Seattle, University of Washington Press).

Cherry, Deborah (2000). *Beyond the Frame: Feminism and Visual Culture, Britain 1850–1900* (London, Routledge).

Clifford, James (1986). 'Introduction: Partial Truths', in Clifford, James and Marcus, George E. (eds). *Writing Culture: The Poetics and Politics of Ethnography* (Berkeley, University of California Press).

Davidoff, Leonore and Hall, Catherine (1987). *Family Fortunes: Men and Women of the English Middle Class, 1780–1850* (Chicago, Chicago University Press).

Davis, Fanny (1986). *The Ottoman Lady: A Social History from 1718–1918* (New York, Greenwood Press).

Duben, Alan and Behar, Cem (1991). *Istanbul Households: Marriage, Family and Fertility, 1880–1940* (Cambridge, Cambridge University Press).

Durakbaşa, Ayşe (1993). 'Reappraisal of Halide Edib for a Critique of Turkish Modernization' (unpublished PhD thesis, Department of Sociology, University of Essex).

Edib, Halide Adıvar (1928). *The Turkish Ordeal: Being the Further Memoirs of Halidé Edib* (London, John Murray).

El Guindi, F. (1999). 'Veiling Resistance', *Fashion Theory*, vol. 3, no. 1, pp. 51–80.

Ellison, Grace (1915). *An Englishwoman in a Turkish Harem* (London, Methuen).

—— (1928). *Turkey To-day* (London, Hutchinson).

Fleischmann, Ellen L. (1999). 'The Other "Awakening": The Emergence of Women's Movements in the Modern Middle East, 1900–1940', in Meriwether and Tucker (1999).

Fortna, Benjamin (2002). *Imperial Classroom: Islam, the State and Education in the Late Ottoman Empire* (Oxford, Oxford University Press).

Frierson, Elizabeth B. (1995). 'Unimagined Communities: Woman and Education in the Late-Ottoman Empire', *Critical Matrix*, vol. 9, no. 2, pp. 55–90.

—— (2000a). 'Cheap and Easy: The Creation of Consumer Culture in Late Ottoman Society', in Quataert, Donald (ed). *Consumption Studies and the History of the Ottoman Empire 1550–1922* (New York, State University of New York Press).

—— (2000b). 'Mirrors Out, Mirrors In: Domestication and Rejection of the Foreign in Late-Ottoman Women's Magazines', in Ruggles (2000).

Garnett, Lucy M. (1890–1). *The Women of Turkey and their Folklore*, 2 vols (London, D.Nutt).

Geertz, Clifford (1984). *Local Knowledge: Further Essays in Interpretative Anthropology* (New York, Basic Books).

Gleadle, Kathryn (2001). *British Women in the Nineteenth Century* (Basingstoke, Palgrave).

Göçek, Fatma Müge (1996). *Rise of the Bourgeoisie, Demise of Empire: Ottoman Westernisation and Social Change* (New York, Oxford University Press).

Graham-Brown, Sarah (1988). *Images of Women: The Portrayal of Women in Photography of the Middle East 1860–1950* (London, Quartet).

Hatem, Mervat (1992). 'Through Each Others' Eyes: The Impact on the Colonial Encounter of the Images of Egyptians, Levantine-Egyptian, and European Women, 1862–1920', in Chaudhuri, Nupur and Strobel, Margaret (eds). *Western Women and Imperialism: Complicity and Resistance* (Bloomington, Indiana University Press).

Kandiyoti, Deniz (1991). *Women, Islam and the State* (Basingstoke, Macmillan).

Keddie, Nikki R. and Baron, Beth (eds) (1991). *Women in Middle Eastern History: Shifting Boundaries in Sex and Gender* (New Haven, CT, Yale University Press).

Kondo, Dorinne (1997). *About Face: Performing Race in Fashion and Theatre* (London, Routledge).

Lefebvre, Henri (1991). *The Production of Space*, trans. Donald Nicholson-Smith (Oxford, Blackwell).

Lewis, Reina (1996). *Gendering Orientalism: Race, Femininity and Representation* (London, Routledge).

—— (2004). *Rethinking Orientalism: Women, Travel and the Ottoman Harem* (London, I.B.Tauris; New Brunswick, NJ, Rutgers University Press).

Lowe, L. (1991): *Critical Terrains*, (Ithaca, NY, Cornell University Press).

Mabro, Judy (1991). *Veiled Half-Truths: Western Travellers' Perceptions of Middle Eastern Women* (London, I.B.Tauris).

MacKenzie, John M. (1995). *Orientalism: History, Theory and the Arts* (Manchester, Manchester University Press).

Massey, Doreen (1994). *Space, Place and Gender* (Cambridge, Polity Press).

Melman, Billie (1992). *Women's Orients: English Women and the Middle East, 1718–1918. Sexuality, Religion and Work* (Basingstoke, Macmillan).

Meriwether, Margaret L. and Tucker, Judith E. (eds) (1999). *A Social History of Women and Gender in the Modern Middle East* (Boulder, CO, Westview Press).

Mernissi, Fatima (1985). *Beyond the Veil: Male–Female Dynamics in Muslim Society*, 2nd edn (London, al Saqi Books).

Micklewright, Nancy (1986). 'Women's Dress in Nineteenth-Century Istanbul: Mirror of a Changing Society' (unpublished PhD thesis, University of Pennsylvania).

—— (2000). 'Public and Private for Ottoman Women of the Nineteenth Century', in Ruggles (2000).

Mills, Sara (1991). *Discourses of Difference: Women's Travel Writing and Colonialism* (London, Routledge).

Montagu, Lady Mary Wortley (1763). *Embassy to Constantinople: The Travels of Lady Mary Wortley Montagu* (1988) ed. Christopher Pick, intro. Dervla Murphy (London, Hutchinson).

Nelson, Cynthia (1996). *Doria Shafik, Egyptian Feminist: A Woman Apart* (Cairo, American University in Cairo Press).

Paker, Saliha (1991). 'Turkey', in Ostle, Robin (ed). *Modern Literature in the Near and Middle East 1850–1970* (London, Routledge).

Peirce, Leslie (1993). *The Imperial Harem: Women and Sovereignty in the Ottoman Empire* (Oxford, Oxford University Press).

Pratt, Mary Louise (1992). *Imperial Eyes: Travel Writing and Transculturation* (London, Routledge).

Quataert, Donald (1994). 'Part 4: The Age of Reforms 1812–1914', in Inalcik, Halil with Quataert, Donald. *An Economic and Social History of the Ottoman Empire, 1300–1914* (Cambridge, Cambridge University Press).

Ruggles, Dede Fairchild (ed) (2000). *Women, Patronage, and Self-Representation in Islamic Societies* (New York, State University of New York Press).

Said, Edward W. (1978). *Orientalism* (London, Routledge).

Schick, Irvin Cemil (2005). 'Introduction', to Melek Hanum. *Thirty Years in the Harem, or, The Autobiography of Melek Hanum, Wife of H.H. Kibrizli-Mehemet-Pasha* (1872) (Piscataway, NJ, Gorgias Press).

Suleri, Sara (1992). *The Rhetoric of English India* (Chicago, University of Chicago Press).

Tickner, Lisa (1987). *The Spectacle of Women: Imagery of the Suffrage Campaign 1907–1914* (London, Chatto and Windus).

Toledano, Ehud R. (1982). *The Ottoman Slave Trade and its Suppression: 1840–1890* (Princeton, NJ, Princeton University Press).

Tucker, Judith E. (1985). *Women in Nineteenth-Century Egypt* (Cambridge, Cambridge University Press).

Yeazell, Ruth Bernard (2000). *Harems of the Mind: Passages of Western Art and Literature* (New Haven, CT, Yale University Press).

Yeğenoğlu, Meyda (1998). *Colonial Fantasies: Towards a Feminist Reading of Orientalism* (Cambridge, Cambridge University Press).

Zonana, Joyce (1993). 'The Sultan and the Slave: Feminist Orientalism and the Structure of Jane Eyre', *Signs*, vol. 18, no. 3, Spring, pp. 592–617.

℘ VIEWING EACH OTHER: ℘

VISUAL DIALOGUES

Many of our sources, as was typical of harem literature and travelogue, promoted themselves as illustrated with photographs or drawings, which, as would have been expected, invariably included images of women. In some cases, pictures of veiled women appeared on the front cover, giving the clearest signal possible of what might be anticipated from the pages inside. Whether this was the authors' decision or that of their editors, it reveals the extent to which all involved understood the power of the visual image. A number of our authors took photographs themselves, which allowed them to establish a different, more collaborative relationship with the people they met.

Throughout the period covered in this book, the fascination with written accounts about and by women in the Middle East was paralleled by a virtually limitless market for paintings and photographs of them. The subject types that appear in paintings by Orientalist artists such as John Frederick Lewis, Jean-Léon Gérôme and Jean Auguste Dominique Ingres (harem women, women carrying water, peasant women) appear in the photographic record as well, indicating the degree to which this was a shared iconography. But the photographic record is considerably more complex than the stereotypical, oft-reproduced views of harem women would seem to indicate. The commercial photographers who worked in the region in the first part of our period produced thousands of views of the Middle East, including a range of diverse views of women. As photography became more accessible to the non-professional, this multiplicity of views increased. Moreover, at the same time as commercial photographers were employing local residents as models for tourist photos, the same photographers were being employed by the locals to produce their own portraits and other images.

The sixteen photographs included here range in date, subject matter and photographic format. The information provided by the images and their captions augments the main introduction and author introductions, as well as introducing new material that links to the themes outlined in the main introduction. The photographs also present the history of photography in the region in a period when photography was an important means by which new social identities were being explored and recorded.

1.

Hundreds of harem photographs were produced in the heyday of commercial tourist photography in the region, from about 1865 to 1890. In this period tourists' guidebooks directed them to photographers' shops where they selected photographs from catalogues that contained a myriad of choices, including monuments, street scenes, landscapes and types. They could also purchase ready-made albums. A survey of commercial harem photographs reveals that a particular set of elements came to be used to signify the harem, as it was constructed in the photographer's studio. This photograph, by the Istanbul firm of Sebah and Joaillier, displays many of those conventions. Textiles, such as the carpet on the floor, are used to define the space, which is furnished with a range of small decorative objects: inlaid table, water pipe and metal vessels of various kinds. The central element is the harem inhabitant (or three, in this case), dressed in appropriately exotic clothes and posed calmly, looking out of the picture.

With three models, this is a more elaborate construction than many harem photographs. Although the photographers' signature does not appear on the image, the backdrop and other props clearly identify this as the work of Sebah and Joaillier. Music, one of the standard activities of harem women, as they were described by Orientalist artists and some travellers, is evoked by the two women holding instruments. The costume worn by the women is a combination of the generic harem outfits often worn in such photographs, and, on the women on the right, the kind of dress (a beautiful embroidered silk *entari* (open robe) with matching *şalvar* (baggy trousers)) that would have been widely worn by wealthy women a few decades earlier.

In many harem photographs, the model at the centre of the scene is presented for examination by the viewer, sitting or reclining on furniture or the floor. This photograph, with a woman extended across the front of the picture frame, arm above her head and apparently relaxed by the tobacco and the music, engages the sexual imagination of the viewer in a much more explicit and direct way than images in which the harem inhabitant is presented in a more self-contained pose.

PLATE 1.
Untitled
The Pierre de Gigord Collection (96.R.14)
c.1880
Sebah and Joaillier
Courtesy Research Library, the Getty Research Institute, Los Angeles

2.

Excursions by harem women to the Sweet Waters of Asia, a park on the Eastern shores of the Bosphorus, were described by many Western visitors. The day-long excursion generally included a picnic, music and time for relaxing and enjoying the pleasant surroundings. Numerous groups would make the trip on any given day (a carriage is just visible in the distance on the right), and vendors would gather there to sell *semit*s (sesame bread rings) and other snacks to the visitors.

The Sweet Waters was especially well known as a gathering place for women and children, but Ottoman men also went there. Some sources mention it as a good site for clandestine (or imaginary) flirtations. It was popular with Western visitors who wanted an opportunity to see Ottoman women. Ottoman women's excursions to the Sweet Waters were a common choice of subject for painters and photographers. There are numerous views in the work of various photographers of women relaxing in the park, of the carriages which conveyed them from their homes to the Sweet Waters, of women travelling in carriages to the park, and related activities.

The circumstances surrounding the production of this particular view of women at the Sweet Waters are not exactly clear. The labelling of the photograph (visible on another print) indicates that it was intended for sale, and, indeed, Kargopoulo was a successful commercial photographer in Istanbul. The image is carefully composed, with the group of women centred in the foreground, other visitors to the park behind them, and hills and architectural elements framing the scene. The central group, six women (on the basis of their dress two of these appear to be servants) and one child, are arranged symmetrically and look directly at the photographer. While they could all be paid models, it is also possible that they agreed to interrupt their holiday to pose for the photographer, whilst discreetly attired in their outdoor dress.

PLATE 2.
Sweet Waters of Asia
The Pierre de Gigord Collection (96.R.14)
1865
Basil Kargopoulo
Courtesy Research Library, the Getty Research Institute, Los Angeles

3.

The figure of the Middle Eastern woman carrying water, although not necessarily as sexualised as that of the harem woman, was a common image in Orientalist painting and photography, as was the Egyptian peasant or *fellah*. This photograph, by the prolific commercial photographer Pascal Sebah, combines two well-known tropes to show Egyptian women differently, in their everyday lives as homemakers and mothers.

Sebah's photograph is one of about 520 images of Egypt that appear in the travel albums of Annie Lady Brassey (see Extract 6). Assembled between 1872 and 1887 to compliment the objects collected for her private museum, seven of the seventy albums contain images of Egypt, mostly from several well-known commercial photographers.

Before the introduction of the Kodak Brownie camera in 1888, tourists purchased the work of commercial photographers to document their travels, either as single images, or as sets already arranged in albums. Active in cities across the globe, wherever there was a market, commercial photographers typically offered their customers hundreds or even thousands of different images. Sebah, like others, provided an extensive repertoire whose diverse presentation of the people and places of the Middle East has been overlooked by late twentieth-century cultural critics, who tend to overstate the currency and circulation of images of languorous harem women and bare-breasted odalisques (see Alloula 1987, and critique by Micklewright 2003). Though such photographs obviously existed and have survived, nude and overtly sexualised images appeared very rarely in the travel albums of British visitors to the region, suggesting that they were neither widely collected nor retained. Lady Brassey, for example, preferred images showing Egyptian women in their everyday activities. Travel books, while generally including illustrations of harem women, usually depict them in relatively chaste and clothed poses. In many cases, such as the images of women in the harem seen in our book, there is little in the photographic image itself that would provide sexual excitement if it were not for their identification as harem women. The frisson of the image is achieved when the represented figure is located in the harem – by settings, accoutrements, pose, caption – thus stimulating the imaginations of viewers well versed in the sexualised stereotypes of Orientalist harem fantasies. In this plate, the figure, though not located in a harem, would have been imbued with some harem associations and with the religious associations attached to the Arab peasantry as inhabitants of the lands of the bible.

Works cited
Alloula, Malek (1987). *The Colonial Harem* (Manchester, Manchester University Press).
Micklewright, Nancy (2003). *A Victorian Traveler in the Middle East. The Photography and Travel Writing of Annie Lady Brassey* (Aldershot, Ashgate).

PLATE 3.
Fellaheen, Cairo
Brassey Albums, Volume 32, p.12
1870s
Pascal Sebah
Courtesy of The Huntington Library

4.

The education of girls and young women was an important political and social issue for much of the nineteenth century in the Ottoman context. During the course of the century, access to education for girls increased, and large numbers of schools were created. While girls in elite families would always have had access to tutors in the subjects their families deemed important (and those subjects shifted over time), by the end of the century, the girls of other classes were able to attend public or private primary schools. The curriculum in those schools, no longer in the control of the religious elite, would have included a variety of subjects. Although many schools were, and had long been, organised by different ethnic or religious communities, the new schools increasingly sought a student body drawn from across the entire population.

This photograph shows two young girls holding their books, dressed in elaborate Western-style dresses, facing the camera with determination if not enthusiasm. It is one of a number of similar views of school children included in the albums presented in 1893 to the American government by Sultan Abdülhamit. The Ottoman gift, fifty-one albums containing 1,824 photographs, was intended as a propaganda tool to convey a very particular view of the Ottoman Empire to the American government. A nearly identical set of albums was presented to the British government a year later, in 1894. The albums contain views of important architectural monuments, scenes of the modern neighbourhoods of Istanbul, schools, and new military installations, hospitals, and the accoutrements of the palace – yachts, horses, palace furnishings, and so on. The firm of Abdullah Frères supplied the majority of the photographs, although other photographers' work is also included.

The albums provide a wealth of documentation about the empire in the last years of the nineteenth century, as well as a clear indication of how the sultan wished to portray his empire to other world leaders. They are also important evidence of the sophistication with which the Ottoman government was able to use photography for their own purposes.

PLATE 4.
Students of the Molla Gürani Preparatory School
Abdul Hamid II Collection 9511.19
Before 1893
Abdullah Frères
Courtesy of the Library of Congress, Prints and Photographs Division

5.

Elizabeth Cooper illustrated her book *The Women of Egypt* with a variety of photographs, some the work of commercial photographers and others that she took. In her text, she refers to the circumstances surrounding her photography, both in general terms, for example when she mentions looking out for an opportunity of getting a snapshot, and in regards to specific images. The woman depicted in this photograph came to Cooper's house looking for work, and agreed to pose for a photograph in exchange for a day's wages.

Although they are hard to track in the economic record and appear infrequently in the work of commercial photographers, women worked outside their own homes in a variety of occupations. Sewing was one task which could be performed on an itinerant basis; other work included day labour in large households, buying and selling inexpensive trinkets on a door-to-door basis, or selling produce or home-produced goods on the street. An important social and economic development beginning at about the same time as this photograph was taken was the opening up of a variety of jobs (in nursing, education, shops and offices) to middle-class women.

Cooper's photographs are obviously snapshots taken with a simple camera. Their composition is less professional, and the subjects are often more relaxed than they might be in a formal studio setting. Cooper's desire to take photographs would have influenced the nature of her interaction with the people around her, as she sought an alternative way of participating in and recording what she saw. The camera also provided her with a reason to be present, or to watch longer in the hopes of taking more pictures. In deciding to use a camera as another means of recording her impressions of what went on around her, Cooper joined the ranks of other amateur ethnographers in this period who wanted to create accurate, scientific accounts of the people and places they visited and whose writing blurs the distinction between travel accounts and more extensively researched studies.

By the time that Cooper was in Egypt, taking photographs had become a much simpler business. The Kodak box camera, developed in the 1880s, was widely available and easy to use, giving individuals much greater control of the kind of pictures they could obtain since they were no longer limited to what commercial photographers produced. As Cooper's pictures demonstrate, the interest of visitors in producing their own pictures also led them to interact in a more dynamic and physical way with the people they wished to photograph.

PLATE 5.
The Sewing Lady
Elizabeth Cooper, *The Women of Egypt*, 1914
Photograph by the author

6.

Grace Ellison, the English feminist and author whose 1915 book, *An English Women in a Turkish Harem*, is extracted below, stayed in the home of her friend Makboulé Hanoum for several months during her visit to Istanbul in 1913. Her visit provided Ellison with first-hand knowledge of harem life, which she deployed in both written and visual form in her book. Travelling with a Kodak camera, she attempted to photograph some of the people she came to know during her stay, often with limited success (see Extract 10). In addition to her own photographs, she used commercial portrait photographs in her book. The inclusion of both commercial and amateur photographs in Ellison's book continues a trend that existed right from the beginning of photographically illustrated books in the mid-nineteenth century, and which allowed the author (or whoever was responsible for choosing the book illustrations) to provide multiple viewpoints in the visual material.

It is not clear whether the photograph reproduced here is the work of a commercial photographer. While the wooden *mashrabiyya* screen behind the two seated figures is the sort of background prop typically used in a commercial studio, its rather haphazard placement in front of a window and the casual pose of the two women would seem to suggest a less formal setting for the photograph. Grace Ellison looks relaxed in the borrowed clothes she wears (as her writing indicates, cross-cultural dressing was a slightly illicit pleasure of her visit), and directs her gaze to the black woman seated next to her. Miss 'Chocolate' (the name given to her by Ellison), who was the household slave assigned to look after Ellison for the duration of her stay, does not return Ellison's gaze, but looks off into the distance. She is also dressed for the street and poses in a more tentative way for the photographer. It is entirely possible that this photograph is the first in which she had appeared, especially if it was produced in a commercial studio.

Ellison takes pains in her book to challenge Western stereotypes concerning Ottoman domestic structures, including slavery. While she clearly appreciates the luxury and lavish hospitality which is possible with a large household staff, she is careful to point out differences between the Ottoman and American systems of slavery. The joint portrait of herself and her slave companion included in the book makes the same point using visual means.

PLATE 6.
Miss 'Chocolate'
Grace Ellison, *An English Woman in a Turkish Harem*, 1915
Photographer unknown

7.

As the caption of this photograph indicates, it was taken in Istanbul by Ellison to illustrate her series of articles in the *Daily Telegraph*. Deciding that it would not be believable to the British public as an authentic image of a harem, the photograph was rejected by the newspaper's editors. The image was then used by Ellison as an illustration in Zeyneb Hanoum's book, which Ellison edited.

If this photograph of a domestic interior is compared with the harem photograph in Plate 1, it is easy to understand why Ellison's photograph was rejected. By the early twentieth century, the British public had at least five decades' worth of Orientalist paintings and photographs on hand to confirm a particular view of the harem. As discussed earlier, a long-standing series of pictorial conventions existed to convey the idea of the harem: textiles covering the floor, and often also the walls and furniture, the inclusion of a specific series of decorative objects such as a water pipe, musical instruments and metal vessels, and furnishings consisting of a low couch and/or cushions on the floor.

The room pictured here, crowded with its chairs, small tables, fussy be-ribboned lamp, numerous framed photographs, and other things, would have looked much too similar to the sitting rooms of *Daily Telegraph* readers to be believable as a Turkish harem. However, we know from a variety of historical sources that the Ottoman elite, especially in Istanbul, began to adopt European furnishings for use in their own homes beginning in the mid-nineteenth century. For one thing, as Ottoman women started wearing closely tailored European-style dresses and corsets, instead of the traditional loosely fitting robes, they were no longer comfortable sitting on low, soft couches. Chairs with firm seats and backs were a much better match for their newly re-fitted, more structured costumes. And, as Ottomans began accumulating photographs of their friends and family, they, along with their European counterparts, would have wished to display these keepsakes.

This photograph, and many others not included here, tell us a great deal about Ottoman interaction with foreign material culture. The movement of goods followed the movement of people, literature, theatre and other manifestations of popular culture, with the Ottomans combining aspects of the old and the new in the continuing re-creation of their living spaces. It was apparently easier for the Ottomans to let go of their old-style rooms than it was for British newspaper editors to let go of their old ideas of the Turkish harem!

PLATE 7.
A Corner of a Turkish Harem of Today
Zeyneb Hanoum, *A Turkish Woman's European Impressions*, 1913
Photograph by Grace Ellison

8.

Zeyneb Hanoum's book (Extract 8) reproduces a series of letters written by Zeyneb Hanoum, her sister and Grace Ellison in the years 1906–12, and is illustrated with a set of photographs which play an essential role in confirming the authorial position Zeyneb Hanoum claims in her writing. While many of the illustrations are portraits of the people whose stories are told in the book, others, like this one, convey a different kind of information.

While the room pictured here was Zeyneb Hanoum's drawing room, in which she presumably spent a great deal of time, for the purposes of the book the room functions like a stage upon which Zeyneb Hanoum is creating the identity she inhabits as an author. The photograph's caption reiterates this function of the image by reminding the viewer that Zeyneb, an Oriental woman, is located, for the moment at least, in a space far from her place of origin. She has carefully filled the room with objects recreating a sense of Orient, but it is a hybrid, modern kind of Orient. Some of the same elements that are used in earlier commercial photographs (Plate 1) to signal 'harem' appear in Zeyneb Hanoum's room: for example the use of textiles on floor, walls and furniture; the inclusion of musical instruments; and even the small inlaid table at Zeyneb Hanoum's side. These harem signifiers are overlaid with European-style furniture (piano, couch, tables, benches), as well as a few embroidered textiles (the gold embroidered velvet covering the couch, and the embroidered towels covering the two benches), which are clearly Turkish in origin, a photomontage on the piano, and a series of knick-knacks and framed pictures. Each object would have been chosen to communicate something about the room's inhabitant, as was her own pose and costume.

Although Zeyneb Hanoum used her room to reinforce her own identity, in fact this room would not have been so different from many other drawing rooms of the period. Most of its furnishings were acquired in Paris, and would have been the same furnishings that others were buying for their own homes. She uses some carefully chosen objects to signal her authenticity, including her own body, draped in a costume of indeterminate origin and cradling an 'exotic' musical instrument. At the same time, she signals modernity by her very presence in Paris and by other objects in the room such as the piano. In the end, we must conclude that her identity, like many of her compatriots, is as hybrid as the decor of her room, an idiosyncratic combination of tradition and modernity, of 'Europe' and the 'Orient'.

PLATE 8.
Zeyneb in her Western Drawing Room, Paris
Zeyneb Hanoum, *A Turkish Woman's European Impressions*, 1913
Photographer unknown

9.

These two photographs are part of an intriguing group of photographs, a series of fifty-nine snapshot-type images, probably made using a simple box camera of the kind generally available from the 1880s. The appearance of these new, simple cameras had a dramatic impact on the ways in which photography could be used, because many more people had access to making pictures and thus to taking control of how they presented themselves and their lives photographically. This group of photographs is the work of an enthusiastic amateur photographer, probably one of the family that is the subject of these photos, and were all taken within a short time of each other – the friends and family members who appear over and over in the photographs remain the same age, and even wear the same clothes in some cases (and on the basis of the clothing in the photographs, they can be dated to 1890–1910).

In one carefully posed view, we see six people, nicely dressed in reasonably fashionable European clothes, seated together drinking tea. Pouring tea is generally the prerogative of the hostess, which is perhaps how the woman seated to the right should be identified. The group is in a shallow space, grouped on and around a couch against a wall between two windows. The wall behind the couch is draped with fabric, with two framed images decorating it.

In a second photograph, we see family members in another pose for the camera. The setting and four of the people are the same, with everyone again arranged around the couch. But this time they are all wearing completely bizarre clothes: the men have on turbans, robes and some kind of draped cloth garment under the robes, with regular belts holding their outfits together. The women are all swathed in what look like lightweight bedcovers or tablecloths. The three older women have scarf-type arrangements on their hair, but not regular *yaşmaks*. In addition to the quasi-exotic dress, stock elements of harem scenes have been included in the image, including a water pipe and small coffee cups.

These photographs remind us again of the way in which different visions, different constructions, of the same subjects coexisted, and collided, in this case, most probably in the studios of commercial photographers in Istanbul. When Ottoman residents of Istanbul visited commercial photographers to have their portraits made they would have been able to examine at their leisure the repertoire of imagery available for sale to tourists, including, of course, harem scenes. Here is one response to those commercial tourist photographs, produced by people who were clearly completely familiar with the standard harem scene and its individual components.

PLATE 9A, 9B.
Family Photographs
The Pierre de Gigord Collection (96.R.14)
c.1890–1910
Photographer unknown
Courtesy Research Library, the Getty Research Institute, Los Angeles

10.

This image shows Musbah Haidar, author of *Arabesque*, as a child of nine or ten. Sitting on her uncle's lap and pictured with her brothers, she is dressed as a wealthy English child would have been. Her dress signals the customary use of Western dress for indoor wear by elite women and girls. Haidar's male relatives are also wearing Western dress (combined with their headgear), including what look like tennis shoes. Her family engaged in sports as leisure at home all the time, and even had a tennis court on their estate. Their enjoyment of athletic activities is a sharp contrast to the images of indolent harem life prevalent in some European literature, painting and photography.

Daughter of a British mother and an Arab royal father, Haidar grew up in an elite, international and politically involved household. Her family situation was unique in Istanbul, setting her apart from other elite young women, a fact reflected in the unusual headdress she wore (the *samade* and *aighal*, a close-fitting cap with elbow-length veil hanging down her back), which made her immediately recognisable in any social setting. Her presence in the photograph among the men of her family illustrates her proximity to political power. Accustomed to being around political discussion at home, and increasingly aware of her own multiple identities, she became an astute political observer and perceptive social commentator.

PLATE 10.
Uncle with his Nephews and Niece
Musbah Haidar, *Arabesque*, 1944 (photograph c.1917)
Photographer unknown

11.

In this photograph, Huda Shaarawi (see Extract 12) is seated at a desk with a book, writing. Dressed in European clothing, she is not veiled. Obviously the work of a professional photographer, as with most portraiture, the presentation of the subject would have been the result of an active collaboration on the part of the sitter and the photographer. Portraiture always involves at least an implicit acknowledgement of the subject's complicity in displaying herself for the viewer, and portraits of women have often emphasised their wealth, beauty or social position. In this case, although presenting herself for our examination, Shaarawi is choosing to foreground her modernity and her intellectual activities (i.e. her writing). Moreover, by positioning herself at a desk she rejects the photographic opportunity that a standing pose would have provided to display her feminine body and clothing more fully to the viewer. Similarly, she does not choose to include her children in the photograph, again rejecting the more traditional mode of female presentation as a wife or mother.

The copy of Shaarawi's portrait reproduced here was inscribed by Shaarawi to Ruth Woodsmall, in whose book the photograph appeared. For Woodsmall to be able to include a signed photograph of one of Egypt's most prominent intellectuals in her book on Muslim women would have been an important indication of Woodsmall's own authority as well as proof of the privileged access to Muslim women which she enjoyed, and which contributed to the truth value of her work. The fact that Shaarawi presented Woodsmall with this signed photograph of herself corroborates the visual evidence of the image, which is that it was intended as a public, professional presentation of a well-known figure.

Woodsmall's possession of Shaarawi's portrait is also representative of the circulation of photographs between European and Egyptian or Turkish women that had been taking place since at least the 1870s when Annie Lady Brassey mentioned that she had been given photographs of the family of the wealthy Egyptian woman that she was visiting. As we know from Brassey and other writers, and the photographic record itself, portraits were popular among the elite of Istanbul and Cairo as they were in England. Exchanging photographs was evidence of a social relationship, perhaps particularly desirable in situations when language was sometimes a barrier to easy communication.

PLATE 11.
Madame Hoda Sharawi [sic], A Moslem Leader of Egypt
Ruth Woodsmall, *Moslem Women Enter a New World*, 1936
Photographer unknown

12.

This photograph presents a large group of women gathered in a public square in Istanbul in 1918. The size of the group and the fact that it is all women, rather than women with their families, indicates that it is an intentionally organised demonstration, not a chance gathering. This reading is strengthened by the fact that some of the women are holding flags and they are all guarded or held back by several military officials. Men are visible at the edges of the group of women, standing in higher places in order to see.

With the defeat of Germany and its Allies at the end of the First World War, Istanbul was occupied by British troops, and it is the entrance of those troops into the city in 1918 that is the subject of this photograph. The British occupation, and the plan by France, Britain and the United States to dismantle and divide the former Ottoman territories created intense anxiety and anger among the Turks, and led of course to the Turkish War of Independence and creation of the republic.

This photograph is a visual indication of the extent to which women had become involved in the political life of their society. Many women had been active during the war, working as nurses or in other ways to support the soldiers or to help the families of those left behind, and their social activism was accompanied by increasing political involvement. As in Egypt, when the crisis of British control of the government spurred Egyptian women to work for nationalist causes, Turkish women here are taking part in a nationalist demonstration. Feminist issues have been set aside for the moment.

The women are nearly all wearing the *çarşaf*, which had become the standard street uniform at this point, covering their dresses with a long skirt, a cape-like upper garment and a head covering. Almost everyone has thrown back the face veil to expose their faces, and almost everyone is wearing gloves – an indication of the fact that by this point gloves, one of the first elements of European fashion to be adopted by Ottoman women in the 1820s or 1830s – had by now become naturalised as a part of modest dress for Turkish women.

PLATE 12.
Turkish Women in Nineteen Eighteen
Halide Adıvar Edib, *Memoirs of Halide Edib*, 1926
Photographer unknown

13.

The subject of this photograph seems ordinary enough: a group of women, all wearing white uniform jackets, sit around two large tables in a classroom, busily engaged in learning how to make hats. But an analysis of this image in comparison to others included here reveals the dramatic and far-reaching social changes that have occurred in Turkey and have led us to this classroom full of women learning the skills of millinery.

First of all, fashion. None of the women who are pictured outdoors in our photographs are wearing hats. (See for example, Plates 1, 2, 5, 6 and 12). They all wear some form of *hijab*, or veil. Naturally the exact shape, colour and fabric of the veil varied with period, place, class and ethnic identity, but hats were not part of Ottoman women's fashion repertoire until after the founding of the Turkish Republic in 1923. In the early years of the republic, as part of his extensive modernisation efforts, Atatürk actively discouraged the wearing of the veil. In the same years, Turkish women began bobbing their hair, as Woodsmall mentions in her text (Extract 14), and as can be seen in this photograph. As the photograph of the 1932 Turkish beauty queen (Plate 15) reveals, bobbed hair and a stylish hat were emblematic of a new image of modern Turkish women.

Plate 4, dated before 1893, shows two young girls who were students at a private elementary school. While education for girls became an important issue in the late nineteenth and early twentieth century, women's education did not become a focus of attention until a bit later. However, with the dramatic social upheavals and population displacements of the First World War and the Turkish War of Independence, the importance of women's education became clear, and more opportunities were developed. While some women attended university, vocational training also emerged as an important means for women to learn new skills, such as millinery, sewing and nutrition.

One reason that vocational training for women became so significant is that, increasingly, women began to enter the labour force. While some women had always worked, as for example, the 'sewing lady' pictured in Plate 5, by the twentieth century labour patterns had shifted. Banks, government offices, shops and small factories all needed employees, and many women wished or needed to work. The millinery class depicted here was one avenue to possible employment.

PLATE 13.
Lifting of the Veil in Turkey Has Made Millinery Classes Popular
Ruth Woodsmall, *Moslem Women Enter a New World*, 1936
Photographer unknown

14.

While educational reform had been an aspect of the Tanzimat reforms of the nineteenth-century Ottoman government, the education of girls was a touchstone of the Kemalist policies of the Turkish Republic. As Plate 4, and the writing of Edib (Extract 13), for example, reminds us, girls had begun attending school in the late Ottoman period, but a much greater emphasis on public education for girls emerged in the first decades of the twentieth century.

This illustration of hundreds of girls on Istanbul Sports Day from Woodsmall's book of 1936 can be paired with the photograph of the two schoolgirls from the Abdülhamit albums of the early 1890s. Both images were aimed at foreign audiences; and both used photographic evidence of progressive female education to communicate the existence of a regional modernity. Yet modernity is inscribed differently on the bodies of these two sets of schoolgirls.

The two girls from the earlier photograph (and many others in the same albums) wear dresses inspired by European fashion, but which are still extremely modest. Their long hair is either curled or neatly braided. In these photographs, the girls face the camera shyly or resolutely, arranged in small groups of two or three, obviously at the behest of the photographer. They represent a wide variety of schools, nearly all of which were parochial in their administration. The students' choice of school would have been determined by their families, based primarily on religious and ethnic factors.

The girls in Plate 14 are all wearing identical fitness uniforms, mandated by the schools that were government run. Education in these public schools was compulsory, and the physical appearance of the girls was closely monitored through the wearing of uniforms, and other means. Physical fitness and personal hygiene were important symbols of modernity for girls and women, and were taught in the schools. In this photograph hundreds of girls are arranged in a neat formation, all positioned identically. The rather tentative photographic control of a few Hamidian schoolgirls of Plate 4 is here solidified to the absolute control of the population of an entire school (or schools). In a similar way the government of the Turkish Republic exerted its control over a new educational system for girls, one in which the students modelled the ideals of the new era.

PLATE 14.
Sports Day
Ruth Woodsmall, *Moslem Women Enter a New World*, 1936
Photographer unknown

15.

With this photograph we come full circle from Plate 1, to a radically different image of the Turkish woman depicted for public consumption. Just how dramatically this image has changed is revealed by a comparison of the two photographs. Some aspects of the photographs are similar: in each case the photograph is intended to convey a particular view of the subjects, who are on display to a potentially very large audience. However, in the case of the harem women pictured in Plate 1, the photograph perpetuated a popular (if inaccurate) stereotype for a commercial market. Plate 15, on the other hand, attempts to substitute a quite different view of Turkish women for the old stereotype and thus represents an explicit propaganda effort from the new Turkish Republic, then in the midst of redefining itself.

In 1932 a Turkish contestant won a European beauty contest. A few decades earlier, Ottoman women would not have appeared unveiled in public – so the entry of Turkish women in beauty contests was a significant departure from tradition. Yet in the 1930s the beauty contest had explicit support from Atatürk, and the press promoted beauty as a sign of civilisation that put Turkey on a par with other modern countries. The republican ideal of female beauty was very different from earlier periods. According to the contemporary press, young girls previously 'displayed a fat and clumsy body with big breasts and fleshly legs … Today's regime requires a healthy and agile body, not a sloppy, clumsy one.' (quoted in Durakbaşa 1999: 154). Being healthy and fit – and thus beautiful – had become a civic responsibility.

Bayan (meaning Ms) Keriman, the Turkish beauty queen, wears modern, stylish clothes, bobbed hair and a hat, and faces the camera confidently. Her win in the beauty contest had been a matter of great national pride. In her photograph she represents the new Turkish woman, an emblem of Turkish modernity. The languid, graceful and beautiful harem inhabitant of the Ottoman period had disappeared, to be replaced by this fit, fashionable and happy modern woman.

Works cited

Durakbaşa, Ayşe (1999). 'Kemalism as Identity Politics in Turkey', in Arat, Zehra F. (ed). *Deconstructing Images of 'The Turkish Woman'* (New York, Palgrave).

PLATE 15.
The Turkish Beauty Queen: Winner of the European Contest
Ruth Woodsmall, *Moslem Women Enter a New World*, 1936
Photographer unknown

16.

Sebah and Joaillier, along with many other photographers, ran successful commercial studios over a long period in Istanbul. Their clients included tourists, resident foreigners, Ottomans, and the government, for whom they produced portraits, documentary photographs, and the full repertoire of tourist images. Harem scenes were a staple of the tourist catalogues, although, as we have mentioned elsewhere, the prevalence of these images in the nineteenth century was much less than we imagine. In addition, we tend to assume that all commercial harem photographs complied with stereotypical poses and compositions, an example of which is the photograph in Plate 1.

When we have the opportunity to look beyond what have become the canonical versions of harem scenes most often published in photo histories, we find some surprising images, like this one. We see all of the set elements that signified the harem – textiles, water pipe, table, and so on – but here they are turned on their head, just as our model is. Instead of a sensuous presentation of a beautifully dressed, languorous woman, we are presented with a woman looking at us upside-down, with a mischievous smile on her face. The picture is silly, even a bit ridiculous.

This photograph, as well as the snapshots of Plate 9, are important reminders that the trope of the harem as it appeared in photographs was fluid, even slippery. In this case the photographer and the model are having fun, playing with the standard version of the harem scene photograph. In the family snapshots in Plate 9, a sophisticated Ottoman family group dresses up in a comic re-staging of the 'traditional' harem. As we see in these examples, Ottoman subjects and photographers were perfectly willing to re-create the harem stereotype of Orientalist literature and art for a commercial market, but they were just as capable of turning that stereotypical image upside down when it suited them.

PLATE 16 (AND FRONT COVER).
Untitled
The Pierre de Gigord Collection (96.R.14)
c.1880
Sebah and Joaillier
Courtesy Research Library, the Getty Research Institute, Los Angeles

1.
JULIA PARDOE (1806–62)

೫ THE CITY OF THE SULTAN; ೩

AND THE DOMESTIC MANNERS
OF THE TURKS IN 1836

Henry Colburn, London
Two volumes, 1837

Julia Pardoe, the earliest of the writers included in this collection, was a prolific author, whose first book was published when she was fourteen. The
second daughter of a military family, she travelled extensively in Europe
with her family, often for health reasons. Her numerous books fall into two
categories: travel writing, which makes up the first part of her writing
career; and historical works, which were part biography, part historical epic,
and were very popular in her lifetime. In her own day, her work was
regarded as charming and lively, based on extensive observation and careful
research.

For *City of the Sultan*, her second attempt at travel writing, Pardoe travelled to Istanbul with her father, arriving there 30 December 1835 and
remaining for about six months. Although (as she mentions in the Preface)
they had originally intended to visit Greece and Egypt in addition to Istanbul, in the end they limited their travels to the city and its environs. Pardoe
acknowledges her disappointment at not travelling further but writes that
she hopes to have given her readers, 'a more just and complete insight into
Turkish domestic life, than they have hitherto been enabled to obtain' (p. x).

Pardoe carried letters of introduction to local residents (as did all travellers in this period, if they hoped to be able to meet anyone at all), and she
made it her business to interact with as wide as possible a social network to
gather the material she needed for her book. The table of contents reveals
that each chapter combines a narrative account of her specific activities and
encounters in the city with the presentation of information relevant to those
activities. For example, in Chapter IX, she describes visits to several different cemeteries around Constantinople, as well as burial practices and beliefs
surrounding death among different religious groups. Though she describes
her focus as 'domestic life', she in fact wrote a reasonably complex social
history of the city, touching on religious practices, consumer habits, festivals, ethnic divisions within the social fabric of the city, and activities and
habits of the court.

The passages selected here address a range of issues, many of which are
reprised by later authors. In the first passage, from Chapter IV, Pardoe
introduces the reader to Pera, the part of the city inhabited by Europeans,

both those who had arrived recently and those who had been living in the city for centuries. Pera was the setting against which most visitors to the city wrote, and it is important to understand its significance. Pardoe is sensitive to the subtle distinctions that existed among the various groups living there, describing the differences in housing, dress and social custom that distinguish Greek from Armenian, for example.

In the second passage, excerpted from Chapter V, Pardoe visits a Greek family, staying for dinner and going with them to a ball. That her father is with her in the family setting points out the different domestic custom among ethnic groups in the city (the sexes would have been segregated in a Muslim family). Pardoe's account of the evening reads as if Jane Austen had visited Istanbul, transferring her own finely tuned class sensibility to the local context. Pardoe's extreme awareness of vulgarity, in dress particularly, was shared by many English women writers and operates as a form of feminine-coded Orientalist criticism.

Next, a series of short excerpts from different chapters illustrates Pardoe's authorial voice and particularly her claim of privileged access, her opinion on the state of Ottoman women, and her positioning of herself vis-à-vis what she is describing.

The longest single passage from Pardoe's book is from Chapter VIII, when the author visits a public bath. She frames her description with references to earlier accounts of the bath – 'fables which have been advanced as facts' – specifically mentioning the writing of Lady Mary Wortley Montagu (1763). But even in her detailed inventory of the bath experience, the sensory overload is such that she finds herself doubting even her own 'reality'. Pardoe's account is important, not just for the evidence of intertextuality it provides, but because it was written in the same period during which extremely well-known paintings of the Turkish bath were being created by the French artist Ingres, and others. Thanks in large part to those paintings, and accounts of male writers, the bath emerged as one of central motifs of Orientalist representation, an element of Middle Eastern life that was hugely overvalued in Western fantasies of segregated life because it allowed such opportunities for fantasy. Pardoe's account, in struggling against this temptation, provides a different view. (In Extract 4, Annie Harvey's description of a visit to the bath published thirty-five years later provides another woman's view of this intriguing yet commonplace aspect of Turkish life.)

Finally, in a passage excerpted from Chapter XXII, Pardoe describes her daring visit to the mosque of St Sophia during evening prayer. She dressed as a Muslim man and in her account emphasised the danger of her adventure, both for herself and her companion, as well as the magnificence and mystery of what she witnessed in the mosque. Other authors included in this volume (Harvey and Grace Ellison, Extract 10) occasionally dressed as Muslim women, but Pardoe's heroic exploits prefigure the much-lauded excursions popularised by later male Orientalists, such as Sir Richard Burton.

Pardoe's work, presented in the form of a personal travel account, is thorough in her focus on the lives of women in early nineteenth-century Istanbul. A comparison of her work to that of Ruth Woodsmall, who wrote in the 1930s (Extract 14), is instructive in understanding how the expectations of research and the presentation of information have changed over the course of a century, and particularly, how the roles of women authors have expanded in that time.

ಬಂ ಄

CHAPTER IV

Merchants of Galata—Palaces of Pera—Picturesque style of Building—The Perotes—Social Subjects—Greeks, European and Schismatic—Ambassadorial Residences—Entrée of the Embassies—The Carnival—Soirées Dansantes—The Austrian Minister—Madame la Baronne—The Russian Minister—Madame de Boutenieff—The Masked Ball—Russian Supremacy—The Prussian Plenipotentiary—The Sardinian Chargé d'Affaires—Diplomacy Unhoused—Society of Pera.

Neither Frank nor Christian is allowed to inhabit the "City of the Faithful;" and the faubourg of Pera, situated on the opposite side of the port, is consequently the head-quarters of the *élite* of European society. Galata, which skirts the shore of the Bosphorus at the base of the hill on which Pera is built, numbers among its inhabitants many very respectable merchants, whose avocations demand their continual presence; but Pera is the dwelling-place of the beau-monde—the seat of fashion—the St. James's of the capital. Here every thing social is *en magnifique:* the residences attached to the different Legations glory in the imposing designations of "palaces"—the gloomy *magazins* of the Parisian *modistes* are as dear and as dirty as can be desired—all the *employés* of diplomacy throng the narrow, steep, and ill-paved streets, while the fair Greeks look down upon them from their bay-windows, projecting far beyond the façade of the building; and the bright-eyed Armenians peer from their lattices "all-seeing, but unseen." The quaintly-coloured houses, looking like tenements of painted paste-board, appear as though a touch would make them meet, and are picturesque beyond description, as they advance and recede, setting all external order, regularity, and proportion, at defiance.

In my rapid definition of European society, I must not omit to mention that the Perotes, or natives of Pera, consider themselves as much Franks as though they had been born and nurtured on the banks of the Thames or the Seine; […]

[…]

After the residence of a few weeks, you can readily determine the origin of every female whom you encounter in the streets of Pera. The fair Perotes, indeed, wear the bonnet, the cloak, and the shawl, which form the walking garb of the genuine European gentlewoman; but, nevertheless, it is impossible not to

distinguish them at a glance; an insurmountable taste for bright colours, an inde-
scribable peculiarity in the adjustment of their toilette, at once mark the Perote;
while the dark-eyed Greek is known by her wide-spreading turban of gauze or
velvet, over which is flung a lace veil, which, falling low upon the back and
shoulders, leaves the face almost entirely uncovered.

[…]

As soon as we were comfortably established round the tandour, a servant
brought in a tray on which were arranged a large cut glass vase, filled with a delicate preserve slightly impregnated with *attar de rose*, a range of crystal goblets
of water, and a silver boat, whose oars were gilt tea-spoons. One of these the lady
of the house immersed in the preserve, and offered to me; after which she
replaced the spoon in the boat, and I then accepted a draught of water presented
by the same hospitable hand; the whole ceremony was next gone through with
my father; and, the tray being dismissed, a second servant entered with coffee,
served in little porcelain cups of divers patterns, without saucers, but deposited in
stands of fillagreed silver, shaped nearly like the egg-cups of Europe.

After this, we were left to our charcoal and cushions until six o'clock; save
that my father smoked a costly pipe with a mouth-piece of the colour and almost
of the bulk of a lemon, in company of our host, a tall, majestic-looking man,
upwards of six feet in height, whose black calpac differed from those of the
Armenians in its superiority of size and globular form. […]

[…]

A Greek dinner is a most elaborate business; rendered still more lengthy by
the fact that the knives, forks, and other appliances which European example has
introduced, are as yet rather hindrances than auxiliaries to most of those who
have adopted them.

[…]

The very aspect of the repast was *appetissant* […] and a delicious dessert
crowned the hospitable meal, at whose termination we hurried to our several
apartments, and were soon immersed in all the mysteries of the toilet.

[…]

Among the ladies [at the ball], the same graduated scale of fashion was per-
ceptible: the elder matrons wore the dark head-dress and unbecoming vest of by-
gone years, half concealed by the warm wrapping pelisse—the next in age had
mingled the Greek and European costumes into one heterogeneous mass, each
heightening and widening the absurdity of the other; and had overlaid the inconsistent medley with a profusion of diamonds absolutely dazzling; while the
younger ladies presented precisely the same appearance as the belles of a third
rate country town in England: their petticoats too short, their heads too high, their
sleeves too elaborate, and their whole persons over-dressed.

I have already remarked on the fondness of the Greek ladies for gay colours; a
taste peculiarly, and almost painfully, apparent in a ball-room; such bright blues,
deep pinks, and glowing scarlets I never before saw collected together; and this
glaring taste extends even to their jewels, which they mix in the most extraordi-

nary manner; their only care being to heap upon their persons every ornament that they can contrive to wear.

[…]

Chapter VI

Difficulty of Obtaining an Insight into Turkish Character—Inconvenience of Interpreters—Errors of Travellers—Ignorance of Resident Europeans—Fables and Fable-mongers—Turkey, Local and Moral—Absence of Capital Crime—Police of Constantinople—Quiet Streets—Sedate Mirth—Practical Philosophy of the Turks—National Emulation—Impossibility of Revolution—Mahmoud and his People—Unpopularity of the Sultan—Russian Interference—Vanity of the Turks—Russian Gold—Tenderness of the Turks to Animals—Penalty for Destroying a Dog—The English Sportsman—Fondness of the Turks for Children—Anecdote of the Reiss Effendi—Adopted Children—Love of the Musselmauns for their Mothers—Turkish Indifference to Death—Their Burial-places—Fasts—The Turks in the Mosque—Contempt of the Natives for Europeans—Freedom of the Turkish Women—Inviolability of the Harem—Domestic Economy of the Harem—Turkish Slaves—Anecdote of a Slave of Achmet Pasha—Cleanliness of Turkish Houses—The Real Romance of the East.

There is, perhaps, no country under heaven where it is more difficult for an European to obtain a full and perfect insight into the national character, than in Turkey. The extreme application, and the length of time necessary to the acquirement of the two leading languages, which bear scarcely any affinity to those of Europe, render the task one of utter hopelessness to the traveller. […]

[…]

[…] Hence arise most of those errors relative to the feelings and affairs of the East, that have so long misled the public mind in Europe; and, woman as I am, I cannot but deplore a fact which I may be deficient in the power to remedy. The repercussion of public opinion must be wrought by a skilful and a powerful hand[.] They are no lady-fingers which can grasp a pen potent enough to overthrow the impressions and prejudices that have covered reams of paper, and spread scores of misconceptions. But, nevertheless, like the mouse in the fable, I may myself succeed in breaking away a few of the meshes that imprison the lion; and, as I was peculiarly situated during my residence in the East, and enjoyed advantages and opportunities denied to the generality of travellers, who, as far as the natives are concerned, pass their time in Turkey "unknowing and unknown," I trust that my attempt to refute the errors of some of my predecessors, and to advance opinions, as well as to adduce facts, according to my own experience, may not entail on me the imputation of presumption.

[…]

[…] It is also a well-attested fact that the entrée of native houses, and intimacy with native families, are not only extremely difficult, but in most cases impossible to Europeans; and hence the cause of the tissue of fables which, like those of Scheherazade, have created genii and enchanters *ab ovo usque ad mala*, in every account of the East. The European mind has become so imbued with ideas of Oriental mysteriousness, mysticism, and magnificence, and it has been so long accustomed to pillow its faith on the marvels and metaphors of tourists, that it is to be doubted whether it will willingly cast off its old associations, and suffer itself to be undeceived.

To the eye, Turkey is, indeed, all that has been described, gorgeous, glowing, and magnificent; the very position of its capital seems to claim for it the proud title of the "Queen of Cities." Throned on its seven hills, mirrored in the blue beauty of the Bosphorus—that glorious strait which links the land-locked harbour of Stamboul to the mouth of the Euxine—uniting two divisions of the earth in its golden grasp—lording it over the classic and dusky mountains of Asia, and the laughing shores of Europe—the imagination cannot picture a site or scene of more perfect beauty. But the *morale* of the Turkish empire is less perfect than its terrestrial position; it possesses the best conducted people with the worst conducted government—ministers accessible to bribes—public functionaries practised in chicane—a court without consistency, and a population without energy.

All these things are, however, on the surface, and cannot, consequently, escape the notice of any observant traveller. It is the reverse of the picture that has been so frequently overlooked and neglected. And yet who that regards, with unprejudiced eyes, the moral state of Turkey, can fail to be struck by the absence of capital crime, the contented and even proud feelings of the lower ranks, and the absence of all assumption and haughtiness among the higher?

[…]

If, as we are all prone to believe, freedom be happiness, then are the Turkish women the happiest, for they are certainly the freest individuals in the Empire. It is the fashion in Europe to pity the women of the East; but it is ignorance of their real position alone which can engender so misplaced an exhibition of sentiment. I have already stated that they are permitted to expostulate, to urge, even to insist on any point wherein they may feel an interest; nor does an Osmanli husband ever resent the expressions of his wife; it is, on the contrary, part and parcel of his philosophy to bear the storm of words unmoved; and the most emphatic and passionate oration of the inmates of his harem seldom produces more than the trite "*Bakalum*—we shall see."

It is also a fact that though a Turk has an undoubted right to enter the apartments of his wives at all hours, it is a privilege of which he very rarely, I may almost say, never avails himself. One room in the harem is appropriated to the master of the house, and therein he awaits the appearance of the individual with whom he wishes to converse, and who is summoned to his presence by a slave. Should he, on passing to his apartment, see slippers at the foot of the stairs, he cannot, under any pretence, intrude himself in the harem: it is a liberty that every woman in the Empire would resent. When guests are on a visit of some days, he sends a slave forward to announce his approach, and thus gives them time and opportunity to withdraw.

A Turkish woman consults no pleasure save her own when she wishes to walk or drive, or even to pass a short time with a friend: she adjusts her *yashmac* and *feridjhe*, summons her slave, who prepares her *boksha*, or bundle, neatly arranged in a muslin handkerchief; and, on the entrance of the husband, his inquiries are answered by the intelligence that the Hanoum[*] Effendi is gone to spend a week at the harem of so and so. Should he be suspicious of the fact, he takes steps to ascertain that she is really there; but the idea of controlling her in the fancy, or of making it subject of reproach on her return, is perfectly out of the question.

The instances are rare in which a Turk, save among the higher ranks, becomes the husband of two wives. He usually marries a woman of his own rank; after which, should he, either from whim, or for family reasons, resolve on increasing his establishment, he purchases slaves from Circassia and Georgia, who are termed *Odaliques;* and who, however they may succeed in superseding the Buyuk Hanoum, or head of the harem, in his affections, are, nevertheless, subordinate persons in the household; bound to obey her bidding, to pay her the greatest respect, and to look up to her as a superior. Thus a Turkish lady constantly prefers the introduction of half a dozen *Odaliques* into her harem to that of a second wife; as it precludes the possibility of any inconvenient assumption of power on the part of her companions, who must, under all circumstances, continue subservient to her authority.

The almost total absence of education among Turkish women, and the consequently limited range of their ideas, is another cause of that quiet, careless, indolent happiness that they enjoy; their sensibilities have never been awakened, and their feelings and habits are comparatively unexacting: they have no factitious wants, growing out of excessive mental refinement; and they do not, therefore, torment themselves with the myriad anxieties, and doubts, and chimeras, which would darken and depress the spirit of more highly-gifted females. Give her shawls, and diamonds, a spacious mansion in Stamboul, and a sunny palace on the Bosphorus, and a Turkish wife is the very type of happiness; amused with trifles, careless of all save the passing hour; a woman in person, but a child at heart.

[...]

I am quite conscious that more than one lady-reader will lay down my volume without regret, when she discovers how matter-of-fact are many of its contents. The very term "Oriental" implies to European ears the concentration of romance; and I was long in the East ere I could divest myself of the same feeling. It would have been easy for me to have continued the illusion, for Oriental habits lend

---

[*] Signifying mistress, or lady.

themselves greatly to the deceit, when the looker-on is satisfied with glancing over the surface of things; but with a conscientious chronicler this does not suffice; and, consequently, I rather sought to be instructed than to be amused, and preferred the veracious to the entertaining.

[…]

I would not remove one fold of the graceful drapery which veils the time-hallowed statue of Eastern power and beauty; but I cannot refrain from plucking away the trash and tinsel that ignorance and bad taste have hung about it; and which belong as little to the masterpiece they desecrate, as the votive offerings of bigotry and superstition form a part of one of Raphaël's divine Madonnas, because they are appended to her shrine.

[…]

How comparative is happiness! I never lay my head upon my pillow, but I am grateful to Providence that I was not born in Turkey; while the fair Osmanlis in their turn pity the Frank women with a depth of sentiment almost ludicrous. They can imagine no slavery comparable with our's—we take so much trouble to attain such slight ends—we run about from country to country, to see sights which we must regret when we leave them—we are so blent with all the anxieties and cares of our male relations—we expose ourselves to danger, and brave difficulties suited only to men—we have to contend with such trials and temptations, from our constant contact with the opposite sex—in short, they regard us as slaves, buying our comparative liberty at a price so mighty, that they are unable to estimate its extent—and then, the hardship of wearing our faces uncovered, and exposing them to the sun and wind, when we might veil them comfortably with a *yashmac!* Not a day passes in which they have commerce with a Frank, but they return thanks to Allah that they are not European women!

[…]

CHAPTER VIII

Bath-room of Scodra Pasha—Fondness of the Eastern Women for the Bath—The Outer Hall—The Proprietress—Female Groupes—The Cooling-room—The Great Hall—The Fountains—The Bathing Women—The Dinner—Apology for the Turkish Ladies.

The first bath-room which I saw in the country was that of Scodra Pasha; and, had I been inclined so to do, I might doubtlessly have woven a pretty fiction on the subject, without actually visiting one of these extraordinary establishments. But too much has already been written on inference by Eastern tourists, and I have no wish to add to the number of fables which have been advanced as facts, by suffering imagination to usurp the office of vision. Such being the case, I resolved to visit a public bath in company with a female acquaintance, and not only become a spectator but an actor in the scene, if I found the arrangement feasible.

The bath-room of the Pasha, or rather of his family, was a domed cabinet, lined with marble, moderately heated, and entered from the loveliest little boudoir imaginable, where a sofa of brocaded silk, piled with cushions of gold tissue, offered the means of repose after the exhaustion of bathing. But I had seen it tenanted only by a Greek lady and myself, and half a score of slaves, who were all occupied in attendance upon us; and I felt at once that, under such circumstances, I could form no adequate idea of what is understood by a Turkish bath; the terrestrial paradise of Eastern women, where politics, social and national, scandal, marriage, and every other subject under heaven, within the capacity of uneducated but quick-witted females, is discussed: and where ample revenge is taken for the quiet and seclusion of the harem, in the noise, and hurry, and excitement, of a crowd.

Having passed through a small entrance-court, we entered an extensive hall, paved with white marble, and surrounded by a double tier of projecting galleries, supported by pillars; the lower range being raised about three feet from the floor. These galleries were covered with rich carpets, or mattresses, overlaid with chintz or crimson shag, and crowded with cushions; the spaces between the pillars were slightly partitioned off to the height of a few inches; and, when we entered, the whole of the boxes, if I may so call them, were occupied, save the one which had been reserved for us.

In the centre of the hall, a large and handsome fountain of white marble, pouring its waters into four ample scallop shells, whence they fell again into a large basin with the prettiest and most soothing sound imaginable, was surrounded by four sofas of the same material, on one of which, a young and lovely woman, lay pillowed on several costly shawls, nursing her infant.

When I had established myself comfortably among my cushions, I found plenty of amusement for the first half hour in looking about me; and a more singular scene I never beheld. On the left hand of the door of entrance, sat the proprietress of the baths, a beautiful woman of about forty, in a dark turban, and a straight dress of flowered cotton, girt round the waist with a cachemire shawl; her chemisette of silk gauze was richly trimmed—her gold snuff-box lay on the sofa beside her—her amber-headed pipe rested against a cushion—and she was amusing herself by winding silk from a small ebony distaff, and taking a prominent part in the conversation; while immediately behind her squatted a negro slave-girl of twelve or thirteen years of age, grinning from ear to ear, and rolling the whites of her large eyes in extacy at all that was going forward.

The boxes presented the oddest appearance in the world—some of the ladies had returned from the bathing-hall, and were reclining luxuriously upon their sofas, rolled from head to foot in fine white linen, in many instances embroidered and fringed with gold, with their fine hair falling about their shoulders, which their slaves, not quite so closely covered as their mistresses, were drying, combing, perfuming, and plaiting, with the greatest care. Others were preparing for the bath, and laying aside their dresses, or rather suffering them to be laid aside, for few of them extended a hand to assist themselves—while the latest comers were removing their *yashmacs* and cloaks, and exchanging greetings with their acquaintance.

As I had previously resolved to visit every part of the establishment, I followed the example of my companion, who had already undergone the fatigue of an Oriental bath, and exchanged my morning dress for a linen wrapper, and loosened my hair: and then, conducted by the Greek waiting-maid who had accompanied me, I walked barefooted across the cold marble floor to a door at the opposite extremity of the hall, and, on crossing the threshold, found myself in the cooling-room, where groups of ladies were sitting, or lying listlessly on their sofas, enveloped in their white linen wrappers, or preparing for their return to the colder region whence I had just made my escape.

This second room was filled with hot air, to me, indeed, most oppressively so; but I soon discovered that it was, nevertheless, a *cooling-room;* when, after having traversed it, and dipped my feet some half dozen times in the little channels of warm water that intersected the floor, I entered the great bathing-place of the establishment—the extensive octagon hall in which all those who do not chuse, or who cannot afford, to pay for a separate apartment, avail themselves, as they find opportunities, of the eight fountains which it contains.

For the first few moments, I was bewildered; the heavy, dense, sulphureous vapour that filled the place, and almost suffocated me—the wild, shrill cries of the slaves pealing through the reverberating domes of the bathing-halls, enough to awaken the very marble with which they were lined—the subdued laughter, and whispered conversation of their mistresses murmuring along in an undercurrent of sound—the sight of nearly three hundred women only partially dressed, and that in fine linen so perfectly saturated with vapour, that it revealed the whole outline of the figure—the busy slaves, passing and repassing, naked from the waist upwards, and with their arms folded upon their bosoms, balancing on their heads piles of fringed or embroidered napkins—groups of lovely girls, laughing, chatting, and refreshing themselves with sweetmeats, sherbet, and lemonade—parties of playful children, apparently quite indifferent to the dense atmosphere which made me struggle for breath—and, to crown all, the sudden bursting forth of a chorus of voices into one of the wildest and shrillest of Turkish melodies, that was caught up and flung back by the echoes of the vast hall, making a din worthy of a saturnalia of demons—all combined to form a picture, like the illusory semblance of a phantasmagoria, almost leaving me in doubt whether that on which I looked were indeed reality, or the mere creation of a distempered brain.

Beside every fountain knelt, or sat, several ladies, attended by their slaves, in all the various stages of the operation; each intent upon her own arrangements, and regardless of the passers-by; nor did half a dozen of them turn their heads even to look at the English stranger, as we passed on to the small inner cabinet that had been retained for us.

[…]

I should be unjust did I not declare that I witnessed none of that unnecessary and wanton exposure described by Lady M. W. Montague. Either the fair Ambassadress was present at a peculiar ceremony, or the Turkish ladies have become more delicate and fastidious in their ideas of propriety.

[…]

During a visit that I made to a Turkish family, with whom I had become acquainted, the conversation turned on the difficulty of obtaining a Firman to see the mosques […]

[…]

[…] I could not refrain from expressing the bitterness of my disappointment, with an emphasis which convinced my Musselmaun hearers that I was sincere.

Hours passed away, and other subjects had succeeded to this most interesting one, when, as the evening closed in, I remarked that —— Bey, the eldest son of the house, was carrying on a very energetic *sotto voce* conversation with his venerable father; and I was not a little astonished when he ultimately informed me, in his imperfect French, that there was one method of visiting the mosques, if I had nerve to attempt it, which would probably prove successful; and that, in the event of my resolving to run the risk, he was himself so convinced of its practicability, that he would accompany me, with the consent of his father, attended by the old Kiära, or House-steward. […]

[…]

What European traveller, possessed of the least spirit of adventure, would refuse to encounter danger in order to stand beneath the dome of St. Sophia? And, above all, what wandering Giaour could resist the temptation of entering a mosque during High Prayer?

[…]

I at once understood that the attempt must be made in a Turkish dress; but this fact was of trifling importance, as no costume in the world lends itself more readily or more conveniently to the purposes of disguise. After having deliberately weighed the chances for and against detection, I resolved to run the risk; and accordingly I stained my eyebrows with some of the dye common in the harem; concealed my female attire beneath a magnificent pelisse, lined with sables, which fastened from my chin to my feet; pulled a *fez* low upon my brow; and, preceded by a servant with a lantern, attended by the Bey, and followed by the Kiära and a pipe-bearer, at half-past ten o'clock I sallied forth on my adventurous errand.

[…]

"If we escape from St. Sophia unsuspected," said my chivalrous friend, "we will then make another bold attempt; we will visit the mosque of Sultan Achmet; and as this is a high festival, if you risk the adventure, you will have done what no Infidel has ever yet dared to do; but I forewarn you that, should you be discovered, and fail to make your escape on the instant, you will be torn to pieces."

This assertion somewhat staggered me, and for an instant my woman-spirit quailed; I contented myself, however, with briefly replying: "When we leave St. Sophia, we will talk of this," and continued to walk beside him in silence. At length we entered the spacious court of the mosque, and as the servants stooped to withdraw my shoes, the Bey murmured in my ear: "Be firm, or you are lost!"—and making a strong effort to subdue the feeling of mingled awe and fear, which was rapidly stealing over me, I pulled the *fèz* deeper upon my eye-brows, and obeyed.

On passing the threshold, I found myself in a covered peristyle, whose gigantic columns of granite are partially sunk in the wall of which they form a part; the floor was covered with fine matting, and the coloured lamps, which were suspended in festoons from the lofty ceiling, shed a broad light on all the surrounding objects. In most of the recesses formed by the pillars, beggars were crouched down, holding in front of them their little metal basins, to receive the *paras* of the charitable; while servants lounged to and fro, or squatted in groups upon the matting, awaiting the egress of their employers. As I looked around me, our own attendant moved forward, and raising the curtain which veiled a double door of bronze, situated at mid-length of the peristyle, I involuntarily shrank back before the blaze of light that burst upon me.

Far as the eye could reach upwards, circles of coloured fire, appearing as if suspended in mid-air, designed the form of the stupendous dome; while beneath, devices of every shape and colour were formed by myriads of lamps of various hues: the Imperial closet, situated opposite to the pulpit, was one blaze of refulgence, and its gilded lattices flashed back the brilliancy, till it looked like a gigantic meteor!

As I stood a few paces within the doorway, I could not distinguish the limits of the edifice—I looked forward, upward—to the right hand, and to the left—but I could only take in a given space, covered with human beings, kneeling in regular lines, and at a certain signal bowing their turbaned heads to the earth, as if one soul and one impulse animated the whole congregation; while the shrill chanting of the choir pealed through the vast pile, and died away in lengthened cadences among the tall dark pillars which support it.

And this was St. Sophia! To me it seemed like a creation of enchantment—the light—the ringing voices—the mysterious extent, which baffled the earnestness of my gaze—the ten thousand turbaned Moslems, all kneeling with their faces turned towards Mecca, and at intervals laying their foreheads to the earth—the bright and various colours of the dresses—and the rich and glowing tints of the carpets that veiled the marble floor—all conspired to form a scene of such unearthly magnificence, that I felt as though there could be no reality in what I looked on, but that, at some sudden signal, the towering columns would fail to support the vault of light above them, and all would become void.

2.
Sophia Lane Poole (1804–91)
🔊 The Englishwoman in Egypt ☙
Letters from Cairo

Charles Knight and Co., London
Two volumes, 1844 (second edition 1845)

Sophia Lane Poole, brother of Edward W. Lane, the well-known British Ori-entalist and expert on Egypt, when presenting her book, *The Englishwoman in Egypt: Letters from Cairo*, employed a strategy familiar in the work of other women travel writers of this period. On the one hand, she claimed authority based on her three years of living in Egypt (she stayed for seven years altogether), and her privileged, gender-based access to Egyptian women. On the other hand, she was careful to explain in the Preface to her book that her decision to visit Egypt was motivated primarily by her desire to see her brother, which would have been a more socially acceptable reason for making such a trip than intellectual ambition or mere curiosity about a foreign land. She also explained that it was originally her brother's idea that she write about her experiences, that he allowed her to use his own notes in her work, and, finally, that he himself selected which of her writings would be submitted for publication. He was even listed as a co-author on the title page of her book. Presenting her accomplishments in the context of his already well-known work simultaneously augmented and undermined the validity of her own (female) authorial voice.

In the first letter excerpted here, Poole writes, 'I have endeavoured to divest myself of prejudice; but altogether to lose sight of our English stand-ards of propriety has been impossible', providing a clear insight into how she is attempting to report on what she sees. She then moves directly into a discussion of the Egyptian women's custom of veiling, introducing it as a social principle that can be traced back to Biblical times. Her attempt to make a link between ancient Egypt and modern Egyptian life reveals the extent to which she considers modern life there as a continuation of or link to the ancient past, a common assumption on the part of many European vis-itors to Egypt. At other points in her writing, she interrupts her description of contemporary events with references to other sources, for example scenes from ancient tomb paintings or *The Thousand and One Nights*, indicating both her access to expert knowledge and the extent to which her impressions of what she is witnessing have been shaped by the expectations that ensued from her reading.

Lane Poole devoted a great deal of time in the book to her own visits to various harems. The material excerpted here is taken from an extended account of her visit to the imperial harem of Muhammad Ali on the occasion of the marriage of his daughter Zeyneb Hanım. Sumptuously organised as a major state event, the wedding provided an opportunity for the Egyptian ruler to invite many guests, including Europeans. Lane Poole attended with her friend Mrs Lieder, the wife of a British missionary in Cairo. The two women were among those chosen to spend a few days in the harem, but the wedding festivities went on for much longer and they travelled back and forth between their homes and the harem several times. Lane Poole was thus able to report both on the events in the harem and, based on her own observations and those of her brother, what went on outside in the streets and public gathering places.

Her careful description of the celebrations, of the elaborate dress worn by different categories of harem women (slaves, brides, royal women, other guests), the various entertainments, meals and her report on the wedding gifts she was shown, tell the reader a great deal, both about Lane Poole's own interests in what she was seeing and about Egyptian society at a specific moment in mid-century. In 1845 the Egyptian ruling elite, while continuing to employ local traditions of gift giving, was also exploring European patterns of consumption and purchasing specific, expensive goods, such as French china. Though harem women still wore traditional dress and jewels, we know from other sources that they were beginning to incorporate individual items of European manufacture such as gloves or parasols into their costume. Likewise, the entertainment and ceremonies associated with the wedding included both traditional elements, such as parades, fireworks, harem dancers, as well as newly imported entertainment, for example, a performance by European actors that Western consuls, European residents and the ulema were taken to see. Although Lane Poole does not necessarily intend to do so, she also provides extremely interesting information about the extent to which English visitors were welcomed by the Cairo elite in the years before England's political and economic involvement in Egypt became more explicit and more entrenched.

Sophia Lane Poole was the middle-class daughter of a country clergyman, and in England would never have had access to the wealthy and elite society that she was able to visit in Cairo. Her privileged access in Cairo, based on her gender and nationality, allowed her the opportunity to observe a range of Egyptian harems. Perhaps because of her own awareness of the fine gradations of social status, she is an acute observer of status in the Egyptian context, always careful to establish her own high rank vis-à-vis other visitors, but also to delineate the social hierarchies among the women whose homes she visited.

ဆ   ෬

PREFACE

The desire of shortening the period of my separation from a beloved brother, was the first and strongest motive that induced me to think of accompanying him to the country in which I am now writing, and which he was preparing to visit for the third time. An eager curiosity, mainly excited by his own publications, greatly increased this desire; and little persuasion on his part was necessary to draw me to a decision; but the idea was no sooner formed than he found numerous arguments in its favour. The opportunities I might enjoy of obtaining an insight into the mode of life of the higher classes of the ladies in this country, and of seeing many things highly interesting in themselves, and rendered more so by their being accessible only to a lady, suggested to him the idea that I might both gratify my own curiosity and collect much information of a novel and interesting nature, which he proposed I should embody in a series of familiar letters to a friend. To encourage me to attempt this latter object, he placed at my disposal a large collection of his own unpublished notes, that I might extract from them, and insert in my letters whatever I might think fit; and in order that I might record my impressions and observations with less restraint than I should experience if always feeling that I was writing for the press, he promised me that he would select those letters which he should esteem suitable for publication, and mark them to be copied. The present selection has been made by him; and I fear the reader may think that affection has sometimes biassed his judgment; but am encouraged to hope for their favourable reception, for the sake of the more solid matter with which they are interspersed, from the notes of one to whom Egypt has become almost as familiar as England.

SOPHIA POOLE.

LETTER I

January, 1845.

After a residence of nearly three years in an Eastern country, in the habit of frequent and familiar intercourse with the ladies of the higher and middle classes of its population, you will probably think me able to convey some general ideas of their moral and social state. To do this, I find to be a task of extreme difficulty; though my opportunities of observation have been such as, I believe, few Englishwomen have enjoyed. In examining the effects of the peculiar position in which females are here placed, I have endeavoured to divest myself of prejudice; but altogether to lose sight of our English standards of propriety has been impossible; and as every state of society in the world has its defects, to avoid comparisons would be unnatural.

[…]

One thing that puzzles me among many others is this: that the main principle of the constitution of society prevailing now among all the Muslim nations, and even among Eastern Christians, seems almost to receive a sanction from the practice of most of those persons whom from our childhood we have learned to regard with the greatest reverence.

In the mention of the veil we trace the Hareem system to the time of Abraham; but to what period its origin is to be referred is, I believe, doubtful. In Abraham's time it seems to have been similar to the system which has hitherto prevailed among the Arabs of the desert, and to have been much less strict that that which commonly obtains among the Arabs and other Muslims established in fixed abodes, in cities, houses, and villages. Rebekah covered not her face in the presence of Abraham's servant, the "eldest servant of his house;" but when she came before the man who was to be her husband, "she took a veil and covered herself. In like manner, the women of the Bedawees, in general, are often careless of veiling the face before servants, and persons with whom they are familiar; and many of them have no scruple in appearing unveiled before strangers.

[…]

LETTER VII

Tuesday, Dec. 16th, 1845.
Having received this evening a third invitation to witness the festivities on the occasion of the wedding of Zeyneb Hánum, and finding that they will commence on Thursday next, I must now devote my whole attention to the task of giving you a description of the novel scenes of which I am about to be a spectator.

Zeyneb Hánum is the youngest daughter of the Páshá, and her affianced husband is Kamil Páshá, lately Kámil Bey, a sort of aide-de-camp and private secretary to Mohammad 'Alee. The Sultán conferred upon him the rank of Páshá when he heard that he was proposed as the future son-in-law of the viceroy of Egypt.

It has occured to me that I should do well to give you a kind of diary of events during the eighth day of the coming fête; for, excepting in such a form, I could not hope to give you a correct idea of an entertainment in every respect strange in its character to our notions of a bridal festival.

Dec. 18th.—About eleven o'clock in the morning I and my kind friend Mrs. Lieder were on our way to the palace in the citadel, in which the festivities were celebrated. We had many interruptions on the way; for several regiments were marching in procession to the Ezbekeeyeh, in which stands the palace of the bride, and to which she is to descend on the eighth day of the entertainment. These regiments were preceded and followed by very respectable military bands. One procession attended a large figure of an elephant, mounted and led by Indians in effigy: the whole (elephant and Indians) to be blown up on the eighth evening, and thus form the finale of the fireworks, which are to be exhibited during every evening in the Ezbekeeyeh. After the elephant, a large ark was drawn, on wheels, attended by musicians and drummers making a deafening noise. Whether the ark is to share the same fate as the elephant, time will show.

The route to the citadel is marked by innumerable new glass lanterns, each containing ten lamps, mostly hung on ropes extending across the streets. When we began to ascend the hill upon which the citadel stands, we found that on either side of the new road temporary pillars, of various fanciful styles of architecture, had been erected, painted in bright colours, and gaily hung with lamps. The principal features of the architecture of the arches of the gateway, and other entrances of the palace were hung with lamps, and the court presented a very picturesque spectacle. Here were festoons of lamps, and many hung fruit-like from the trees; while the whole court was covered over with a red and white awning, producing a subdued light under a bright sunny sky. The garden was strikingly pretty, with the addition of bright lamps hung in festoons wherever they could be so arranged.

After gaining the last entrance, we passed the Hareem curtain, that impassable barrier to men, excepting the lord of the citadel, or any necessary employé; and we found the usual army of eunuchs, and female black slaves, looking out for the arrival of the European ladies, who had been invited. Passing through the lower saloon, we found the white slaves of many Hareems, gorgeously attired. With a full tide of these to accompany us, we proceeded up the staircase, and being directed, on reaching the upper saloon, what course to pursue, we made our way through a dense crowd towards the seat of honour.

There we found the bride seated, raised upon cushions of pale pink satin, splendidly embroidered with gold. Her young brother, Mohammad 'Alee Bey, was seated by her side. On her left hand stood her Highness Nezleh Hánum, the eldest daughter of the Páshá, showering small gold and silver coins among the crowd. This circumstance accounted for the presence of, perhaps, three thousand persons, many of whom seemed very eager in striving to obtain the bounty. The coins thrown in the Hareem were pieces of five and three piastres, and silver paras mixed up with barley and salt. The reason for throwing the barley I could not learn, but the salt was intended to prevent the influence of the evil eye.

On the right hand of the bride sat the mother of Sa'eed Páshá, and Nezleh Hánum appointed me a seat next to her, and Mrs. Lieder beyond me. When the shower of gold and silver ceased, the bride left the saloon, oppressed with the weight of gold and jewels, and supported by four slaves. The moment she rose, we were almost deafened by the sounds of many tambourines, and the shrill quavering cries of joy called zagháreet. The expression of her countenance was very sad, and gave rise to a report that she disliked her affianced husband. With her the crowd partially dispersed, and Nezleh Hánum sat down, and as she received her own pipe, ordered that pipes should be offered to us; but we both declined them. I was surprised by the splendour of the mouthpieces. That which was offered to me was beautifully set with diamonds, and the stem was rich with lacing of gold thread. Her Highness' pipe was the most costly I have ever seen. It was of the same description as ours; but the amber mouthpiece, splendid with diamonds, was as rich as art could make it; and the lower part of the pipe was beautifully decorated with a profusion of diamonds. The little tray in which the pipe-bowl rested was of exquisite enamel.

Coffee was served to us in the elegant manner of the high Hareem. A silver chafing-dish, suspended by chains, and containing live charcoal, upon which boiled the coffee in a tiny pot, was carried by a slave magnificently attired; while another bore the small round silver tray, with the little coffee-cups and their exquisite jewelled stands. All were costly; but those handed to her Highness were most splendid. The zarf, or stand of the coffee-cup, was spirally inlaid with diamonds, on a ground of delicate enamel.

The saloons are built in the form of an oblong cross: the whole is matted, and the ends are furnished with divans of pale dove-coloured satin, massively embroidered with gold, and finished with a fringe of gold twist about a foot deep. The walls and ceilings throughout are painted in good taste: the arabesque and gilding of the ceilings are chaste and beautiful; and though the paintings, representing generally Turkish summer palaces, are evidences that the artists employed had no knowledge of perspective, yet they are so well arranged to represent a sort of pannelled wall, the gilding above and on either side of these paintings is delicately and tastefully applied, and owing to the age of the decorations, the prevailing colour is a pale bluish grey, so that the whole is harmonious, or, to use an artistic term, all is in good keeping.

There is a lower saloon of the same form, and these may be considered as saloons of reception. The private apartments are entered from the corners of the center of the cross, thus making up a rectangular figure. One compartment of the cross is occupied by the grand staircase; and the best situation for seeing all that took place was in the compartment opposite to the staircase in each saloon.

The views from the window of that palace are beautiful and highly interesting. During the time of extreme confusion occasioned by showers of gold, I turned towards a window and was much impressed by the contrast the view presented with the scene within. The cemetery of Káïd Bey lay beneath, at some little distance in the desert. Never did the majestic beauty of that group of mosques and tombs so charm me, and never did the deep solitude and solemn stillness ever reigning among those monuments seem to me so deep and still. The city lay stretched to the left; and beyond it the green carpet spread by the inundation bordering upon the land of Goshen—the view is most imposing.

I have not yet told you of the magnificent dress of the bride. She wore a yelek and trowsers of red Cashmere embroidered with gold in a florid style, equally gorgeous and elegant, and interspersed with pearls, with a saltah (or jacket) of red velvet lined with ermine, and almost covered with embroidery of gold and jewels. Her head-dress was absolutely grotesque, and of prodigious width: a pale yellow crape kerchief was bound across her forehead, and so arranged on either side as to resemble wings. On the front of this band, and on the spreading blue tassel of her tarboosh, were arranged a variety of diamond sprays, a tiara, and a crescent and star, the whole being surmounted by a small yellow bird, resembling the bird of Paradise excepting in colour, from which spread two long and curving tail feathers, one bending down on the right, and the other on the left. She wore also a superb diamond necklace, of which I will have more to say hereafter. Her hair was partly braided, partly dishevelled, and turned up and mingled with the blue tassel, without any regard to form or effect. Her girdle was a Cashmere shawl embroidered and fringed with gold. Nezleh Hánum was attired in a yelek and trowsers of white satin, very delicately embroidered with gold and coloured flowers. Mohammad 'Alee Bey wore a tight military jacket embroidered with gold and tags of pearls, and full cloth trowsers. He left us soon after the bride had returned to her private apartments, that he might preside at a dinner given to the students of the Páshá's colleges. He is the youngest son of Mohammad 'Alee, now just twelve years old. We should think it strange in Europe that a boy of that age should sit at the head of a table to which some hundreds were invited; but I doubt not that he presided well, for a Turk of almost any age has a keen sense of propriety, and wonderful self-possession.

Benches were now brought forward, and six female slaves approached us, each bearing a different instrument of music, while a little band of other performers, each with a tambourine, accompanied them. The six took their seats, three on each bench, and the tambouriners stood behind them, and on either side. The musicians played and sang several Turkish airs extremely well, during about half an hour, when the crowd again thickened, and another bride advanced towards the seat of honour, preceded and followed by the girls beating their tambourines. Her head-dress was as grotesque as that of the Páshá's daughter, bedecked with a profusion of diamonds, and surmounted by black and yellow feathers. Her saltah, too, resembled that of Zeyneb Hánum, and so did the shawl she wore as a girdle, but her yelek and trowsers were of striped Cashmere embroidered with gold. She threw herself at the feet of Nezleh Hánum, and at those of the mother of Sa'eed Páshá, and then took her seat in the distinguished corner. Crowds then poured in, and Nezleh Hánum again threw a profusion of gold and silver coins among the multitude. The bride sat about ten minutes, looking completely wretched, and then retired, supported and accompanied in the same manner as her predecessor; and after having, with considerable difficulty, carried her burden of embroidery and jewels across the saloon, she fainted. Alas! poor brides! Mysterious as is the future to every girl on the eve of marriage, how tenfold grievous must be the apprehensions of her who knows nothing, but by report, of her affianced husband.

When the second bride had disappeared, and the crowd had swept away, leaving still a goodly company of hundreds, the musicians again sang and played until Nezleh Hánum rose to quit the saloon. The girls with tambourines preceded and followed her, beating their instruments as when they accompanied the brides. We now felt disposed to reconnoitre, and were soon joined by the mother of Mohammad 'Alee Bey, who gave us her usual charming welcome, and led us to the retiring room which had been apppointed for the European guests. She is really a very sweet, sunny-faced person, always in a pleasant, polite humour, and apparently always happy. She invited us to see the bridal presents, which had that morning arrived from the bridegroom, and we accompanied her into an adjoining room, where many costly and beautiful jewels, dresses, services of plate, &c., were displayed, and where others were being unpacked. The jewel-box was covered with red velvet, and decorated outside with sprays of diamonds. We were shown about twelve dresses of velvet, gros de Naples, and satin, most spendidly embroidered with gold, all in the florid style before mentioned, bordered with gold lace, plaited, and so disposed as to form a fringe of flowers and leaves nearly three inches deep. In similar dresses some of the slaves were attired on that day. Within each dress was folded a magnificent Cashmere shawl. The slippers and mezz (or inner shoes) were beautifully set with diamonds, and the straps of a pair of bath clogs were exquisitely decorated with the same precious stones. The clogs were inlaid with mother-of-pearl, and gold tassles hung from the straps. I was much pleased with two scent bottles which were completely covered with diamonds. There were four dinner-services of silver, and a curious silver tea-service, composed of a sort of vase or urn, and silver cups and saucers of the ordinary tea size. I remarked several trays of French china, and very elegant china dishes of basket-work for fruit. [...]

[...]

LETTER VIII

December, 1845.

On the departure of the European guests, we had left the room in which we had been sitting to say "good-bye" to our friends and acquaintances; and when we returned, a very curious scene presented itself. Six of the fattest old ladies of the Hareem were running after each other in a circle, in the centre of the room, disguised in chintz coats nearly fitting their round persons, with high fool's-caps on their heads. Their game consisted of snatching at each other's caps, and throwing them down, and and scrambling for them; while they continued their circle, running, jumping, and tumbling. It was very absurd, for the good ladies were particularly unwieldy.

A theatrical exhibition followed, in which a scolding wife was represented by a pretty girl, while six other girls, in male attire, took part in a conversation, which, being in Turkish, I could not understand. The spirit, however, of the farce seemed to be that one of the six personated the pretty girl's husband, and the other five her paramours. They successively endeavoured to approach her, while she appeared to encourage their addresses, but were each chased round the part of the saloon appropriated to these performances by the husband, caught, and then thrown down by him; or rather, after a little wrestling, they one after another obediently rolled on the floor, and then got up and walked away. When this was over, her Highness rose, the tambourine girls preceded and followed her as before, and we all retired for the night.

We were conducted to a room which was furnished round with divans, and in the centre was arranged a very large and long musquito-curtain, of blue silk, under which, agreeably with the custom of the country, were placed, on the mat which covered the marble pavement, three large mattresses and pillows, with sheets and quilted coverlets. I mention these particulars to show you how carefully our comforts were considered; for the Easterns themselves generally sleep on their divans. We who were to share these beds were five persons; and we were all much tired, but too hungry to go to bed. Under such circumstances, I felt bold enough to ask for some supper for my companions and myself, and did so, and my request was most good-naturedly received and granted. A piece of cloth of gold was laid on the mat; a pretty Arab stool was placed upon it, and a silver tray, containing several little dishes, was brought. We supped right merrily, and the report of our good cheer taking wind, we were joined by two ladies, visitors, from another room, a mother and her daughter. I had during the day exceedingly admired those charming persons. They were Easterns, and were magnificently dressed, and wearing splendid diamonds; their whole attire was in perfect taste. When they joined our little supper-party they were in dishabille; but they were quite as beautiful with the simple white kerchiefs bound round their fair brows; and the plain cotton waistcoat and full trowsers, which formed their nightdress, became them admirably.

We were glad to go to bed, but our room was a throughfare, having doors opposite to each other; and persons were passing and repassing during nearly the whole night; consequently the night was far too lively to admit of much sleep. We were not aware, until the morning, that one, at least, of our comfortable quilted covers (which were as light and nearly as warm as eider-down) was of lilac satin, and beautifully adorned with a rich raised embroidery of gold.

Rising with the sun, we all felt that we should be glad if one of the many attendants who entered our room for the purpose of bidding us Good morning, should propose to bring us breakfast, when the pretty coffee-apparatus arrived, and tiny cup of coffee was for each the portion. One of our companions asked for some bread, and two flat cakes were brought and divided amongst us. Finding that the English really liked an early breakfast, our attendants most good-naturedly promised that everything "should be very nice for us, and plentiful, on the following day; but they had not been aware that any one ate in the morning." [...]

[...]

[...] we proposed seeing and hearing what might be going forward in the great saloon below. On our arriving at the marble staircase, we heard the Arab female band in full concert; and when we reached the first landing, and turning, saw nearly the whole saloon, how heartily we wished that such a fairy-like scene could be transferred to canvas, and that thus our friends in England might be able to form some idea of Eastern magnificence. Trite as is the remark, I cannot help observing that the sight which here presented itself to me most strikingly reminded me of the "Thousand and One Nights." On the staircase stood here and there a slave gorgeously attired; and, at the foot of the staircase, grouped as if for artistic effect, were ladies and slaves, whose dresses displayed such a combination of rich and delicate colours, and such a variety of magnificent embroidery, while on their heads and waists glittered innumerable jewels, that they unknowingly presented so splendid an effect as beggars all description. In the centre of the great saloon sat a circular group of Arab musicians on cushions on the mat, with every variety of instrument used in this country, all beautifully picturesque in form, and daintily inlaid with mother-of-pearl and dark wood. These women were all wearing the white head-veil, bound across the forehead and under the chin in the sphinx-like fashion so generally adopted by the Arab women, and hanging entirely over their backs. You will imagine that in their picturesque simplicity of attire they formed a striking contrast and pleasing relief to the gorgeous splendour of the ladies of the Hareem. Beyond this circle was the opposite compartment of the saloon, extending far away, with its rows of windows, and crimson satin gold-embroidered divan across the end. Upon that divan sat all the elder members of the Páshá's family; Nezleh Hánum being in the right-hand corner. Forming a row on each side of the compartment were the ladies of Efendees belonging to the Páshá's household. The elders were simply attired; but the Effendees' wives were very splendidly adorned, and the attendant slaves magnificently apparelled.

Finding that we were expected to join the party in that part of the saloon, we did so, and looked back with admiration on the scene through which we had passed. The dresses of the day before were laid aside for others infinitely more costly and beautiful; indeed the splendour displayed on that second day in the hundreds of rich dresses and decorations, could hardly, I think, be surpassed; and curiously enough, *every* article of dress was different from those worn on the day before; even the diamonds were changed for others which were more costly, in many cases. The dancing-girls, the little group of six, in pink Cashmere trimmed with gold fringe, alone retained their former dresses during the whole festivity, and their doing so had a very pleasing effect, for they were identified by their pretty dresses, and the very uniformity amidst so much variety was pleasing to the eye.

[…]

Intending to return home on that day (Saturday) to spend Sunday at home, and to see my dear ones, and finding my kind friend in the same mind, we both prepared for departure, as soon as the brides had repassed; and now at home, I must tell you of the entertainment the Páshá gave his male guests, and of the out-door fantasia. By the way, this word fantasia is one of the most useful of all words here; every decoration, however applied, every entertainment, musical or otherwise, is styled a fantasia.

Mohammed 'Alee Páshá entertained a different select dinner-party on the several days of the festivities. Among the persons invited by him were the consuls, and many of the European travellers and residents in Egypt. On one day the principal 'Ulama dined with him; and in the evening, after dinner, he led these grave and distinguished personages into an apartment which had been fitted up as a theatre, to witness there the performances of a company of European actors! It was the first time, they say, that any of them had been present at such a scene; and we may reckon their adventure among the greatest of all the European innovations which occured during the festivities.

On the morning of the first day of the festivities, while I was preparing to go to the citadel, the bridegroom's presents, which I have described to you, were conveyed to Zeyneb Hánum with some pomp from her future abode in the Ezbekeeyeh. A friend who witnessed it described it to me as follows:—One of the Páshá's military bands headed the train, followed by a regiment of lancers. Then came a number of military officers on foot, bearing on their heads trays of sweetmeats; and, after these, the carriages in which the jewels, plate, dresses, &c. were deposited. Each carriage was drawn by four horses, and covered with green velvet fringed with gold. On either side of each walked three officers in scarlet and gold. Some more officers bearing trays of sweetmeats followed the carriages, and another regiment of lancers and a military band closed the procession.

On each night there are theatrical performances at the citadel, and tickets are sent to Europeans and to as many Easterns as can be accomodated. Three hundred cooks are employed daily to prepare excellent food for the poor in the palace of the Ezbekeeyeh. The long route from the Ezbekeeyeh to the citadel, extending about two miles, is hung with large lanterns, each containing ten well-lighted lamps, and the Ezbekeeyeh, the citadel, and many of the principal houses were illuminated. The great irregular place called the Ezbekeeyeh, where the palace of the bride is situated, being of large extent, nearly half a mile in its greatest length, and about a third of a mile in its greatest width, is the chief scene of the out-door amusements. Its conversion, from a spacious lake into a pleasant garden, surrounded by a canal, and crossed by several roads, is almost complete. Here, near to each extremity of its main road, which traverses it from west to east (from the side of the palace of the bride, and the exterior of the city, towards the heart of the metropolis), are erected two large and lofty triumphal arches. The road between them is bordered by illuminated pillars, and by small globe-shaped lanterns of red and white paper. Many hundreds of this kind of lamp are also hung upon cords between the trees which border the whole tract of garden-ground and the several roads: and a large screen which conceals the front of the principal part of the bride's palace is hung with a vast number of similar lights. The general aspect of the place at night is singularly beautiful and picturesque.

During each day wrestlers, rope-dancers, and musicians entertain the people in several places; but the great focus for amusement is the Ezbekeeyeh. Every night there is a display of an abundance of rockets and other very good fireworks; therefore while I am in the Hareem I have the satisfaction of knowing that my dear children have amusements which they much enjoy. At the top of a very high soaped pole in the Ezbekeeyeh a shawl and ten pounds have been placed, to be the property of any one who can climb to the top. Many and earnest have already been the attempts of the poor people to obtain this boon; but they have fallen down like stones after gaining a certain height. During each day there are frequent discharges of artillery from the citadel and other parts, and the cannons thunder over the city at least four times each day.

[…]

[…] On the morning of this day (Wednesday), the last day of the festivities in the Hareem, almost all the European ladies who had dined in the palace on the first day came again, and many more arrived from Alexandria. It was the seventh day, that on which the hands of the bride are dyed with henna after taking the bath, according to ancient custom, and the day before she is introduced to the bridegroom. […]

[…]

We were all then invited to dinner, and about three hundred sat down to table. Nezleh Hánum presided. After dinner, Turkish and Arab dancing, and the delightful singing of the 'A'lmehs, in turns amused the company. Crowds continued to pour in until midnight, when about twenty slaves came forward, each bearing in her hands a dress in a piece of cloth of gold. These, it was said, were presents to be dispensed in honour of the principal bride. One branch of the double staircase was then cleared for her descent, while the other was densely crowded, and the procession (termed the procession of the candles) commenced. A number of eunuchs slowly descended the staircase first, each bearing a large painted wax candle, about four feet long: then a blaze of innumerable candles appeared at the head of the stairs, and flowed gently down, like a river of light. This effect was produced by a number of slaves, each bearing seven or eight wax-lights, fixed in a basket decorated with gaily-colured flowers, on a small green jar, containing, I am told, a paste of henna for dyeing the hands, to give them a deep orange-red hue, which many, by a second and different application, change to black. The jars they held in their hands, and raised high over their heads. Among these slaves walked the bride, blazing with diamonds; her jewels reflecting the hundreds of lights around her. She was preceded and attended as usual by the dancers, and by girls beating their tambourines. When all the candle-bearers reached and crossed the floor of the lower saloon, the noise produced by the shrill cries of joy and the beating of the tambourines was almost deafening.

The bride remained about a quarter of an hour, and then with her attendant band, and numerous candle-bearers, she crossed the saloon, and ascended the staircase. […]

3.
Emmeline Lott (dates unknown)
ɞ The 'English Governess' ଔ IN Egypt
HAREM LIFE IN EGYPT AND CONSTANTINOPLE

T.B. Peterson & Brothers, Philadelphia
1865

Beginning in the second half of the nineteenth century, elite families in Cairo and Istanbul hired European tutors or governesses for their children. Clearly a sign of status and culture, the tutors and governesses were supposed to teach the children foreign languages and music, as well as to introduce them to European customs. The governesses who lived with the families of their charges were well positioned to observe domestic life, and some took advantage of their privileged access to write about it. Emmeline Lott's book is one such work, with its full title, *The 'English Governess' in Egypt. Harem Life in Egypt and Constantinople*, intended to signal the truth and authenticity of her account.

Lott was hired to look after Ibrahim Paşa (b. 1860), the son of the Khedive Ismail Paşa, Viceroy of Egypt (r. 1863–79), arriving when her charge was a young boy of about five. In the book, Lott mentions being interviewed for the job in London, and then having an agent of some sort, Mr B., in Cairo, with whose family she stayed for a short time upon her arrival from London. There was, therefore, already by mid-century a system in place by which the Egyptian royal family obtained what they wanted from Europe, whether fashion, furniture or employees. While similar business arrangements would have been in place for the Ottoman royal court, they did not employ governesses for the royal children in the same way, as Leyla Saz Hanımefendi's account demonstrates (Extract 11). The royal children in Istanbul had foreign tutors, but their constant companions were members of high-ranking Ottoman families. At the time that Lott was writing, the Egyptian royal family (which was not Turkish in its origin since its founder, Muhammad Ali, came from Albania) had a different, much more direct relationship to Europe – in terms of politics, culture and consumer goods – than the Ottoman court.

Although we do not know very much about Lott, she was evidently a woman who needed to earn her own living, whether by serving as a governess or by writing (she was the author of at least one other book). She is always at pains to establish her status, especially in relation to those she considers inferiors, such as the German 'peasant servants' with whom she ate while in the palace. Lott also mentions at numerous points in her narrative that she insisted upon receiving what she refers to as 'proper respect', a further indication of the extent to which matters of class and status occupied her attention. Elsewhere in her book she refers to an occasion in her childhood when she was found in the private grounds at Windsor Castle, yet another means of emphasising her own status as someone whose family had access to the English royal residence.

As a piece of harem literature, Lott's work is of interest for a number of reasons. She is clearly aware of what others have written about the harem, often correcting mistaken information, or referring to works that she assumes her readers will also know. She repeatedly stresses her first-hand knowledge of her subject and the reliability of her account. She is overwhelmingly negative in her interpretation of nearly everything that she sees, taking the general stereotypes that other authors invoke and casting them in the worst possible light. Thus, the childlike simplicity and charm of Turkish women in Harvey's account (Extract 4) is rendered as indolence and stupidity in Lott's writing. Nonetheless, her amazingly detailed and precisely dated account provides a very good look at certain aspects of harem life in the Egyptian royal family in the year 1865, especially the extent to which European consumer goods had been adopted in the palace. We learn from Lott that the Egyptian royal palace did not contain very much European furniture at this point, compared to later years, but that, in 1865, Egyptian princesses were using tooth powder from Paris to clean their teeth. Lott's detailed information is valuable as a means of understanding what was going on in Egypt at the time that she wrote, but the broader analysis and her interpretation of what she saw tell us about her own attitudes and perceptions.

Two longer passages from her book are excerpted here, the first describing her arrival at the palace, and the second, some time later, recounting her visit to her agent, Mr B., to complain about her situation. In the first excerpt, as Lott is led through the palace to meet her charge and the ladies of the court, she provides a careful description of the palace interior. She finds her own room completely inadequate since it has virtually no furniture and none of the Western conveniences that she requires. She apparently worried that being forced to live in this state, without the Western goods that guaranteed gentility, would undermine her status. As she meets and observes the inhabitants of the palace, she is unable to take herself outside her own culture, to understand any of what she is seeing.

Not surprisingly, Lott was not successful in adapting to her new position and residence. By the time she visited Mr B., she had developed a long list of the degradations to which she was constantly subjected: the lack of furniture, the inadequate diet (she hated the local cuisine), the polluted air of the palace, and so on. She was not given total control of her charge or allowed to treat him as a European child would have been. At this point in her narrative, she addresses the Western reader directly ('Well, kind reader'), a textual strategy she employs to highlight the dire circumstances in which she found herself. Lott's stay in Ismail Paşa's palace was not long, but her experience did provide her with the material to produce what was marketed as an authoritative account of harem life.

སྐ ཕ

The Lady Superintendent now took me by the hand, led me up two flights of stairs, covered with thick Brussels carpet of a most costly description, and as soft and brilliant in colors as the dewy moss of Virginia Water. The walls were plain. Then we passed through a suite of several rooms, elegantly carpeted, in all of which stood long divans, some of which were covered with white and others with yellow and crimson satin. Over the doorways hung wide satin damask curtains, looped up with heavy silk cords and tassels to correspond, with richly gilded cornices over each, and the windows which overlooked the Nile had Venetian shutters attached to them outside. Against the walls were fixed numerous silver chandeliers, each containing six wax candles, with frosted colored glass shades, made in the form of tulips over them. On each side of the room large mirrors were fixed in the wall, each of which rested on a marble-topped console table, supported by gilded legs. The only other articles of furniture that were scattered about the apartment were a dozen common English cane-bottom *kursi*, "chairs."

Across one apartment a line was suspended, on which hung the Princess's jackets, wardrobes being totally unknown within the precincts of this "Enchanted Castle." Against the walls of another were piled up the beds, which heap was covered over with a rich silk coverlet. On the divan was placed a silver tray (as the use of both toilet tables and washhand-stands was totally unknown) containing the Princess's toilet requisites. These merely consisted of a plain black india-rubber dressing-comb, a white ivory-handled hair-brush, a very large-sized smalltooth-comb, two tooth-brushes, a glass box, containing tooth dentifrice from Paris, a small round silver bowl, into which poured the perfumed (rose) water with which Her Highness, the mother of the Grand Pacha, dressed her hair, the substitute for oil or pomatum (neither of which is ever used by any of the Viceregal family), and a large bottle of essences, all of which were covered over with a transparent crimson silk gauze cloth, bespangled with gold crescents, and bordered with gold fringe an inch deep.

In another apartment stood a large mahogany cupboard, containing the fumigating powders which are burned in the rooms, dried fruits, soaps, essences, boots, shoes, quantities of cast-off wearing apparel, Her Highness's cash-box, a small black ebony casket inlaid with gold, packets of cigarette papers, tobacco, pipe-bowls, silver braziers and dishes, zurfs, both in japan, china, and silver. Jewelry cases, candles, and a complete miscellany of sundry articles: in fact, it was a "curiosity shop."

At the extremity of those rooms I was led into a smaller apartment, where, on the divan (so called from the Persian word *dive*, signifying "fairy, gem") which was covered with dirty, faded yellow satin, sat the Princess Epouse. She is a wee dwarf of a handsome blonde, with fine blue eyes[,] short nose, rather large mouth with a fine set of teeth, expressive countenance, but rather sharp and disagreeable voice; her hair was cut in the Savoyard fashion, with two long plaits behind, which were turned round, over the small brown gauze handkerchief she wore round her head, in which were placed, like a band, seven large diamond flies.

She was attired in a dirty, crumpled, light-colored muslin dress and trousers, sat *à la Turque*, doubled up like a clasped knife, without shoes or stockings, smoking a cigarette. Her waist was encircled with a white gauze handkerchief, having the four corners embroidered with gold thread. It was fastened round, so as to leave two ends hanging down like the lappet of a riding-habit. Her feet were encased in *babouches*, "slippers without heels."

By her side sat the Grand Pacha Ibrahim, her son, so styled after the manner adopted by the renowned Mahomet Ali with the Princess Nuzley, *"Nuzley Hanem."* He was dressed in the uniform of an officer of the Egyptian infantry. On his head he wore the fez; across his shoulder hung a silver-gilt chain, from which was suspended a small silver square box beautifully chased with cabalistic figures of men, beasts, and trees, enclosed inside which was another smaller box made of cypress wood, which contained verses of the Koran. He was about five years old, of dark complexion, short Arab nose, and rather tall for his age, and looked the very picture of a happy, round-faced cherub. When I approached towards the divan, he gave full proof that his lungs were in a healthy state, as he set up a most hideous shriek, buried his black head in his mother's lap, who laughed most heartily at the strange reception His Highness had thought proper to bestow upon his future governess.

In front of the divan, behind, and on each side of me, stood a bevy of the ladies of the Harem, assuredly not the types of Tom Moore's "Peris of the East," as described in such glowing colors in his far-famed "Lalla Rookh," for I failed to discover the slightest trace of loveliness in any of them. On the contrary, most of their countenances were pale as ashes, exceedingly disagreeable; fat and globular in figure; in short, so rotund, that they gave me the idea of large full moons; nearly all were *passée*. Their photographs were as hideous and hag-like as the witches in the opening scene of Macbeth, which is not to be wondered at, as some of them had been the favorites of Ibrahim Pacha. But *que voulez-vous?* It is their *"Kismet"* to remain for ever within the four walls of the Harem. It has descended to them from primeval days—the days of the Patriarch Abraham.

Some wore white linen dresses and trousers. Their hair and their finger-nails were dyed red with *henna*; many of them looked like old hags, in the most extended acceptation of the expression. Some wore the *tarboosh*, round which they bound colored gauze handkerchiefs. They had handsome gold watches tucked into their waistbands, which were similar to that of Her Highness's, which hung suspended from their necks by thick, massive gold chains. Their fingers were covered with a profusion of diamond, emerald, and ruby rings; in their ears were earrings of various precious stones, all set in the old antique style in silver; while others only wore plain gauze handkerchiefs round their heads. They had been favorites in their youth. Behind stood half-a-dozen white slaves, chiefly Circassians, attired in colored muslins, their dress and trousers being of the same pattern. Their head-gear was similar to that of the ladies of the Harem, and the ornaments which adorned their persons were equally as costly.

The Mistress Superintendent introduced me to the Princess Epouse who kept me standing a considerable time, while she fixed her eyes steadfastly upon me and smiled.

[. . .]

I was then conducted into the Princesses' suite of apartments, which consisted of two large saloons, covered with magnificent Brussels carpet but completely besprinkled, as it were, with spots of white wax, which had been suffered to fall from the candles which the slaves carry about in their fingers. Around them were placed divans covered with red satin damask; the windows and door hangings of the same materials, a very large mirror, reaching down from the ceiling, which was painted with flowers and fruits, with the crescent, and numerous warlike instruments, and music placed in each corner, to the top of a marble table supported on gilded legs, on each of which stood a silver chandelier containing eight wax candles, with red-colored glass shades covered with painted flowers.

Out of each of these rooms doors opened into seven others, which are the dormitories of the young Princesses the daughters of the Viceroy, and the ladies of the Harem.

On the right hand side of the first room was the small bedroom which was assigned to me as my apartment, and which was to serve me, like

"The cobler's stall,
For chamber, drawing-room, and all,"

and into which my guide conducted me. It was carpeted, having a divan covered with green and red striped worsted damask, which stood underneath the window, which commanded a fine *coup-d'œil* of the gardens attached to the Palace and the Viceroy's pavilion. The hangings of the double doors and windows were of the same material. The furniture consisted of a plain green painted iron bedstead, the bars of which had never been fastened, and pieces of wood, like the handles of brooms, and an iron bar, were placed across, to support the two thin cotton mattresses that were laid upon it. There were neither pillows, bolsters, nor any bed-linen; but as substitutes were placed three thin flat cushions; not a blanket, but two old worn-out wadded coverlets lay upon the bed. Not the sign of a dressing-table or a chair of any description, and a total absence of all the appendages necessary for a lady's bedroom—not even a vase. Certes, there stood within that narrow cupboard-like uncomfortable-looking chamber a Parisian chest of drawers (rather a wonder, for the Turkish and Egyptian ladies invariably place their body-linen, &c., in the *youks*, cupboards constructed in the walls of their rooms), having a marble top, and a shut-up washhand-stand, to correspond with an elegantly-painted ewer and basin of porcelain.

I gazed at the accommodation assigned to me with surprise; and yet what could I have expected, as every apartment which I had passed through was totally destitute of everything that ought to have been placed therein? Not a foot-stool, no pianos, nor music-stools; not a picture adorned the walls. Being "The Bower of Bliss" of a descendant of the formidable Mahomet Ali, who so boldly repudiated the Prophet Mahomet's doctrine "that pictures were an abomination," it was but natural for me to imagine that I should find some beautiful paintings decorating the principal apartments. But no, none hung there. Not a single article of *vertu* graced the rich console tables.

In short, not any of the splendid rooms of the Enchanted Palace of the Crœsus of the nineteenth century contained anything, either for ornament or use, except the bare decorations. In fact, the whole of them seemed to me nothing more than places in which to lie down and in which to vegetate, aided by eatables and drinkables, and sleep. They were even destitute of *soofras*, "tables," whose shapes are very rude, height about a foot, breadth as wide as a plate; just large enough to hold a Turkish coffee-cup, "*findjar*," or the bowl of a pipe, and, although inlaid with some variegated pieces of mother-of-pearl, are only pretty, not having anything rich or elegant about them; still, none were to be seen. Accustomed to the elegant manner in which drawing-rooms of the nobility of my own country are set off with elegant *fauteuils*, superb occasional chairs, *recher-ché* nicknacks, as well as a whole host of most costly things, they presented a most beggarly and empty appearance. The whole of the Harem looked like a house only partially furnished; in short, like a dwelling which either the poverty or the niggardness of its proprietor had prevented from being properly furnished.

At first I thought this proceeded from parsimony; for well do we know that a miser—and the Viceroy, like his strange character of a father, Ibrahim Pacha, who was one of the most notorious usurers of his day—loves bright golden sovereigns as dearly as his life: but I afterwards learned that it was *a la mode Turque*, for elegance is quite eschewed by all true Ottomans.

It most decidedly evinces a great superiority in remarkable characters, who have revelled in the midst of profusion, to be able—like that departed warrior of the nineteenth century, Arthur Duke of Wellington, who expired in his small apart-ment at Walmer Castle, plainly fitted up with that camp furniture which had been his only luxury throughout his most memorable campaigns—to resign, without a murmur, almost every luxury and convenience. It exhibits a healthy independ-ence of externals; but it is a state of things that brings women down to the level of the brute.

Retracing our footsteps Anina led me into that vast regal-looking chamber, the Hall of Audience of the Castle of Indolence; for it was much more spacious and loftier than the Long Room in the Custom House in London. The floor was beau-tifully enamelled, as it were, with that native product of the East, the glowing alphabet of that mystic code of signals, the language of flowers, woven on the finest carpeting which the looms of Belgium ever wrought. The lofty ceiling was as exquisitely painted with Egyptian landscapes as the Imperial saloons of Versailles, and an immense gilt chandelier hung suspended from the rich corniced roof. The walls were papered with floral designs, all in unison with that lovely bouquet, that blossomed, as it were, beneath the impious footsteps of my unbelieving self. The hangings of the lofty doors and noble windows, overlooking those perfumed gardens which had never before been trodden by any "dog of a Christian," were of the most costly description. They were composed of rich yellow satin damask curtains, overtopped with elaborately-gilded cornices, and looped up with massive silk cords and heavy bullion tassels. From the walls projected silver chandeliers, ornamented with colored tulip-shaped shades, the transparent wax candles in which, when lighted, threw forth a most agreeable pink shade over the whole of this superb and princely reception saloon. Long divans, covered with rich satin damask, bespangled with the eternal gold and silver crescents glittering about in all directions, like stars

> "In the etherial firmament on high,"

were placed under the whole length of the windows.

Here, indeed, might be seen a few signs of elegance and refinement, as numerous richly inlaid console tables, which, in point of workmanship and design, might vie in splendor with those in the Pitti Palace at Florence, supported on richly-gilded legs, were scattered about, on which stood several beautifully-painted Sèvres and Japan china vases, filled with most lovely nosegays!

[. . .]

But, oh! horror of horrors! the European innovation of a dozen common English cane-bottomed chairs, on which I afterwards beheld some of the ladies of the Harem endeavor to establish themselves, and at which exhibition not only myself, but the Viceroy and the Grand Pacha could not refrain from laughing outright! as one of their legs hung down, looking most miserably forlorn, while the other sought in vain for room to double itself up upon the chair like a hen at roost. This was not most assuredly, in keeping with the magnificent decorations of this palatial hall; and this constituted all the furniture. It looked bare, vacant, and miserably empty.

Upon re-entering the apartment, I beheld the Princess Epouse (the second wife), and whom I designated, in contradistinction to the other two wives, my Princess, as I was attached to her suite, seated on the Divan, doubled up like a clasp-knife, attired in Turkish costume, very plainly dressed, wearing the gauze handkerchief wound round her head, and fastened with a band, containing seven (the Moslem's magical number, as they believe there are no less than seven heavens) large diamond pins, forming as many of those scourges of Egypt, flies.

She was smoking a cigarette, for cigarettes have of late years almost superseded the use of pipes in this Elysium of Love. Perhaps the expense of those costly amber-mouthed and jewel-studded stems used by the élite of the Turkish and Egyptian ladies of rank, may have contributed in no slight degree to that innovation—for economy in the East appears to be the order of the day. Her Highness was smoking it most cleverly: she really seemed to puff away at it as if it were her amusement, and so it evidently was; but yet I soon discovered that my Princess, like the generality of all honorable Turks, was the *slave* to tobacco in the form of cigarettes. I cannot help thinking that such constant use of the weed vitiates their character, and renders stagnant the small stock of stability with which the Almighty has endowed the Ottomans of both sexes. Well, there she sat, just like one of the porcelain figures which ornament the chimney-pieces in Germany. Not a muscle did she move—she looked like wax-work, and her figure would have made an excellent addition to Madame Tussaud's celebrities.

How much did I regret that I had not been taught the art of taking photographs, for then I could have daguerreotyped the whole of the inmates of the Harems of Egypt and Constantinople. It was an opportunity missed of portraying, from life, the caged beauties of the East. This is much to be regretted, as no other European lady is ever again likely to have the chance. By her side sat the darling of her soul, the Grand Pacha Ibrahim, his person unadorned, by any jewel except the blue turquoise bead in the tassel of his fez.

[. . .]

As I approached, the Princess Epouse rose from the divan, motioned to me to occupy her seat, and thus was I officially installed as governess to the Grand Pacha Ibrahim, the infant son of Ismael Pacha, Viceroy of Egypt.

[. . .]

CHAPTER VII

As soon as the Princess Epouse had quitted the *oda* "apartment," I was surrounded by the entire motley group of slaves, both black and white. Most of them assumed singular gestures; some knelt and kissed my hands, others my knees, and many of them squatted down at my feet. The ladies of the Harem patted me on the back, a sign of their pleasure at seeing me; and almost all kissed my cheeks.

All of a sudden I was electrified at hearing upwards of fifty voices exclaiming simultaneously, "*Koneiis! Quiyis! Koneiis!*" "Pretty! Pretty!" While a whole chorus shouted forth, "*Gurzel! Gurzel!*" "Beautiful; Beautiful!"

Some of them took up the black straw-hat which I had taken off and laid down upon the divan at my side. This they passed from hand to hand, gazing with pleasure and delight at that specimen of English manufacture. After this they examined the whole of my costume from head to foot. What seemed to attract their notice the most was the crinoline I wore, which was by no means a large-sized one; and yet many Turkish and Egyptian ladies of the present day may be seen in the streets of Alexandria and Constantinople walking about in that appendage.

At the earnest request of some of the ladies of the Harem, I rose from my seat, and walked up and down that noble hall, in order that they might see how European ladies generally paced up and down their rooms.

Anina, thinking that I must require some refreshment after my journey from Cairo, clapped her hands, which is the Turkish and Egyptian manner of calling domestics, when two white slaves left the room, but soon returned, accompanied by two other black slaves, who carried in their hands a silver tray, on which was placed a *kebab*, a small piece of mutton on a silver skewer, which had been broiled upon charcoal almost to a cinder. It was highly spiced and sugared. A flat cake of white Arab bread, as salt as brine, was placed by it. There were no cruets, nor sauce, nor gravy of any kind, but a knife and plated fork. This they placed upon a *soofra*, at the side of the divan.

While I was endeavoring to partake of this specimen of viceregal hospitality—for I had been so surfeited with food cooked *à l' Arabe* at the banker's, that my heart turned against it—they kept gazing at me in as much astonishment as a child looks at the wild beasts at their feeding time in the Zoological Gardens in the Regent's Park, and watched the manner in which I used my knife and fork and ate my unpalatable refreshment, as if I had been a wild animal out of the depths of an Indian forest.

[. . .]

The next morning, as soon as the Prince had returned from his usual walk, I obtained permission from the Princess Epouse to pay a visit to Mr. B.'s, at Cairo. Orders were accordingly given by the Grand Eunuch for a state barge to be prepared to convey me across the Nile, and a messenger was despatched to Cairo, to order a carriage to be sent down to the landing-place, on the Cairo side, as there are no carriages or horses kept at the Harem or Pavilion.

After I had been kept waiting several hours, I embarked in the barge, landed on the other side of the Nile, entered the Viceregal carriage, and forthwith proceeded to the banker's.

Fortunately I found Mr. B. at home. He received me very kindly, and listened attentively to my description of the inconveniences to which I had been subjected.

As I found it utterly impossible to adopt any regular system as to the educational surveillance of the Grand Pacha, I deemed it prudent to explain in detail to Mr. B. the difficulties which I had to encounter.

The irregularity which prevailed in the domestic arrangements of the Harem had totally frustrated all my endeavors to carry out any regular system. Sometimes I received orders from the Grand Eunuch which were issued at the caprice of the Princess Epouse, who, as a matter of course, was perfectly ignorant as to the manner adopted in Europe of training up young children, to take the Grand Pacha out walking at six o'clock in the morning; on other occasions at seven, eight, and nine o'clock. And when once the little Prince was in the gardens, it was exceedingly difficult to get him to return. His will was law; and no matter how singular and unreasonable his whims were, still he must be indulged in them.

I drew up a scheme for his education, and endeavored to obtain the Viceroy's sanction to its execution; but that Prince explained to me that he did not wish the Prince to be taught from books or toys, as he would pick up English quickly enough by being constantly with me; so that I abandoned all idea of educational training.

Then I explained to Mr. B. the numerous degradations to which I was subjected, and called his attention to the fact that I was unprovided with either chairs or tables; that I was obliged to use my trunks as substitutes for such necessaries, which were liable to, and actually did, before I retired from His Highness's service, produce spinal complaint.

Again and again, as I had previously done, when remaining as a guest, nay, I should rather add as a caged bird, under his hospitable roof, I pointed out to him that not only did I find the Arab diet so nauseous to my taste as to oblige me to live chiefly upon dry bread and a little pigeon or mutton, but that, owing to the want of more nourishing food, and especially European cooking, I found my strength gradually sinking day by day; and that the constant use of coffee, and the total deprivation of those stimulants, such as malt liquor and wine, to which I had always been accustomed, and of which it is absolutely necessary that Europeans should partake in warm countries to counteract the hostile debilitating effects of the climate, would, I fear, soon throw me on a bed of sickness.

Besides, I was constantly being sent out with the Prince into the gardens during the intense heat of the day, the thermometer often ranging from 99° to 100°; it really seemed as if the Princess Epouse considered that I had been thoroughly acclimatized before I entered the Harem.

Then the very atmosphere that I breathed was continually impregnated with the fumes of tobacco, into which large quantities of opium and other deleterious narcotics were infused, which so affected my constitution that my spirits began to flag, and I felt a kind of heavy languid apathy come over me, that scarcely any amount of energy on my part was able to shake off.

The irksome monotony of my daily life had produced a most unpleasant feeling in my mind. Not only had I lost much of my wonted energy, but a kind of lethargy seemed to have crept over me; a most indefinable reluctance to move about had imperceptibly gained ascendancy over my actions;—to walk, to speak (and here I must not forget to mention that my voice had become extremely feeble)—to apply myself to drawing, reading, or in fact, to make the slightest exertion of any kind whatever, had become absolutely irksome to me.

It was not the feeling of what we Europeans call *ennui* which I experienced, for that sensation can always be shook off by a little moral courage and energy; but it was a state bordering on that frightful melancholy, that must, if not dispelled, engender insanity. And my experience of such feelings is not to be wondered at, if my position in the Harem is thoroughly examined.

CHAPTER XII

Well, kind reader; there I was, totally unacquainted with either the Turkish or Arabic tongues; unaccustomed to the filthy manners, barbarous customs, and disgusting habits of all around me; deprived of every comfort by which I had always been surrounded; shut out from all rational society; hurried here and there, in the heat of a scorching African sun, at a moment's notice; absolutely living upon nothing else but dry bread and a little pigeon or mutton, barely sufficient to keep body and soul together. Compelled to take all my meals but my scanty breakfast (a dry roll and a cup of coffee) in the society of two clownish disgusting German peasant servants; lacking the stimulants so essentially necessary for the preservation of health in such a hot climate; stung almost to death with mosquitoes, tormented with flies, and surrounded with beings who were breeders of vermin; a daily witness of manners the most repugnant, nay, revolting, to the delicacy of a European female—for often have I seen, in the presence of my little Prince.

> "A lady of the Harem, not more forward than all the rest,
> Well versed in Syren's arts, it must be confessed,
> Shuffle off her garments, and let her figure stand revealed,
> Like that of Venus who no charms concealed!"

Surrounded by intriguing Arab nurses, who not only despised me because I was a Howadji, but hated me in their hearts because, as a European lady, I insisted upon receiving, and most assuredly I did receive, so far as the Viceroy and the Princesses, the three wives, were concerned, proper respect. The bare fact of my being allowed to take precedence of all the inmates of the Harem, even of the *Ikbals*, "favorites," galled them to the quick; and there is no doubt that they were at that time inwardly resolved to do their utmost to render my position as painful as possible, nay, even untenable. Then my only companions were the ladies of the Harem, whose appearance I have already described as being totally at variance with that glowing myth-like picture that Tom Moore gives of retired beauty[,] so erroneously supposed to be caged within the precincts of the *Abodes of Bliss*, in his exquisite poem of "Lalla Rookh," for therein I failed to find

> "Oh, what a pure and sacred thing
> Is beauty curtained from the sight
> Of the gross world, illumining
> One only mansion with her light."

They were composed of old *Ikbals*, favorites of Ibrahim Pacha, and some of those who had ceased to rank as such, or as the slaves emphatically termed it, to *please* the "Baba Efendimir."

I was struck with their use of the expression, "please the Viceroy," for it was one that had been used to me, when I had an interview in London with Mr. C. H.'s sister prior to my leaving for Egypt, by that lady. At that time I did not heed the expression; now that the *Ikbals* had used it I understood their significance of its meaning, and I was perfectly convinced in my own mind, that, taking it in that sense, they meant that I should *not* please His Highness, no matter how long I remained in the Viceregal service.

4.

ANNIE JANE HARVEY (D.1898)

℘ TURKISH HAREMS AND ℘ CIRCASSIAN HOMES

Hurst & Blackett, London
1871

Turkish Harems begins with the arrival in Istanbul of the yacht *Claymore*, bearing Annie Jane Harvey, along with her husband, sister and a large crew. Already well-travelled, Harvey had produced *Our Cruise on the Claymore, with a Visit to Damascus and the Lebanon* (1861) from a previous voyage with her husband and she subsequently wrote a travel book about Spain, as well as several works of fiction (published under the pseudonym of Andrée Hope). Harvey moved in fashionable, elite circles of British politicians and intellectuals, and was a fairly prolific if not vastly well-known writer. *Turkish Harems* was dedicated to Harvey's particular friend Lady Elizabeth Russell (renowned for her political, intellectual London salon), for whom she also wrote a privately published memoir in 1876. While in Istanbul, Harvey was the guest of the British embassy, and her family also enjoyed a close relationship with the British consul in Lebanon while they were visiting there.

Although the majority of the book is about her travels in Russia, it is packaged as harem literature, using the evocative words 'harem' and 'Circassian' in the title to attract readers. Offering a mix of travelogue and harem account, the descriptions of harem visits and Ottoman women are combined with Harvey's careful observation of landscape, towns, street scenes and aspects of domestic life such as food traditions and cooking. As an experienced author, Harvey was aware of the conventions of travel literature, prefacing her book with a brief wish 'that her accounts, though they inadequately express the beauty and charm of these distant countries, may interest those who prefer travelling for half-an-hour when seated in their arm-chairs'. Like Lady Brassey's better-known books that had their origins in letters written home (Extract 6), Harvey's work was apparently based on diary entries made during her travels. Unlike Brassey's limited interest in the lives of women abroad, Harvey positioned herself to write extensively about the Turkish women she met.

The material included here from Harvey's books is taken from three chapters (I, IV and V) and provides engaging detail about her attempts to get to know Ottoman women and to understand their home life. She offers repeated cautions about the potential unreliability of other Western accounts of harem life – warning against authors who do not understand what they see, or have little opportunity to observe the true nature of Ottoman domestic life. In contrast, her close relationships with Ottoman women are used to endorse the truth status of her account, a citational model familiar to readers of harem literature, and travel accounts more generally.

In Chapter I she introduces the topic of harems by noting European women's increasing difficulties in gaining access to visiting Ottoman women, as well as acknowledging the important role played by the wives of European diplomats in brokering invitations. Her much longer account of harem life in Chapter IV begins with a reminder of the challenges of getting to know Turkish women since 'everyone feels shy, and everyone is stupid ...'.

Harvey's narrative details her visit to one household as well as a trip to a public bath, providing a paradigm of the harem visit that is described in greater or lesser detail by so many travellers to Istanbul or Cairo in this period. She talks about harem etiquette and the problems of communicating without a shared language. In the absence of sustained conversation, a typical range of activities included smoking (still a novel experience for many European visitors), eating, showing off children, touring the house and examining each other's clothes, sometimes even trying them on.

The pleasures of cross-cultural dressing are a common feature of both men and women's travel accounts, although their reasons for doing it, and the circumstances are sometimes quite different. Men often used it for disguise (in her 1861 book, Harvey describes the arrival on the yacht of a 'Bedouin Arab' who turns out to be their friend Mr Graham still in his 'travelling dress', p. 9). Women travelled in disguise less often (an exception to this is Pardoe in Extract 1), but frequently used cross-cultural dressing-up sessions as a way of interacting with their Ottoman hosts, particularly when conversation was restricted by language (Ellison, Extract 10). Ottoman women were sometimes intensely curious about European dress and wanted to be able to examine it for themselves, even try it on. Western visitors liked to dress up in 'Turkish' clothes, notably the flattering *yaşmak* (as they often did in the photographer's studio). Ottoman and Egyptian women also would dress up with their own friends, as a means of passing the time, sometimes even documenting their costumes with photographs (one such image appears in Huda Shaarawi's memoir).

In the last set of excerpts, from Chapter V, Harvey writes about the visits that women frequently made to the park at the Sweet Waters of Asia, a popular gathering place for women (see Plate 2). In addition to her description of the music and sweets that were an important part of the outing, she is alert to the class distinctions that governed how women were able to behave in public, noting that middle- and lower-class women seemed to have more fun. In the end, she concluded that, despite the many advantages of their situation, Ottoman women were hampered by their lack of education and by seclusion, and their alleged freedom was actually very limited. It is important to remember that she was writing just after an early version of the Married Women's Property Act (passed in 1870). Earlier English women writers, who had no property rights, were often envious of Ottoman Muslim women's rights to own property and the other legal protection they enjoyed.

The childlike simplicity and charm of Ottoman women noted by Harvey was a prevalent stereotype, commented on by other women observers such as Vaka Brown (Extract 7) and Ellison.

ဢ Cઢ

Every year it is more difficult for passing travellers to gain admittance to the harems. Of course the members of the principal families object to be made a show of, and equally of course the wives of the diplomatists residing in Constantinople are unwilling to intrude too frequently upon the privacy of these ladies. A Turkish visit also entails a somewhat serious loss of time, as it generally lasts from mid-day to sunset.

When royal and other very great ladies arrive at Constantinople, certain grand fêtes are given to them in different official houses, but these magnificent breakfasts and dinners do not give Europeans a better knowledge of Turkish homes than a dinner or ball at Buckingham Palace or the Tuileries would give a Turk respecting the nature of domestic life in England or France.

The wives of several diplomats had given us letters of introduction to many of their friends at Constantinople, and so kindly were these responded to by the Turkish ladies that we found ourselves received at once with the greatest cordiality, and before we left the shores of the Bosphorus had made friendships that we heartily trust we may be fortunate enough to renew at some future day.

After a stay of several months, our conviction was that it would be difficult to find people more kind-hearted, more simple-mannered, or more sweet-tempered than the Turkish women.

[. . .]

Of course a jealous and perhaps neglected wife may occasionally make a pretty young odalisk's life somewhat uncomfortable, but harsh usage and cruelty are almost unknown; and in general the wife (for now there is seldom more than one) is quite satisfied if her authority is upheld, and if she remain the supreme head of the household. If content on these matters, she rarely troubles herself about the amusements of her husband.

A Turkish woman also rapidly becomes old, and after a few years of youth finds her principal happiness in the care of her children, in eating, in the gossip at the bath, and in the weekly drive to the Valley of the Sweet Waters.

A Turkish wife, whatever her rank, is always at home at sunset to receive her husband, and to present him with his pipe and slippers when, his daily work over, he comes to enjoy the repose of his harem.

In most households also the wife superintends her husband's dinner, and has the entire control over all domestic affairs.

The greatest charm of the Turkish ladies consists in the perfect simplicity of their manners, and in the total absence of all pretence.

When we knew them better, the childlike frankness with which they talked was both amusing and pleasant; but many of them nevertheless were shrewd and intelligent, and had they received anything like adequate education, would have been able to compete with some of the most talented of their European sisters.

As mothers, their tenderness is unequalled, but their fault here is over-indulgence of the children, who, until ten or twelve years of age, are permitted to do everything they like.

Many of the ladies whose acquaintance we made showed a remarkably quick ear, and great facility in learning various songs and pieces of music that we gave them. Their voices were sweet and melodious, and it was surprising with what rapidity they caught the Italian and Neapolitan airs that they heard us sing.

The great bar to any real progress being made towards their due education, and the enlargement of their minds, is the seclusion in which they live.

Men and women are evidently not intended to live socially apart, for each deteriorates by the separation. Men who live only with other men become rough, selfish, and coarse; whilst women, when entirely limited to the conversation of their own sex, grow indolent, narrow-minded, and scandal-loving. Like flint and steel, the brilliant spark only comes forth when the necessary amount of friction has been applied.

Whatever degree of intimacy may be attained, it is rare that foreigners obtain a knowledge of more than the surface of Turkish life and manners. Strangers, therefore, should speak with much caution and reserve; but still, even a casual observer must perceive that polygamy and the singular laws regarding succession are productive of innumerable evils amongst the Turks.

[...]

CHAPTER IV
THE HAREM

The first visit to a Harem is a very exhausting business, for everyone feels shy, and everyone is stupid, and the stupidity and shyness last many hours.

We were fortunate, however, in paying our first ceremonious visit to the Harem of R—— Pasha, whose wife enjoys, and deservedly, the reputation of being as kind in manner as she is in heart. Madame P. was so good as to go with us as interpreter. We were afterwards accompanied by a nice old Armenian woman, well known amongst the Turkish ladies, as she attends many of them in their confinements, and is always summoned to assist at weddings and other festivals, besides being often trusted as the confidential agent for making the first overtures in arranging marriages.

[. . .]

Etiquette requires that a spoonful of the sweetmeat should be eaten, and the spoon then placed in the left-hand bowl. Some iced water is drunk, and then the tips of the fingers only should be delicately wiped with an embroidered napkin presented for the purpose.

A calm and graceful performance of this ceremony marks the "grande dame" amongst Turkish ladies, and many a foreigner has come to grief from being unacquainted with these little details.

[. . .]

Now came more slaves bringing coffee. One carried a silver brazier, on which were smoking several small coffee-pots; another had the cups—lovely little things, made of exquisitely transparent china, and mounted on gold filigree stands; a third carried a round black velvet cloth, embroidered all over in silver. This is used to cover the cups as they are carried away empty.

Narghilés were now brought, and for some minutes we all solemnly puffed away in silence. For myself, personally, this was an anxious moment, for I very much doubted whether my powers as a smoker would enable me to undertake a narghilé, very few whiffs being often enough to make a neophyte faint. I looked at my sister; she was calmly smoking with the serenity and gravity of a Turk. The hanoum's eyes were fixed on vacancy. She had evidently arrived at her fifth heaven at least. The pretty daughter was looking at me, but I did not dare look at her; so, as there was no escape, I boldly drew in a whiff. Things around looked rather indistinct; however, I mustered up my courage and drew in another. It was not as disagreeable as the first, but the indistinct things seemed to get even fainter, and were, besides, becoming a little black, so I took the hint, and, finding nature had not intended me for a smoker, quietly let my pipe go out. Narghilés are now seldom used in harems except for occasions of ceremony. On all subsequent visits cigarettes were brought, which were much more easily managed.

When the pipes were finished we began to talk, and mutually inquired the names and ages of our respective children. The hanoum has three—the eldest son, H—— Bey, the daughter named Nadèje, and a little fellow about five years old, who came running in very grandly dressed, and with a great aigrette of diamonds in his little fez—evidently mamma's pet.

H—— Bey wanted very much to talk. But, alas! our Turkish words were sadly few, and conversation through an interpreter soon languishes and becomes irksome. [. . .]

[…]

Upon our expressing a wish to know how the "yashmak," or veil, was arranged, Nadèje immediately had one put on, to show how it ought to be folded and pinned; and as by this time we had become great friends, it was good-naturedly proposed that we should try the effects of yashmak and "feredje," and the most beautiful dresses were brought, in which we were to be arrayed.

Further acquaintance with the yashmak increases our admiration for it. The filmy delicacy of the muslin makes it like a vapour, and the exquisite softness of its texture causes it to fall into the most graceful folds.

Some of the feredjes, or cloaks, were magnificent garments. One was made of the richest purple satin, with a broad border of embroidered flowers; another of brocade, so thick that it stood alone; another of blue satin worked with seed pearls.

The jackets, "enterrees," &c. &c., were brought in piled upon trays and in numbers that seemed countless. A Parisian's wardrobe would be as nothing compared with the multitude and magnificence of the toilettes spread before us.

The jewels were then exhibited. Turkish jewellers generally mount their stones too heavily, and the cutting is far inferior to that of Amsterdam; but the hanoum had some very fine diamonds, really well set. One aigrette for the hair was exceedingly beautiful. The diamonds were mounted as a bunch of guelder-roses, each rose trembling on its stem. We also much admired a circlet of lilies and butterflies, the antennæ of the butterflies ending in a brilliant of the finest water. There was also a charming ornament for the waist, an immense clasp, made of branches of roses in diamonds, surrounded with wreaths of leaves in pearls and emeralds, a large pear-shaped pearl hanging from each point.

[. . .]

On a Friday, or other holiday, many hundreds of people congregate at the Sweet Waters both of Europe and Asia. The women, arrayed in gorgeous dresses, recline on carpets beneath the trees, little spirals of smoke ascend from the numerous pipes, the narghilé bubbles in its rose-water, the tiny cups of coffee send forth a delicious fragrance, the perfume of fresh oranges and lemons fills the air. The still more exquisite sweetness of orange blossoms is wafted towards us, as a gipsy flower-girl passes through the groups, carrying many a mysterious bouquet, of which the flowers tell a perhaps too sweet and too dangerous love-tale to the fair receiver.

Then a bon-bon seller comes, laden with his box of pretty sweets. Many are really good, especially the sweetmeat called Rahat-la-Koum, when quite fresh, and another, made only of cream and sugar flavoured with orange-flower water.

Every now and then the wild notes of some Turkish music may be heard from the neighbouring hills—the band of a passing Turkish regiment; or perhaps the monotonous but musical chant of some Greek sailors falls on the ear, as they struggle to force their boat up the tremendous stream of the Bosphorus.

Seen from a little distance, and shaded by the flattering folds of the "yash-mak," Oriental women almost always look pretty; but when, as they often do, the fair dames let the veil fall a little, and the features become distinctly visible, the illusion is lost at once.

The eyes are magnificent, almond-shaped, tender and melting, but, with very few exceptions, the nose and mouth are so large and ill-formed, that the face ceases to be beautiful; the superb eyes not compensating for the want of finish in the other features.

As a class, the Armenians were the best-looking, but the women's head-dress was remarkably becoming. They wear a thin coloured handkerchief, with a broad fringe of gauze flowers, tied coquettishly on one side of the head, long plaits of hair being arranged round it like a coronet.

As in Western countries, the middle and lower classes seemed to enjoy themselves the most. They sat on the grass, and talked to their friends. They could eat their fruit and drink their coffee *al fresco*, while some of the Sultan's odalisks, and other great ladies, shut up in their arabas and carriages, performed a slow and dreary promenade up and down the middle of the valley.

Very weary did some of these poor things look, but the guard of black slaves on each side the carriage forbade any hope of an hour's liberty. Happily, excepting in the Sultan's harem, it is now becoming the fashion for the ladies to descend from their carriages and to pass the afternoon beneath the trees.

Many other Eastern fashions are also becoming modified. The huge yellow boots are disappearing, French ones taking their place; parasols and fans are also used, and all the fashionable ladies now wear gloves.

[. . .]

When we had been a few weeks at Constantinople, and had visited some half-dozen harems, we began to think we knew something about Turkish life, and it was not until we had been there some months, and become acquainted with the families of most of the principal pashas, ministers, &c., that we discovered how little we really knew about it.

But although we might change our opinions respecting many domestic customs and manners, time and more intimate knowledge of their character only increased our liking and admiration for the Turks, both men and women.

Benevolence and kindness are the principal characteristics of both sexes. During the whole period of our stay in Turkey we never saw even a child ill-treat a hapless animal.

Travellers, especially women, are seldom sufficiently conversant with the laws of a country to be able to expatiate with much accuracy on such matters. Turkish laws are said to be bad; perhaps they are so, but certainly there are few cities in Europe where the streets can be so safely traversed, both by night and day, as those of Constantinople.

Turkish manners, also, are peculiarly agreeable. Turks are not ashamed to show that they wish to please—that they wish to be courteous; happily they have not yet adopted that brusquerie of manner that is becoming so prevalent in the West.

The fault is perhaps an overabundance of ceremony and etiquette. Even in their own houses, in the seclusion of home, the master of a family is treated with a respectful deference which would astonish many Christian sons, who unhappily often now only look upon their father as the purse-holder, out of whom they must wring as much money as possible.

In the Selamluk* no person seats himself without the permission of the master of the house; in the harem the same etiquette is observed, the hanoum, or first wife, reigning there supreme.

---

* Apartments belonging to the men.

We had often heard that Eastern women enjoyed in reality far more liberty than their Western sisters, and in some respects this is certainly true; but in point of fact the liberty they possess in being able to go in and out unquestioned, to receive and pay visits where they choose, does not at all compensate for the slavery of the mind which they have to endure, from being cut off from the education and mental improvement they would gain by association with the other sex.

Mental imprisonment is worse even than bodily imprisonment, and by depriving a woman of legitimate ambition, by taking from her the wish for mental culture, she is reduced to the condition of a child—a very charming one, probably, when young, but a painful position for her when, youth having departed, the power of fascination decays with the loss of beauty; and though in some instances it is well known that the natural talent of the woman has had the power of retaining her husband's heart, still it too often happens that, after very few years of love and admiration, he turns to one still younger and fairer to charm his hours of leisure.

Not only did we constantly see Madame R—— and her charming daughter Nadèje, and the wives and relatives of the ministers, &c., whose acquaintance we made, but we had the honour of being invited to pay visits to most of the members of the imperial family; and the more we saw of the Turkish ladies the more we liked the kindly, gentle-hearted women who received us with such friendly hospitality.

In the royal palaces there was of course more splendour, more gold, more diamonds, more slaves—especially the hideous black spectres, who are often so revoltingly frightful that they look like nightmares. But in all essentials a description of a visit to one harem serves to describe the receptions at all.

During our visits to their wives the pashas often requested permission to enter the harem, and we were delighted to make the acquaintance of F—— Pasha, a statesman distinguished throughout Europe by his enlightened views, his generous nature, and by the improvements his wise legislation has effected for his country. Successive visits, both to his lovely palace on the Bosphorus and to us on board the yacht, turned this acquaintance into a friendship which we valued as it indeed deserved.

It was sometimes amusing to see the astonishment of the women when they found we did not object to converse with the pasha. They could hardly understand that we would allow him to enter the harem during our stay there.

In deference to their feelings we, however, always drew down our veils before the master of the house entered, a proceeding which we were aware materially increased their respect for us, and for our sentiments of reserve and propriety.

More intimate acquaintance with our Turkish friends enabled us to see how often they were annoyed and disturbed, probably quite unintentionally, by the proceedings of their European guests.

Madame F—— is a charming person, clever and intelligent to an unusual degree. She is said to possess great and legitimate influence with her husband.

She invited us one day to a large party, consisting of most of the "lionnes" of the Constantinopolitan world.

Some of these ladies were very pretty, and perhaps rather fast. Many of them had adopted several French fashions, wearing zouaves and Paris-cut bodies instead of their own pretty jackets and chemises, a change we thought much for the worse. The great mixture of colours, also, which looks so well in the Turkish full dress of ceremony, seemed much out of place in a semi-French costume.

Our Paris bonnets produced quite a furore. So much were they admired that we lent them to be tried on by the whole assembly. Each fair Turk thought she looked lovely in the ludicrous little fabric of lace and flowers, though we would not be so untruthful as to say they were half as becoming as their own fez, with the grand aigrettes of diamonds, which they place so coquettishly on the side of their pretty heads.

These ladies were wonderfully "well up" in all the gossip of Constantinople. They were perfectly cognisant of all the little details of every embassy and legation, knowing every member of them by sight.

They have a game which is played for sugar-plums. Various diplomats or well-known persons are imitated by some peculiarity they have, such as a mode of walking, talking, bowing, &c. The spectators have to guess who is meant, every failure being paid for by a certain number of bon-bons.

Of course the descriptions are unflattering; the more they are so the greater being the laughter excited. Many of the described would have been astonished could they have seen how cleverly they were caricatured. There was a luckless secretary of one of the smaller legations who seemed a favourite victim, as he certainly had many "odd" ways.

5.

MELEK HANUM (DATES UNKNOWN)

℘ THIRTY YEARS IN THE HAREM; ℘

OR, THE AUTOBIOGRAPHY OF MELEK-HANUM, WIFE OF H.H. KIBRIZLI-MEHMET-PASHA

Chapman and Hall, London
1872

℘ SIX YEARS IN EUROPE: ℘

SEQUEL TO THIRTY YEARS IN THE HAREM. THE AUTOBIOGRAPHICAL NOTES OF MELEK-HANUM, WIFE OF H. H. KIBRIZLI-MEHMET-PASHA

Chapman and Hall, London
1873

Melek Hanum (as she appears on the title pages of her books) was a member of the Ottoman elite. Along with other Middle Eastern women included here, her background was multi-ethnic: her mother's family was Greek, her father Armenian, and, after her first marriage to a British doctor ended in divorce, Melek Hanum married a Muslim Turk, converting to Islam at that point. While her family circumstances apparently allowed her access to elite society, they did not provide for her financial security, so Melek Hanum was required to make her fortune through advantageous marriage. Ambitious, politically astute and apparently quite unscrupulous, she worked incessantly to advance the career of her second husband, Kibrizli Mehmet Paşa. Eventually convicted (wrongly, she insists) of ordering the murder of a servant, she was divorced from her husband (who went on to have a distinguished political career) and was sent into exile in Konya. After a number of years, her son from her first marriage, now grown, appeared and helped her escape to Istanbul, where she was reunited with her daughter. Finally they fled to Europe. This dramatic life story is told in Melek Hanum's first book, *Thirty Years in the Harem*. The sequel, *Six Years in Europe*, recounts their continued hardship and penury once they had left the Ottoman dominions; rendering her, as she explains at the end of the book, with no recourse but to publish her autobiography as a means of supporting herself.

As an author, Melek Hanum is sensationalist and self-serving, plotting her story as melodrama: a feisty but wronged woman who does her best under adverse circumstances. To some extent this was perhaps an accurate

reflection of her situation, since her case clearly attracted considerable interest, or at least notoriety. While her writing is interesting on details of
domestic life and slavery, it is not necessarily very reliable since she tends to
generalise from the example of the imperial household. However, Melek
Hanum is very good at demonstrating how elite women were able to exercise political influence, if they chose to. The first passage excerpted here
recounts her own success in dispensing political favours (and the financial
rewards that she accrued) when her husband was serving as the Ottoman
governor in Jerusalem. Throughout the books, she is very concerned with
money: listing her husband's salary, the value of gifts received and given,
and the price of housing, for example. She always cites pressing reasons for
having to involve herself in pecuniary affairs, but clearly delights in her
power and political influence and the money it earned her.

Subsequent passages in her first book, and in its sequel, tell the story of
the complicated series of events which unfolded after her husband (in part
due to Melek Hanum's efforts) was appointed to the important position of
ambassador to the English court and which eventually led to her ruin and
exile. Peopled with deceitful servants, loyal eunuchs and treacherous political enemies, Melek Hanum's account of her life home alone in Istanbul with
her husband away (at this time wives did not accompany their male relatives
who were sent on diplomatic missions to Europe) is theatrical, yet evocative
of the social and economic constraints confronting women who were forced
to operate without the protection of male relatives.

Melek Hanum's work is clearly 'harem literature' of the most sensationalist type, yet it is also very much like popular melodramatic English fiction
of the 1860s, for example, Wilkie Collins's *The Woman in White*. Immediately upon its publication her first book found a ready audience, and
eventually went into further editions. *Thirty Years in the Harem* was
reviewed in *The Levant Herald*, an important English-language newspaper
in Istanbul, where much of Melek Hanum's story had taken place:

> … It is firstly and above all an autobiography… and yet, as her story
> does in point of fact comprise thirty years of harem life it cannot by
> any means be said that the somewhat catch-penny title which she, or
> probably her publishers, have chosen for it, is a misnomer. To the gen-
> eral reader, indeed, the main attraction of the volume will doubtless
> consist in the glimpse which it incidentally affords of the … *Harem*.
> The book can make no pretensions to literary merit: it is written in a
> gossipy and often slipshod style, in much the same words that we
> might suppose to have dropped from the lady's own lips as a hanoum
> in the course of a confidential chat with an inquisitive Frankish lady
> visitor … This *sans gêne* and apparent unconsciousness of addressing
> an aggregate public engages our faith in the unstudied truth of the
> details thus given of life behind the *perdé* … A perusal of the work
> must impress the reader with a fact which often suggests itself to the
> Frank resident here, how far from being the mere cypher that Western
> notions assign to it, is the role of the weaker sex in Turkey … In truth
> it may be said that the might of female influence in the making and
> marring of public man, and the conduct of public affairs is far greater

in this country than in chivalrous Christendom. It is not without some
seeming show of reason that Melek Hanoum claims to have laid the
foundation of the fortunes of her late eminent husband: her acumen,
tact, and indomitable will, undeterred, we may add by over nice
scruple, are abundantly evident throughout. *Levant Herald*, Constantinople, 16 September 1872, vol. 4, no. 15. p. 62.

The review provides fascinating information about how the book and its
audience were perceived in 1872. For example, in noting that the book was
an autobiography, yet sold as harem literature, the writer indicated an awareness of the genre overlap that the book represented, and also pointed out that
the publishers used 'harem' in its title as a marketing strategy. Moreover, the
reviewer also credits Melek Hanum's account of female influence and her
understanding of the Western readership. The truth value of the book is
assessed both on the basis of the textual strategies of the author ('apparent
unconsciousness of addressing an aggregate public') and the specialist
knowledge of the *Levant Herald*'s readership ('the Frank resident here').

℘   ℭ

[From *Thirty Years in the Harem*]

During these fêtes I remained in the [governor's] palace [in Jerusalem], where
the ladies of the principal dignitaries of the city came to call on me; it is usual in
the East to do so at the time of the chief solemnities of the year. My fair visitors
belonged to the most diverse nationalities: Moors, with light hair and fair com-
plexions; Arabs, with their expression full of pride; Georgians and Circassians,
with regular and pleasing features. All brought their narghilés, or pipes; they
seated themselves in a circle round me, and we passed our time agreeably, chatting together with the utmost freedom; for all etiquette is banished from
conversations among women.

Sometimes they spoke to me about their protégés. "Could you not contrive,"
said one, "to procure my brother his exchange? he is *caïmakam* (lieutenant-
colonel) of a *sandjak* (department), and I am very anxious to have him appointed
to a better post." "Perhaps," added another, "madame will be able to get me the
place of this caïmakam, of whom such complaints are made." "It rests with you,"
observed the first speaker, "to do me this service; I assure you that you won't
find us ungrateful; if you succeed, we will give you a beautiful present."

To all this I gave no answer; but the next day I would call the steward or the
secretary. "Such a person," I would say, "has been recommended to me, and I
have a promise that my good offices shall not go unrequited: do what you can to
procure a favorable exchange, and you shall have your share of whatever I may
receive."

The official whom I thus addressed, knowing that his place depended upon me, would seize the first opportunity to speak to his master. "Your excellency," he would say, "the caïmakam of such and such a sandjak is giving cause for much complaint; he is said to be accessible to bribes, and to be careless in the discharge of his duties."

"I have heard some reports about him, but I did not think they were serious."

"These reports are, unhappily, too well founded; and, although they may be somewhat exaggerated, would it not be better to have, at so important a post, some person in whom you could place entire confidence? I know, for example, some one of the greatest zeal in your excellency's service; he is thoroughly competent, and, if you will allow him to wait upon you, I feel assured that you will be pleased with him."

The interview being held and the Pasha satisfied, the exchange is effected, and I receive what has been promised me. In two years I disposed in this manner of more than fifteen important posts in favor of persons whom I had never even set eyes on.

Another means of procuring funds for myself was by engaging in commerce, a thing expressly forbidden to Pashas, but which I carried on in person, without the intervention of the governor in any respect.

The inhabitants are bound to furnish horses, mules, or camels for the public service, and this without any remuneration. My agents demanded of the peasants, on my behalf, their beasts of burden; and they fearing lest, by a refusal, they should draw upon themselves the anger of the Pasha, lent the animals, which were employed in conveying from Jaffa the corn I had purchased there. This was sold at Jerusalem at a considerable profit, although it was offered at a somewhat lower price than that asked by the merchants, who were obliged to defray the heavy expenses of transport.

As may be seen, the promises which the ministers make to the European powers, and the orders which they give in consequence to the various authorities, are eluded, and all the more readily since the Porte has no real intention of making them respected. If a European consul had lodged any complaint at Constantinople about the trade in which I engaged, what answer would be returned? "What you complain of calls for no censure; the merchants of Jerusalem sell grain to the people at exorbitant prices; the governor's wife, in order to assuage the misery of the inhabitants, finds means to sell wheat at a reasonable rate, and the peasants associate themselves in this good work by lending their animals; there is nothing to find fault with in that."

[…]

On my return I found the Pasha was absent, having gone to put down an armed dispute that had arisen between two Arab villages.

One day, when I was quietly resting in the harem after the fatigue of my journey, I heard a great tumult in the court-yard of the palace, where the Pasha's court of justice and other offices were situated. My apartments communicated with this court-yard by a large staircase outside. I saw through the window a furious crowed of Arabs raising terrible shouts. I inquired for the steward, the cavas-baschi, and the other officers, in order to ask them the cause of such a disturbance. They, fearing for their lives if they showed themselves to these people, had done their best to conceal themselves.

Seeing that, if the Arabs were allowed their own way, they might proceed to extremities, I quickly made up my mind, and half covering my face with a shawl, presented myself at the head of the staircase:

"What is the matter, my friends, that you raise such an outcry? Tell me what you want, and although the Pasha is absent, I will do what I can to oblige you."

"The matter!" said one of them, who appeared to be one of the ringleaders. "They have lately established, at the gates of the city, a duty upon all the merchandise we bring in, in such a manner that we are obliged to pay before we have sold any thing; moreover, the license to collect this tax has been conferred upon a Frenchman; so that we are toiling to enrich an infidel. We wish the duty to be removed."

"I am on your side," I answered; "I had pledged the Pasha not to impose this tax, but an order from the Sultan compelled him to do so, and he was forced to obey; the Frenchman of whom you complain is not responsible. Moreover, we have written to Constantinople to ask for the suppression of this levy; in two or three days we shall receive a reply; there is every reason to believe that the Padishah, who is a father to his subjects, will grant the abolition which we have solicited."

At these words they all cried out, "God bless the wife of our governor! Allah protect our Pasha! Long live our Sultan! Amin! Amin!"

"In praying for your master, you do well," I replied; "always continue to act thus, and you will obtain whatever is just. Return to your homes, and as soon as the answer arrives it shall be proclaimed."

They withdrew, satisfied at the result of their proceeding. As for me, I was better pleased to see them depart than I cared to show. I returned to my apartments attended by their clamorous blessings.

The next morning I summoned the cavas-baschi, and asked him the names of the principal authors of the disturbances of the day before. He named fifteen. I immediately directed him, as usual in such cases, to seize them—an order which was executed before they left their homes. They were forthwith sent into exile, and were not permitted to return until their spirit had been completely subdued. It may be that some among them were innocent, but in such affairs it seems preferable to run the risk of inflicting some slight suffering both on the innocent and the guilty, rather than to excite popular passions by proceeding in the regular course of justice in order to apportion the blame attaching to each. In the East these nice distinctions are not attended to; guilty and innocent are arrested, and chastisement inflicted upon them.

[…]

CHAPTER XVI

It was in the month of Ramazan, in the year 1848, that my husband was appointed ambassador to the English Court. This appointment was occasioned by the threatening attitude assumed by Russia by her intervention in the Austro–Hungarian difficulty. The Porte, alarmed at the progress made by this Power, thought it necessary to form an alliance with the West, and particularly with Great Britain. This delicate mission was intrusted to Kibrizli-Mehemet-Pasha, who was intimately associated with Reshid-Pasha, the promoter of this new policy.

Independently of the political reasons which influenced this nomination, Reshid had certain entirely private motives for the selection of my husband; he wished to secure the friendship and support of the Palmerston Cabinet, and to bring financial operations to bear upon the London market. In other words, he offered England commercial and financial advantages in exchange for the support which that Power would undertake to give to his own policy and personal control. The negotiations which preceded this appointment did not take place altogether unknown to me. On the contrary, my share in the transaction materially assisted its prosperous issue. With this view I used my personal influence with the grand vizier, to induce him to nominate my husband to the post, in preference to any other candidate. Kibrizli-Pasha used immense exertions to achieve his object, but he thought it prudent to send me alone, in advance, as a negotiator, for he feared lest he should compromise himself in vain. Experience had taught him that nothing was impossible to a woman.

[…]

Since religious prejudices and custom forbid Mussulman wives to accompany their husbands into a Christian country, I was, of course, unable to go with my husband to his embassy. [Secluding herself and rarely leaving the house, Melek Hanum's spirits became very low.]

[…]

My boy, Djehad-Bey, was naturally of a sickly and feeble constitution, so that he had always been a subject of great anxiety both to me and to his father. Soon after the Pasha left for London, Djehad's health grew worse from day to day, so that the physicians at length lost all hope of his recovery. This crowned my despair, for I knew that nothing could console his father for such a loss. The Pasha dearly loved this child, whom he regarded as his future heir. The death of his elder son, Moharem-Bey, had already caused him lively sorrow, and now, if Djehad died, he would be inconsolable. But, independently of these considerations, which only affected me indirectly, sinister notions meanwhile filled my breast with alarm. Selfishness, making its voice heard amidst grief and disappointment, caused me, I must confess, to dread the consequences which the loss of Djehad might produce as regards my position. It seemed to me that the loss of his heir would impel the Pasha to take another wife, and to put me on one side, after the fashion in vogue among other Turks. When once this idea found a place in my brain it was impossible to get rid of it; on the contrary, all my efforts could not prevent its increasing more and more, until it at length attained the proportions of a vampire that persecuted me by night and by day.

[…]

Skillfully feigning to share my uneasiness and to take to heart my interests, while discussing the probabilities that might arise out of the death of my poor boy, this woman [her housekeeper, Fatmah], far from striving to tranquilize my spirits, increased my agitation by the assurance that my suspicions regarding my husband's intentions were only too well founded, for she herself knew, on good authority, that the Pasha had resolved to marry again in case his son died. Such an event, she remarked, would inevitably bring about my destruction, as a woman like myself would never tolerate such an affront.

Having succeeded, by such words as these, in convincing me of her devotion, and exciting in my breast the most violent emotions, Fatmah then proceeded to give me advice, and to tell me that it was needless to give way to despair, for that in this world a remedy could be found for every ill. Pressed to explain herself more particularly, Fatmah added:

"Well, madam, you have only to buy a child of some unhappy creature, and to put him in the place of your own. The Pasha's absence affords a golden opportunity which should not be lost."

This counsel cheered me to such a degree, that at that moment I did not hesitate to recognize in the treacherous Fatmah a savior who would restore my tranquillity and assure my happiness. But now, when I calmly reflect on the impropriety of which I was guilty in associating with such a woman, I can scarcely understand how I could have had a mind so perverted and so blinded as to be unablè to see that Fatmah's project was a piece of sheer madness.

To have recourse to a feigned confinement, in order to put forth as my own an infant that was the offspring of another, was a simple impossibility, for the very agents whom I should have to employ to execute such a piece of jugglery would be the first to reveal the secret and compromise me before the world.

But a phantom of the imagination that seemed to be pursuing me, and the dread I entertained of a catastrophe, so utterly blinded me, that I believed every thing to be possible. And so, with inconceivable simplicity, it appeared to me that nothing could be easier than to give one's self out to enceinte, and to borrow an infant, just as one may borrow a costume, or set of jewels, or any thing else. As for the agents whom it was necessary to employ in the performance of this precious trick, it never entered into my head that they would take the earliest opportunity of betraying me.

And, in the mean time, I was the woman whose intellect was vaunted and admired by every one; she whom all were ready to consult as if she were an oracle! But such is the weakness of the human mind, which from the loftiest height may fall into the abyss of insanity and blind infatuation! It is an acknowledged truth that the more spirit one has, the more follies one commits. That my folly was inexcusable I admit, and it is this conviction that has led me to endure with resignation the twenty years of suffering to which I have been condemned. But this fault, which had its source in a feeling of jealousy, very natural in a woman, attained, thanks to the spite of my enemies, the proportions of an infamous crime. They who thirsted for my blood transformed, I say, a simple fault into a crime, and punished me by social degradation, by exile, by the confiscation of every thing I possessed, and by condemning me to a life of misery and shame. It is time, however, to take up the thread of my story at the point from which I have digressed. Fatmah succeeded in obtaining my consent, and all the needful measures were taken to prepare for the birth of the pretended infant. The critical period having arrived, Fatmah went in search of a child, and bought one from a poor woman, who was glad to get rid of what she found too heavy a burden.

It must here be mentioned that Fatmah was not alone in the enterprise, for it would have been impossible for her to accomplish her work without previously securing the aid of another agent. With this view, she thought fit to take into her confidence one of the eunuchs, named Beshir, in order that he might have a hand in the clandestine introduction of the infant. However, all the pains they took were absolutely useless, inasmuch as the sickness of my son Djehad all of a sudden took a favorable turn, and his recovery was not long delayed. And so, after all, the only result of this affair was that I found myself charged with an additional burden, and became the victim of those of whom I had been the accomplice.

[…]

[Fatmah was bribed to leave and Beshir was appeased, but Fatmah returned during a religious celebration, even though Melek Hanum challenged her right to be present.] As I saw clearly, by the tone of this response, that Fatmah would have no hesitation in creating a scene in the midst of the guests, I thought it prudent to retire; not forgetting, however, to summon Beshir, and caution him to say nothing to the woman, for I did not wish to have a disturbance in the house. I gave him to understand that Fatmah would only stay a very short time, and consequently he need not think any thing at all about her.

Counting on the efficacy of the measures I had taken, I entered the room where my guests were assembled, and gave myself up to duties of hospitality.

But, while the company were regaling themselves with the charms of music and of song, Fatmah was engaged in the prosecution of her sanguinary designs. Skillfully evading observation, she proceeded gently to open the door that separated the selamlik from the harem, and admitted one of the servants, named Omer, who, as her lover, was to bear a hand in the contemplated assassination. Fatmah then succeeded, by a ruse, in inveigling Beshir into the bath-room; there the two assassins sprang upon the unfortunate Arab, hurled him to the ground, and suffocated him. Such was Fatmah's rage against her victim, that she resolutely took his life herself by sitting on his face, while Omer contented himself by throwing him down and holding his hands.

CHAPTER XVII

Scarcely had Beshir heaved his last sigh when the doors of the harem were broken open, and an infuriated crowd invaded the apartment, with cries of "Murder! murder! Vengeance! vengeance!" Terror seized on every one. The guests took flight from the fury of the mob. The insurgents made their way to the room whither I had retired, with three of four of my slaves, who had remained faithful to my cause. The wretches, on entering, did not scruple to bespatter me with the blood of Beshir, and to menace me with sabres, sticks, and other weapons which they brandished in the air.

I must here pause to remark that among this swarm of invaders there were not more than five or six members of my household; the remainder, numbering perhaps thirty or thereabout, were strangers, whose presence at this moment is quite incomprehensible. It would appear as though they had been collected together in order to give a theatrical effect to the tragedy.

Order could only be restored through the intervention of the police, who lost no time in appearing on the scene of the disaster. The police agents hastened to make out their official report by submitting the assassins to examination. When they came to inquire into the motives for the commission of the crime, a scene of violence ensued. On the one hand, those who sought my destruction boisterously called upon Fatmah and Omer to inculpate me alone; on the other, these preserved an obstinate silence. This strife was carried on for some time without inducing the culprits to depose that it was solely by my orders that they had killed the enurch. It was only through a hint that by this means alone could they hope to escape capital punishment, that the two murders were induced to avow I had ordered them to put Beshir to death. As soon as the depositions were taken, the prisoners were conducted, under escort, to the office of the Minister of Police to take their trial.

During the course of these tragic events, my enemies, and those of my husband, tried their utmost to achieve our ruin. My enemies were delighted to have at last found the means of crushing me forever, and putting it out of my power to injure them. The political enemies of my husband, on their part, hastened to take advantage of the opportunity afforded them of separating us, and so destroying our combined action. Without me, Mehemet-Pasha was a half-disabled foe, for it was well known what a part I had had in his promotion. It was through me that an understanding had been established between him and the grand vizier, and it was by my efforts that his nomination to the post of Minister for Foreign Affairs had been spoken of with favor. Such an event, his opponents well knew, would be a death-blow to them. These said enemies were the Valideh, the Sultan's mother; Mehemet-Ali-Pasha; Mehemet-Pasha, Minister of Police; Rifaat, and a host of other Pashas more or less influential.

Impelled by such motives, these people made as great an uproar as possible, and spread false reports of my alleged crimes and atrocities. The journals, native and foreign, were filled stories designed to gratify public credulity, and to exhibit my character under the most revolting aspect. This was an easy task, for I had no one to take my part.

Finding that by such means they had produced the desired effect, my enemies had recourse to legal proceedings, and procured my arrest. Four days, indeed after Beshir's death, I received a summons to appear before the Minister of Police to answer the charges that had been brought against me. Tearing myself from my children, and from those about me who had remained faithful, I got into my carriage, and was driven to the office. I was then confined in a house which the Government had prepared and furnished for the occasion. My keepers were two female servants and a domestic, in the confidence of the minister, and upon whom he could rely. As to the treatment I had to undergo from them during my imprisonment, I may say that while, on the one hand, they affected to lavish on me those attentions which were due to woman in my position, on the other hand they resorted to every means of intimidation.

[…]

While these things were going on in the office of the Minister of Police, intrigues outside were running their free course. The enemies of Reshid-Pasha's cabinet were making superhuman efforts to crush, at one blow, myself and my husband. Taking advantage of the prevalent public feeling, they endeavored to make my affair a ministerial question, and impeached Reshid-Pasha for shielding me.

The grand vizier, indeed, saw that it was impossible to save me from the hands of my enemies, for such a course would have been fatal to his administration.

Compelled to yield before such a coalition, Reshid found himself under the necessity of a abandoning me to my fate.

However, he did his best to save Kibrizli-Pasha from being involved in my ruin, for, by so doing, he neutralized the efforts of those who were seeking to disable one of his colleagues. With this object, therefore, he forthwith summoned my husband to Constantinople, held sundry long conferences with him, and succeeded in persuading him of the necessity of appeasing the clamors of the opposition by repudiating me.

This sacrifice, as I learned afterward, cost the poor Pasha many tears, but political exigencies prevailed over sentimental and all other considerations, and my husband was forced to bow to the will of his chief. My divorce was immediately notified to me by the emissaries of the Minister of Police, who handed me back my dowry, a mere trifle, and made me sign a receipt. […]

[…]

[CHAPTER XVIII]

Months, years passed away without any change in my situation, which would have been sad and wearisome in the extreme but for the generous hospitality of the worthy governor.

I need scarcely say that, during my stay at Koniah, the mental depression which weighed upon me as an exile could not be alleviated, either by the sympathy or generous kindness which the good Hafiz-Pasha and his family bestowed on me. I can say that, though exiled in body, my spirit was at Constantinople with the objects of my affection, my children and my husband. Day and night my thoughts carried me to my native land, and I felt almost inconsolable; frequently, in a fit of despair, I turned my eyes to heaven, and cried, "My God, when will my afflictions cease?—when shall I find peace?" The fervency of my prayers brought about my deliverance in an almost miraculous way, for the Almighty sent me a protector in my son Frederick, who came unexpectedly to my assistance, comforting me in my sorrow, and reviving me in the midst of my enemies.

The reader will remember my stating at the beginning how I had left at Rome my daughter Evelyn and Frederick, my eldest son. Since my marriage with Kibrizli-Pasha I had entirely lost sight of these dear children, who had been placed in convents, and brought up under the care of their aunt.

It happened, however, that Frederick, on his return to Constantinople, hearing of my persecution and exile, determined on joining his fate to mine. Driven almost to madness by the love of a mother he had scarcely seen, he threw himself at the feet of Mehemet-Ali-Pasha, the then Minister of War, 1854, and implored him to allow him to join his mother, she to whom he owed his existence.

The Pasha, touched by this proof of filial affection, acceded to his prayer, and immediately issued the orders necessary to enable him to proceed to Koniah. Mehemet-Ali also gave him out of his private purse the sum of thirty pounds to provide him with the funds for the journey.

I had gone one day to visit one of my friends, who lived near to the tomb of the patron saint of Koniah, and was resting myself near a window, when we heard a knock at the door. My friend hastened to ascertain who it was, but, instead of coming back to me, she remained talking in a low voice with the stranger, whoever it might be.

Animated by a feeling of curiosity, I looked toward the door, and saw through the opening an elegant-looking young man, dressed in uniform, who suddenly walked into the room and up to the place where I was sitting.

This strange apparition, and the boldness shown by the youth, alarmed me, and involuntarily I recoiled, and was about to rise from my seat, when the stranger threw his arms around my neck, crying out,

"Don't you know me, mother? I am Frederick."

These words quite overcame me, for at that moment of supreme excitement I could scarcely believe my eyes, or trust my ears. Frederick, whom I had left almost an infant, and whom I considered as lost to me forever, could it possibly be the handsome young fellow before me? Was it a dream, the past thirteen years, or was it reality?

My poor boy, enraptured by the sight of a mother upon whom he could at last gaze, kissed me over and over again, holding me in his arms, and seemed never tired of looking at me. He took out his purse, containing his whole wealth, and placed it in my hands, saying,

"Take it, mother; you are poor, but I love you."

From that moment the fairest prospects seemed opening before me; I was no longer a desolate and deserted woman without a defender or helper. The news of my dear son's arrival produced a great sensation at Koniah, all my friends sharing in my joy.

Frederick, who had assumed the name of Osman-Bey, remained with me a month, and on his return to Constantinople did his best in order to have me recalled from exile. It was owing to intelligence I received from him that decided me on endeavoring to make my escape, so as to join him at Constantinople, and from that time he has ever been my protector and comfort, and the support of my old age.

ℬ ☙

[From *Six Years in Europe*]

CHAPTER XXI

[...] My [financial] embarrassments augmented as time rolled on, nor did I see any prospect of avoiding a catastrophe. In my dilemma I solicited advice of M. Decourdemanche.

"Why not write a book?" said he. "Yours has been an eventful life; you must have much to relate that would interest the public. What say you to my proposition?"

I had only one objection to make to it; my inability to write any European language. The alternative of dictation offered a ready solution of this difficulty, and it was agreed that if his friend Monsieur Paton, of the "Gaulois," could arrange for the publication of the work, in that journal, in a series of *feuilletons*, I might earn a few thousand francs very honourably.

I ought to state that the most pressing necessity alone induced me to yield to this proposition. The idea of writing a book had never once crossed my mind, and I felt great reluctance to make myself the heroine of a romance which turned on details of family life, and involved disclosures I would rather not have to make. There is, however, no reasoning with necessity and clamouring creditors. I therefore yielded to its ignorance of all laws.

Under these circumstances I commenced the dictation of my memoirs, in the form suggested, the eldest son of M. Decourdemanche—whom I shall call Monsieur Alphonse—acting as amanuensis. He devoted about two hours every evening to this work, and as I could not suspect that either he or Monsieur Paton entertained any relations with my husband and his kinsfolk and friends at Constantinople, I kept nothing back. [...]

[...]

But a bitter disappointment awaited me. A few days later Monsieur Alphonse informed me that Monsieur Paton had taken the manuscript to the Turkish Embassy, and been prevailed upon not to issue the narrative, as originally agreed, but to set the book aside, and write instead, a series of articles on the subject of the intended introduction of the railway system into Turkey, for which the sum of ten thousand francs would be paid him; and that for the services he had already rendered to the Turkish government, the order of the Medjidi would be conferred upon him. In this way I learnt—to my astonishment—of the relations of Monsieur Paton and his friends with those I had every reason to regard as my enemies, and as spies upon my actions.

[...]

I at once made application to two other popular daily newspapers, the editor of one of which went so far as to advertise the publication of the work, under the title of "Memoirs of a Turkish Lady." Three or four days after, the editor informed me he had changed his mind, and if he published the work at all, it would not be until the next year. He declined to give me any explanation of his course, and I had to submit to another disappointment. I was also unsuccessful in the other instance, and was so discouraged that I shut up the manuscript in my trunk, and abandoned the idea of publishing it.

[...]

[Estranged from her daughter, Melek Hanum finds that Ayeshah has recently married her enemy, M. Alphonse.] This was the last blow. The cup was full. Husband, daughter, wealth, position, prospects, gone! I turned sick! Hope died within me: smitten out of my heart suddenly, at once, by this final stroke. The bitterness of the hour was aggravated by the thought that my enemies had at length triumphed, and were rejoicing over my defeat. I felt that nothing now remained to me that I at all cared to live for. Bewildered, scarcely conscious, I allowed my friend to lead me away, like a passive infant. She took me back to the sea-side, where a raging fever seized me, and where, for a period of five months, I hung between lunacy and death.

It was my fate to recover. With convalescence came thoughts for the means of supplying the necessaries of existence. I remembered the rough record of my life, lying useless in my trunk. I had no ambition to appear before the world as an author, but daily needs are imperative, and my sole, immediately available resource lay in that trunk. I sought a publisher, and found one. I leave "Thirty Years in the Harem" and this present narrative of my experiences in Europe to tell their own tale. Their sole merit is their truthfulness. Between me and my persecutors I leave the reader as Judge.

6.

ANNIE LADY BRASSEY (1839–87)

ഔ A VOYAGE IN THE 'SUNBEAM' ଌ

OUR HOME ON THE OCEAN FOR ELEVEN MONTHS

Longmans, Green and Co., London
1878

ഔ SUNSHINE AND STORM ଌ
IN THE EAST

OR CRUISES TO CYPRUS AND CONSTANTINOPLE

Longmans, Green and Co., London
1880

ഔ UNPUBLISHED JOURNAL ଌ

1883
Hastings Public Library, UK

Annie Lady Brassey was a wealthy English woman, traveller, amateur bota-
nist, philanthropist, writer – in many ways a typical product of her class and
period, but equally a woman of extraordinary achievements. She travelled
with her husband and children aboard their own yacht, and to a large extent
was isolated from the native inhabitants of the lands to which they journeyed. While on land they moved, as much as possible, within the confines
of empire. That is, they stayed with British colonial officials, socialised with
the British elite whenever they were available, visited at Government
House, and interacted in a very limited way with local, non-British society.
As their travels are described in Brassey's five books, and judging from the
contents of both Brassey's museum collections and the photograph albums
she assembled, her goal in their travel was, at least partially, the accumula-
tion of knowledge about the world. For her, knowledge seems to have
consisted of facts about plant life, geology, biology and, to a much lesser
extent, native arts and crafts.

Brassey's writing about Cairo and Istanbul included here spans a nine-
year period, from 1874 to 1883, and is excerpted from two of her published
books and her unpublished journal. All of Brassey's books adopt the same
structure. She presents a chronological edited version of the daily accounts

of the family's activities, including their excursions, unusual events that occurred on the ship, social events on land and sea, and a great deal of information about the appearance and condition of the places they visited.

Brassey's writing displays some of the characteristics that other authors have identified in the work of Victorian women travel writers. Her books are often introduced with a short preface by her husband, who, in the way that male relatives apparently felt it necessary to do in this period, speaks in a disparaging manner of 'these simple pages', but also lauds his wife's faithful recording of her impressions, and her perseverance. He therefore reminds the reader that the author was simply recording what she saw, not carrying out exploration or research, and that, unlike the accepted paradigm of male genius, she laboured long and hard at her work. While Brassey supported British imperial politics, she did not present her own travel narrative as a journey of conquest or penetration. She does participate in the project of imperialism in her desire to inform her readers about all that she saw, positioning herself as an explorer whose gains are in knowledge rather than territory.

A Voyage in the 'Sunbeam', the second of Brassey's travel accounts, was by far the most successful, in part perhaps because of the novelty of the journey it described: a family with four young children travelling around the world for eleven months on their private yacht. The book appeared in its first edition in 1878, and was reprinted many times. The passage from the *Sunbeam* excerpted here recounts some of Brassey's brief 1877 visit to Cairo with her children, where they saw the pyramids and visited the old city. The Brasseys stayed at Shepherd's Hotel, as did many British visitors in this period. From their vantage point in the modern city they regarded the old city as a kind of museum, which they wished would remain unchanged.

We also include passages from *Sunshine and Storm in the East*, Brassey's third book, published in 1880. The book is divided into two parts, the first of which concerns Istanbul and the Ionian Islands in 1874, and the second describing Cyprus and Istanbul in 1878; the book's title refers to the great differences that Brassey noticed in Istanbul between their first and second trips.

The selections here focus on Brassey's interactions with Ottoman women, and her observations concerning their lives. She is an acute observer of detail, noting the dress, coiffure and accoutrements of the women as they were moving more and more towards European fashion. Because of her own social position, she visited very high-ranking Ottoman women, who spoke French or English, so the language barriers that other writers noted were not a problem, and they were able to converse freely on a variety of topics. The last excerpt from the book is from Brassey's second visit to Istanbul, in 1878, describing a party she hosted on their yacht for her Ottoman women friends, which reveals Brassey's ongoing acquaintance with women in the upper echelons of the Ottoman elite over a number of years, their interest in her and in her daughters, and the changes in Ottoman social mores during the past four years.

Brassey's books were based on the letters she wrote home in the form of a journal that was copied and distributed among a number of people by her secretary. Some of her journal, from the collection of the Hastings Public Library, is also excerpted here. Her account of the family's daily activities and the people with whom they interacted while they were in Cairo in 1883 is invaluable as a means of understanding what constituted travel for wealthy English speakers in this period. A description of Brassey's visits to two Egyptian women of her acquaintance is notable for the information it provides about their interior furnishings and their fashions in 1883, as well as other details – for example, Princess Mansour presented Brassey with photographs of herself and her family, indicating the extent to which photography had been adopted by the Egyptian and Ottoman elite by this point. Brassey is a careful observer whose writings about the women she met in Cairo and Istanbul give a sense of the nature of her engagement with their world, but more interestingly, show the extent to which some elite Ottoman women maintained active social ties with European women, which spanned many years and crossed continents.

ಉ   ೞ

[From *A Voyage in the 'Sunbeam'*]

Wednesday, October 28*th.*—To-day we paid visits to some harems. The two nieces of the Viceroy of Egypt, Princess Nazli and Princess Azizieh, on whom we first called, were at their farm in the country. Madame Ikbal Kiasim, daughter-in-law of Fuad Pasha (the greatest statesman Turkey ever had), after keeping us waiting some time, sent first a slave and then a French *dame de compagnie* to tell us she was in her bath, and was therefore very sorry she could not receive us.

At Madame Hilmeh Bey's (granddaughter of Fuad Pasha) we were more fortunate. She was at home, and received us in a French *robe de matinée*, a blue cashmere beautifully embroidered with wreaths of roses, *crêpe lisse* ruffs and frills, a pile of dyed golden hair (naturally black) rolled and twisted and curled in the latest fashion. She laid down a French novel to rise and greet us—rather a contrast to the last harem I had been in at Tunis. All the women of the higher classes of the present generation are tolerably educated, have European governesses, and read European books—principally novels, I fancy—and all bemoan their present hard fate very much. It is a great mistake of the Turks to think that they can educate their wives and daughters, and still keep them in confinement and subjection. To hear this poor little woman talk of her own and her lady-friends' feelings, you would think the revolution must soon come. The children of the present day in Turkey are brought up to think the system of yashmaks and confinement a most tyrannical custom, and not to be endured. Still I am afraid education does not prevent their using the cowhide frequently and very cruelly on their slaves. During our visit to-day two slaves, attired in semi-English semi-Turkish dress, brought us in first some sweetmeats and a glass of water each, and afterwards a cup of coffee. Our hostess apologised for not sharing it with us, owing to its being Ramazan. After dinner at Misseri's, we went to the Turkish theatre, where we saw what appeared to be a very amusing piece, though of course we could not understand a word. The dresses were all Turkish, the actresses all Armenians. Ten years ago the Armenian women were veiled as carefully as the Turkish women, and it was difficult to tell them apart. Now it is equally difficult to tell the former from Europeans, either in dress or manners.

[...]

In the afternoon [...] we went in caïques down the Golden Horn to the Sweet Waters of Europe. It was a pleasant row of about two hours, the latter part up a narrow river bordered with velvety turf and shaded by magnificent plane-trees. In the spring and summer, when the whole place is crowded with caïques and carriages, and the Turkish ladies are seated in groups under the trees on their carpets, eating sweetmeats and drinking coffee, it must indeed be a gay scene. At the Sultan's kiosk we got out and walked to the palace, a little higher up. The whole place swarmed with peacocks. There were hundreds of them in every direction, walking about the greensward, perched on the trees, on the walls, on the housetop, or running in and out of the mansion specially provided for them, adjoining the palace. They are great favourites of the Sultan, and, as such, are well cared for. The carriage met us here, and we drove back to Constantinople. Just as we were starting up the hill, our dragoman asked us if we had our revolvers. As it so happened, we had not thought it necessary to bring them; but though it had become quite dark before we reached the town, we did not meet with any molestation.

Saturday, October 31*st.*—After breakfast we set off in the gig to visit the new Palace of Tcheragan, as Aarif Pasha had arranged for us to do. We saw all over the harems, consisting of hundreds of rooms, with floors covered with matting, distempered walls, and very elaborate curtains, each furnished with a large four-post bed and numerous divans, covered with splendid satin brocades, all differing in pattern from each other, as well as from the curtains. Only one wardrobe, and not a single chair, was to be found in the whole palace. However handsome their clothes may be, the women just lay them in a heap on the floor. We wanted to look at the Sultan's apartments, which are the best worth seeing; but unfortunately he was coming to make a personal inspection, so we were obliged to retire with our curiosity ungratified.

[...]

We were to have ridden round the walls again; but as it was a pouring wet day, we wasted some time in debating and hoping it would clear. The expedition round the walls had to be abandoned, and in the afternoon Evie and I went to pay some visits in the harems, having previously sent notice of our intention, as the Turkish ladies like to be fully prepared to receive visitors. We first went to the Princess Azizieh's, and, having passed through several doors and climbed up innumerable stairs, found ourselves in her reception-room, commanding a beautiful view over the Bosphorus. The Princess received us in an elaborate blue velvet *toilette de matin,* trimmed with undyed ostrich feathers, her hair being very much frizzed. she is a decidedly stout but pretty woman, with lovely eyes, teeth, hair, and expression. Soon after our arrival a long jasmine stick pipe, with a beautiful amber mouthpiece, studded with diamonds, was brought in by the slaves and handed round. Sweetmeats followed on a gold tray, in gold dishes, thick with large diamonds and rubies, and finally coffee in egg-shell china cups, encased in exquisite gold filagree stands, pierced with holes, each hole filled with a large diamond, set clear and swinging, so that the effect was most brilliant. The Princess had a pleasant little French companion, Madame Boyer, and she herself, for a Turkish lady, talked very well; so the visit was pleasant, though a long one. It is considered an insult to your hostess to remain less than an hour, and we stayed longer. The Princess had some of her slaves dressed up, that we might see their costumes. One little black page, about nine years old, in a gorgeous Albanian dress, stiff with gold lace and embroidery, and a remarkably full white petticoat, was very droll. The Princess herself smoked cigarettes the whole time, and was interested about the yacht, which she is extremely anxious to see. She asked many questions concerning our manners and customs in England, our travels, and London and Paris, both of which cities she is dying to visit, though she has very little chance at present of doing so, I fear—poor thing! The conversation turned, as usual, on the wrongs of the Turkish women, and the most ardent longings for freedom and liberty were expressed by all.

Madame Kiasim unfortunately being again engaged, our next visit was to the Princess Nazli, sister of the Princess Azizieh, quite as pretty, perhaps even better educated, certainly more advanced in her ideas, and speaking English as perfectly as her sister does French. Her rooms are as beautifully fitted up in light blue satin and brocade as her sister's are in the same materials of a red colour. The furniture was all French, and very handsome, but here many books and flowers might be seen, and the place had altogether a more European and home-like look. The Princess, who wore a plaid dressing-gown, received us kindly. The numerous slaves were not particularly well dressed, but the pipes, the sweetmeat and coffee services were resplendent with rubies, diamonds, and precious stones. She, like her sister, smoked all the time, and conversed pleasantly and frankly, telling us many details of the interior of Turkish life, and of her own history. Her father, Mustapha Fazil, is only twenty days younger than his brother the Viceroy of Egypt, and was his heir-apparent till the Sultan changed the order of succession and made it pass to the Viceroy's eldest son—a step which he is anxious to take in his own case, but which, I should think, would never be allowed by the Mussulmans. Princess Nazli, who is a grand-daughter of Mehemet Ali, was engaged to her cousin, the heir-apparent, and all her trousseau was prepared, when the Viceroy was seized with a sudden fear of being poisoned if surrounded by too many near relations; so the match was broken off, and she was engaged to Halil Pasha, who, when his father died, is said to have had two millions and a half sterling left him in gold, packed in boxes. He went to Paris, spent a million and a half in that most fascinating of cities, then returned, married the Princess, and settled down to spend the remaining million.

Izzet Bey, who married the sister, seems much nicer, though he is not so rich. He is the son of a most charming mother, a Circassian slave, who was brought up and educated by Fuad Pasha, and was ultimately chosen by him to become his son's wife. Fuad Pasha accompanied the Sultan to England and Paris in 1867. Among many other reforms, he wished to bring about the freedom of women. He even said, in a memorable speech on a public occasion, that Turkey would never take its proper place till the walls between the Selemlek (or men's apartments) and the harem were broke down, and the softening and purifying influence of women was allowed to be felt. Consequently his relations, the ladies of the harems I have visited to-day, are allowed more liberty than any others in Turkey.

[…]

CHAPTER VII
VISITS FROM TURKISH LADIES. FEAST OF BAIRAM.
WALLS AND PALACES OF CONSTANTINOPLE

Here woman's voice is never heard; apart,
And scarce permitted, guarded, veil'd, to move.

Sunday, November 8th.—Our experiences of last Sunday had not inclined us to make another attempt at church. We therefore had service on board, and afterwards went to look at Mr. Preziosi's sketches. He is an artist who has lived here for many years, and some of his costume pieces and landscapes are beautiful. We had a large and unexpected party to lunch. Having asked a few friends, several others dropped in, amongst them Mr. Chlebowski, the Polish artist.

Monday, November 9th.—A wet morning, but we had an early breakfast and were off to the bazaars, which are all under cover, though very dark and muddy. We spent a long time there and made a good many purchases. This being the last day of Ramazan, the traders were all so anxious to get money to spend at the Feast of Bairam that there were wonderful bargains to be obtained, and the things were much cheaper than when we were here last. The Pigeon Mosque was more crowded than ever with stalls, and our wanderings took up so much time, that I was obliged to go straight on board to receive some Turkish ladies. Izzet Bey, grandson of Fuad Pasha, and husband of the Princess Azizieh, came first, and stayed to receive his mother, Madame Kiasim, a wonderfully handsome young-looking woman, about forty-five, but not appearing thirty. In the cabin, when, with doors closed, she took off her feridjee and yashmak, she looked exactly like a Frenchwoman, being beautifully dressed in two shades of brown, with a black lace bonnet, and having all the manners and conversation of a European. Her remarks about books, pictures, and things in general were extremely clever and sensible, and it was difficult to imagine how she had gained her knowledge, or to believe that she was only an educated slave, bought when young by Fuad Pasha to play with his son, and afterwards married to him on account of her superior talent, tact, and manner, as well as of her extreme beauty. She was accompanied by a white slave and a black eunuch.

The Princess Azizieh sen her little black slave in Albanian costume, on purpose to please Muriel, she herself being too unwell on come on board. This was a great disappointment to her, for she had experienced considerable difficulty in procuring leave to come, these being the first visits ever paid by Turkish ladies to a European. The Princess Nazli arrived next, dressed in delicate blue satin and Brussels lace, with pale pink feathers in a blue satin pork-pie hat to match. She had also her white slave and black eunuch in attendance, and was immensely interested in everything she saw, admiring most things greatly. She smoked nearly all the time, but did not seem to approve either of our coffee or our tea. After visits of more than two hours' duration, our guests departed, I think highly gratified; at all events, they had had quite a novel experience, and, fortunately, the day was so fine that they had no nervous fears in going backwards and forwards in the boat.

[...]

We had a busy morning on board. Several friends came to luncheon, and others arrived soon afterwards. Then came Princess Nazli, Princess Azizieh, and Madame Ikbal Kiasim, each with her suite, and by appointment, to see the yacht and to have tea with me. Their costumes were more Parisian and their yashmaks thinner than ever, and the slaves, having forsaken their beautiful Eastern costumes since we were here before, looked more fashionable, but not half so pretty. Some had visited the yacht previously, some had not, but all were interested in seeing our curios from various parts of the world. They drank tea and coffee, smoked innumerable cigarettes, and stayed until nearly 6 p.m., though some of them were rather overcome by the motion of the vessel as it was anything but a smooth day. The last four years seem to have added greatly to the amount of liberty they enjoy. They are now much less particular about seeing gentlemen, and, once in the cabin, laughed and talked with the greatest freedom and enjoyment. Some of the princesses had been on board the 'Antelope' and the 'Alexandra,' to see some torpedo experiments, and were quite pleased to meet Admiral Hornby (who was on board the yacht) again. A few months ago Princess Nazli went to Egypt, and was not allowed to return to Constantinople. She put on a thick yashmak and feridjee, borrowed a thousand francs, and travelled back with her English maid, who has now been with her for five years. As soon as they had made a clear start they threw off yashmak and feridjee and travelled as two English ladies, until they reached Constantinople, when they again assumed the Oriental costume. Within comparatively recent years such a proceeding on the part of a Turkish married lady would have been rewarded by the bowstring, the sack, and the Bosphorus. [...]

ॐ   ॐ

[From *Sunshine and Storm in the East*]

At half-past six we reached Cairo, and were conveyed in a large *char-à-bancs* to what was formerly Shepherd's Hotel, now partly rebuilt and much altered for the better. Even in that short drive we could see that the face of the capital of Egypt had altered as much as the country, though I am not sure that it is so greatly improved. After a refreshing dip in cool marble baths and a change of garments, we went down to the large *table-d hôte*. Then we sat in the veranda looking on the street until we became tired of doing nothing, after which we started for a stroll in the Ezkebieh gardens close by. They are beautifully laid out for evening promenade; but although the flowers are lovely, and the turf, thanks to constant waterings, is deliciously green, all the large trees have been cut down. There is no seclusion, no shade, which seems a pity in a country where the greatest desire of life is shelter from the noonday heat. To-night both Arab and French bands were playing within the inclosure, and it was pleasant enough listening to Offenbach's music under the beams of the full moonlight. Few people appeared to appreciate it, however, for the gardens were nearly empty; but then the season is over, and every one has fled before the coming heat.

Saturday, April 28th.—We had settled to start at six o'clock this morning to visit the Pyramids, an excursion which had been for some little time eagerly looked forward to and talked about by the younger members of our party. The morning was cold and gray, a strong northerly wind was blowing, and the change from the weather which had prevailed but a few hours previously was altogether most striking and unexpected. We drove rapidly through the streets and the outskirts of the town, where old houses are being pulled down and new ones rapidly built up, and where a general air of new bricks and old rubbish pervades the scene. Then we crossed the Nile by a handsome iron bridge, and saw the Palace of Gezireh, where the Prince of Wales and his suite were lodged. We passed the railway extension works, and, to the great delight of the children, saw two elephants busily employed, one of which was being made to lie down to enable his mahout to dismount. Soon the little ones gave a shout of 'The Pyramids!' and there before us stood those grand monuments of a nameless founder, which for centuries have stood out in the sands of the desert, while the burning African sun and the glorious African moon have risen and set on their heavenward-pointing summits for countless days and nights. Even the earth has changed her position so much since they were erected that the pole star no longer sheds its light in a direct line through the central passages, as it did when first they were designed.

We drove along under avenues of now leafless trees to the foot of the hill on which the Pyramids are situated. Here everybody was turned out to walk except Muriel and me, and a tremendous tug the horses had to drag even us two up to the real foot of the Pyramids. On arriving we were at once surrounded by a crowd of Arabs. They are certainly a fine-looking lot of men, rather clamorous for backshish, and anxious to sell their curiosities, real or imitation. They were, however, good-natured, civil, and obliging, and amused me much during the hour I spent alone with them while the rest of the party were ascending and descending the Pyramids. Many could speak several languages quite fluently, and almost all of them took a good deal of interest in the war, and the prospects of success on either side; while many had a fair knowledge of the geography of Europe. While all the rest were on the top of the one large Pyramid, a man ran down from the summit and up to the top of the next smaller one (which is, however, more difficult to ascend) in 'eight minutes for a franc.' This feat was repeated several times by different men, but it really occupied nearer ten minutes.

We ate some bread and wine, bought a few curiosities, and then drove back to the city, feeling very cold and shivery, and regretting the wraps we had left behind. We reached the hotel just in time for twelve o'clock *table-d'hôte* breakfast, and, after an acceptable rest, sallied forth again, this time on donkeys, to see the bazaars and the sunset from the citadel. We went across squares and gardens and through wide streets, for, alas! Cairo is being rapidly Haussmannized. For the capitalist or resident Cairo may be improved, but for the traveler, the artist, the lover of the picturesque, the quaint, and the beautiful, the place is ruined. Cairo as a beautiful and ancient Oriental city has ceased to exist, and is being rapidly transformed into a bad imitation of modern Paris, only with bluer skies, a more brilliant sun, and a more serene climate than it is possible to find in Europe. Only a few narrow streets and old houses are still left, with carved wooden lattices, where you can yet dream that the 'Arabian Nights' are true.

ℬ   ℛ

[from Lady Brassey's Diary]

Sunday, February 4th, 1883—Tom and the children breakfasted with the Duke of Sutherland, who arrived yesterday and has kindly asked us all to go with him by special train to Tel-el-kebir tomorrow, which will just give Tom a chance of visiting that place before he returns to England.

Later on we went to a rather small and very stuffy church, where we heard Dean Butcher preach. He has just come from Shanghai, where he says he looked out anxiously for us in the "Sunbeam", in 1877. After lunch we paid several formal visits, so that Tom might leave cards and write his name down before returning to England, and then went for a drive along the Shoobrah road, where all the rank and fashion, European and Egyptian, disport themselves on Sunday afternoon. The ladies of the hareem, royal and otherwise, are all to be seen in their smart carriages, with attendant "sais", and sometimes with outriders. Then, there were English and Egyptian mounted officers, in uniform, and people riding horses, donkeys and patient camels, besides a large number of pedestrians.

Altogether it was a gay, varied, and animated scene, as we passed along the road to the Shoobrah gardens, which looked deserted and out of order. We found it pleasant enough, however, wandering about under the trees, or sitting down to eat the oranges or smell the sweet flowers which some of the numerous gardeners brought us. But we did not stay long, for though the sun was hot the wind was cold, and we were anxious to get back before sunset.

Friday, February 9, 1883

[…] When at Port Said, I was sorry to hear that my old friend at Constantinople, Princess Nazli, was not quite pleased with something I had said about her in one of my books. I could scarcely imagine what it could be, as, on looking through "Sunshine and Storm" again, I was unable to find anything that I thought would have been likely to annoy her. I left a card at her house a day or two ago and was pleased to get a nice little note from her yesterday asking the children and me to go and see her at half-past one today. There is a longish drive through a garden to her house, and the usual three gates of admittance to a Hareem have to be passed. The Princess received us most cordially and I was pleased to find, when I asked her, that, as is often the case in such matters, the idea of her being offended with me existed only in the mind of my Port Said friend. Her first remark was "I am not going to smoke, or ask you to smoke, for I see in your book that you do not like it. I am quite changed since I saw you last, quite Europeanised." As a matter of fact, I believe she smokes just as much as ever, but has so far emancipated herself from the rules of the Hareem that she receives gentlemen visitors and gives dinner-parties at which gentlemen are present, much to the horror and annoyance of the Khedive, who keeps her as a sort of semi-state prisoner, and will not allow her to return to Constantinople, as she dearly longs to do. Being entirely dependent on the Khedive for her financial resources, I suppose she is obliged to do more or less as he wishes, though I fancy it is a good deal less than more. The Princess asked after everybody who was on the yacht at Constantinople, and was specially sorry not to see Sir Thomas and Mr. Bingham.

Sunday, February 11, 1883

[…] Later in the day I went with Lady Dufferin to have tea with Princess Mansour, sister of the Khedive. We were received at the inner door of the palace by seven or eight white female slaves, all richly dressed in rather dull brown striped silk dresses, with a good deal of white lace about them, and made in semi-European fashion. I don't think the costume suits them nearly as well as the more gorgeous Eastern garments they used to wear a few years ago. Slaves and French fashions do not harmonize at all. At the top of the stairs we were met by more slaves, and, a few rooms farther on, by the Princess's companion, who conducted us into the presence of the Princess herself. She seemed pleased to see Lady Dufferin and Lady Helen again, and was very polite to me. Her costume consisted of a black satin dress with a long train, and close by her was an enormous bearhound, bigger than that of Sir Roger Palmer, which is so familiar to all who visit

English dog-shows. Two full sized greyhounds played about the room, and in their gambols with their huge companion threatened destruction to the ornaments and numerus small tables, of which there were many in the apartment. I was surprised to see dogs in such a place; but the Princess Mansour does not allow herself to be bound by the ordinary rules of a hareem. The companion told us that the dogs caused great alarm to the Egyptian visitors, and were always kept out of the way when any were expected. After tea, at which all sorts of sweetmeats and cakes, and the thickest of buffalo cream, were produced, the Princess showed us over her house, which is not only richly, but tastefully and originally furnished, in a mixture of Egyptian and French styles, with more nick-nacks and little ornaments than I had ever before seen in an oriental residence.

[...] After a pleasant but somewhat lengthy visit, the Princess gave us her own, her husband's, and her children's photographs, and we took our departure, with the same ceremony with which we had arrived. A visit to a hareem always interests me, and as a rule I leave it with a feeling of profound pity for the generally objectless and uneventful lives of the inmates.

Lady Dufferin had kindly asked me to dine with them again, on this our last evening in Cairo. Nobody else was there except the Duke of Sutherland and Mr. Pourtal. It was Tom's birthday, and we therefore drank his health. I wonder where he is now; how far on his journey home!

The kindness of my host and hostess made an agreeable termination to the week (or rather eight days) I have spent in Cairo; a week that has been rendered pleasant and interesting by the friends I have met, and the people with whom I have been brought into daily contact. It is a period too that will afford much food for reflection in the future, as having been passed in a land that has been and still is going through a great crisis, in company with those whose names will form part of their country's history.

7.
DEMETRA VAKA BROWN (1877–1946)

ᔓ HAREMLIK ᔕ

SOME PAGES FROM THE LIFE OF TURKISH WOMEN

Houghton Mifflin Co., Boston and New York; Constable, London
1909

Demetra Vaka was born and spent her young life on the island of Prinkipo
(Büyükada) in the Sea of Marmora, near Istanbul. She came from an ethnically Greek Ottoman family and was raised in the Greek Orthodox faith.
Educated at Greek schools in Istanbul and then in France, the early death of
her father meant that she had few financial resources. In 1895 she emigrated
to the United States of America to avoid the limited opportunities available
to a girl in her home community. Her entrée to New York was as companion
and governess to the family of the Ottoman consul (also a Greek). Staying
on alone when the consul was recalled, Vaka Brown worked initially as a
journalist on the Greek-language press in New York, leaving to teach in private schools. She married Kenneth Brown, an American writer, in 1904 and
moved with him to Virginia. Though this seemed a life of comfort and ease,
Vaka Brown was bored and frustrated. Returning to New York, her husband
suggested that she convert her Ottoman experiences into a saleable com-
modity. Aiming to correct American misunderstandings about Turkey, Vaka
Brown's stories of her Turkish childhood first appeared in middlebrow
American magazines. *Haremlik*, published in 1909, was her first book and
began what was to become a trilogy on the life of Ottoman women. Vaka
Brown continued to publish books and journalism on the Balkans and the
Middle East. Specialising in regional politics, she was recognised at the time
as an authority on the 'Eastern Question', valued as both a political and a
social commentator.

Haremlik is based on a visit home in 1900, prior to the Young Turk revolution of 1908 and before Vaka Brown was married. At the start of the book
she depicts herself on the boat pulling into Istanbul, keen to revisit her old
haunts with 'a mind full of Occidental questioning'. The book tells of a
series of visits to Muslim Ottoman women, many of whom had been her
childhood friends. Although Vaka Brown presents herself as a modern independent Westernised woman, she was aware that her friends, drawn from the
Muslim elite, led lives that were materially more comfortable than hers,
even if she enjoyed greater personal freedoms. This ambivalence about the
limited opportunities of Western 'liberation' is coupled with a nostalgic
investment in the pleasures of elite segregated life that dated back to her
childhood, when her Turkish friend Djimlah's luxurious harem was regu-

larly a refuge from the rigours of her Greek school and the money worries that plagued her at home.

Vaka Brown's contradictory responses to the changes evident in Ottoman society at the turn of the century are seen in the passages extracted here about Ottoman feminism. In the first section, taken from Chapter VI, she recounts a discussion with her friend 'Houlmé' about the changing marital expectations of Muslim women. Houlmé had been given a Western-style education and was affianced to her much-beloved cousin. But, reared on the Western ideal of romantic love, she had, to her regret, asked her grandfather to sent her fiancé to Europe so that she could be sure he had returned to her through choice. Anxiously missing him, she declaims to Vaka Brown that it was Western fiction that had ruined her happiness. Western, particularly French, literature recurs in the next chapter as the cause of Turkish women's foolish ideas. Vaka Brown was not alone in diagnosing the evils of French literature (see also Zeyneb Hanoum, Extract 8). But, though her patronising tone threatens to reduce Turkish women's social activism to trivial matters of romantic fantasy, this should not distract from the fact that at this time many progressive Ottomans were preoccupied with their restricted rights in matters of personal choice.

Like other commentators from the period (see Ellison, Extract 10), Vaka Brown did not want to encourage Ottoman feminists to copy the West – especially if they were motivated by inaccurate and sensationalist renditions of Western society. In contrast to Houlmé's classic 'caught between two cultures' dilemma, the feminists at Zeybah Hanoum's meeting are represented as misguided and childish. Despite its sarcasm, her account highlights the dynamism and variety of Ottoman feminist opinion. The women of her acquaintance are shown to be versed in the literature and history of several Western nations – not the isolated, ignorant playthings generally held to inhabit harems. Their cultural and political agency is also illustrated by their symbolic use of Western and Ottoman clothing. Despite ridiculing their special grey *çarşafs* as silly self-promotion, Vaka Brown reveals her own Orientalist attachment to the veil as picturesque exotica when she notes with acid satisfaction that those who had changed into contemporary Paris fashion were uncomfortable when trying to lounge on traditional divans for the after-lunch entertainment.

For all that she criticised the women for unnecessarily romanticising their campaign, Vaka Brown was herself a fanciful writer, characterising herself later as the 'troubadour' of the old ways. Her uncertain status as an émigré Ottoman, not ethnically Turkish but never entirely Western, explains many of the contradictions seen in *Haremlik*. Asked at the meeting to prescribe a programme for Ottoman feminists, Vaka Brown's relativist analysis demonstrates her mixed loyalties: aware of the limitations of Westernised modernity she used her experiential understanding of the advantages held by Ottoman women to recommend that they embrace the assistance offered by Ottoman men and the legal rights provided by Islamic law. Herself both separate and similar, Vaka Brown could see how these elements exceeded the support available to women in the West. Endeavouring to be a reliable informant for her Western readers without becoming one with the attractive world of the elite Muslim harem, her nostalgia for the rapidly obsolescing harem was about more than domestic arrangements: the multi-ethnic Ottoman Empire to which she gave allegiance was also to disappear in the shift to the homogeneous Turkish Republic.

℘ ℘

"Houlmé," I said, "for some of you, Occidental education is like strong wine to unaccustomed people. It simply goes to your heads. Look at Djimlah, your sister; she certainly is as educated as you are, but she could never behave the way you or Chakendé Hanoum did.

"True," Houlmé assented. "My sister is educated as far as speaking European languages goes, but she has never been touched by Occidental thought. To her, her husband is her lord, the giver of her children. To me, and to those who think as I do, a man must be more. He must be to his wife what she is to him, all in all. Is not this what the Occidental love is? I did not use to think this way till I read your books. I wish I had never, never known. I do not like to hurt the feelings of my venerable grandfather, for I am the only child of his only daughter, as Murat is the only child of his only son, and I know that he did by me what he thought best. Sometimes, however, I should like him to know that with his new ideas he has made me miserable by allowing me to acquire thoughts not in accordance with our mode of living."

"Houlmé, if your cousin came back, and you became his wife and had any daughters, how would you bring them up?"

"I have thought of this very much indeed," was her answer, "and I should like to talk it over with Murat when he becomes my husband. I do not think Turkish parents have any right to experiment with their children. I should not like to give to my daughters this burden of unrest. I should like to bring them up as true Osmanli women."

"Then you disapprove of the modern system of education that is creeping into the harems? Were you to be free to see men and choose your husbands, would you still disapprove?"

"Yes. It took you many generations to come to where you are. Back of you there are hundreds of grandmothers who led your life and worked for what you have to-day. With us it is different: we shall be the first grandmothers of the new thought, and we ought to have it come to us slowly and through our own efforts. Mussulman women, with the help of Mahomet, ought to work out their own salvation, and borrow nothing from the West. We are a race apart, with different traditions and associations."

"Is this the thought of the educated women of the harems to-day?" I asked.

Houlmé's face saddened as she said:—

"No, young Hanoum, I am alone in this thought as far as I can make out. The others say that we must immediately be given freedom and liberty to do as we like with ourselves. Indeed, they look upon me with mistrust as if I were a traitor."

"Have they any definite plans of what they want to do?"

"I doubt whether *you* would call them definite plans, but I should like very much to have you come with me to our next meeting, which will be in two days. There are forty of them now and I think that they will do more harm than good, as they are going about it in a very irrational way. Their motto is, 'Down with the Old Ideas.' Naturally they refuse to obey their parents and their husbands."

"How old are they, on the average?"

"The youngest of them all is seventeen and the oldest forty. They are all unmarried, with the exception of five who have left their husbands."

"You are not in sympathy with their movement though you belong to it?"

"No, young Hanoum, for I am afraid that it is more romanticism that guides them than thought for our beloved country. I call them to myself, 'Les Roman-esques des Harems,' though they call themselves 'Les Louises Michel.'"

"Goodness gracious!" I exclaimed, "Louise Michel was an anarchist!"

"So are they," said Houlmé; "and because I tell them that through anarchy we can do nothing, they will not hear me."

I told her that I should certainly be glad to go with her to the meeting of the reformers, and she promised to take me soon.

We did not go inside the house that night. Bringing some pillows and rugs out on the balcony, we slept there until the morning light drove us in.

[. . .]

In my room I was surprised to find a new *tchitcharf* of silver-gray silk. "What is this for?" I asked Houlmé.

"You cannot go to the meeting unless you have this color on. It is the emblem of dawn, the dawn we are about to bring to the Turkish women's life."

A few minutes later Houlmé and I, in company with an old slave inside the carriage with us, and an old eunuch, who was the shadow of Houlmé, sitting on the box by the coachman, were driving to Hanoum Zeybah's house, where the meeting was to be held. It was half-past ten o'clock when we reached there, and we were the last to arrive. Inside the door stood two gray phantoms, to whom we gave the password, "Twilight."

In a large hall stood the rest of the gray symbols of dawn, all so closely veiled as to be unrecognizable. Without a sound they saluted us in the Turkish fashion; and then we were all conducted to a large room. It was very mysterious and con-spirator-like. The nine windows of the room were tightly shuttered, that no ray of unromantic sunlight should fall upon the forerunners of a new epoch. We all sat crosslegged and motionless on a bare settee which ran around two sides of the room. Over our heads hung a banner of sky-blue silk, embroidered in silver with "*Freedom for Women!*" Beneath that hung another of black, bearing the words "*Down with the Old Ideas!*" in fiery red. There were no chairs. The beautiful oak floor was partially covered with Eastern rugs, and on some fat cushions in the middle of the room sat out hostess, the originator and president of the society.

President Zeybah clapped her hands three times and announced that the meeting was about to begin. It did begin, and continued for more than an hour.

The president produced a manuscript with gilt edges from a European satchel at her side, and read her contribution to the club.

"Women, fellow-sufferers, and fellow-workers," she read "we come here to-day to dig a little farther into the thick wall which the tyranny of man has built about us. By nature woman was meant to be the ruler. By her intuition, her sympathy, her unselfishness, her maternal instinct, she is the greatest of the earth. One thing alone brute nature gave to man—strength! Through that he has subjugated woman. Let us rise and break our bonds! Let us stand up *en masse* and defy the brute who now dominates us! We are the givers of life; we must be the rulers and lawmakers as well. Down with man!"

In this strain, and in a deep voice befitting a ruler and a lawmaker, the president read from her gilt-edged paper, and ended up with the proposition that six members of the club should be chosen by lot to kill themselves, as a protest against the existing order of things. The proposition, which was made in all seriousness, provided, however,—with a *naïveté* that might have imperilled the gravity of a meeting of American women,—that the president of the club should be exempt from participation in the lot-drawing.

This plan for making tyrant man sit up and take notice was received with a murmur from the veiled listeners, rather more of approval than of disapproval. The question, however, was not discussed further at the moment, and the president called on another lady to read her paper.

The first speaker having proved that women were great and were only kept from recognition by the brute force of man, the second one went ahead to prove that women were capable of doing as good work as men in certain cases, by citing George Sand, George Eliot, and others. A third one asserted that women were mere playthings in the hands of men, and called on them to rouse themselves and show that they were capable of being something better.

I was utterly disgusted at the whole meeting. I might just as well have been in one of those silly clubs in New York where women congregate to read their immature compositions. There were totally lacking the sincerity, the spontaneity, and the frankness which usually characterize Turkish women.

When the meeting adjourned, we passed into several dressing-rooms, where the veiled and secret conspirators against the dominion of man all kept luncheon gowns. When the assemblage came together again, the majority of them were corseted and in Paris frocks, and all were quite unveiled, the mystery of the meeting having been mere pretense and affectation. These forty-odd women, ranging in age from seventeen to forty, were drawn from the flower of the Turkish aristocracy. Luncheon was served in a large room overlooking the Golden Horn. We were seated at four round tables, and during the meal the great cause was forgotten, and they were again spontaneous Turkish women.

After luncheon we passed into the reclining room, where Eastern dances and music were given for our pleasure. I was happy to notice that as we lay about on the couches, the Parisian-gowned ladies were distinctly less comfortable than the rest of us. After the music was over, the heavy conversation was started again by our hostess, who was never happy for long unless she considered that she was shining intellectually. She was not yet thirty, but had found time already to divorce two husbands.

"What I like most about American women," she said to me and to her disciples, "is the courage they have in discarding their husbands. Why should a woman continue to live with a man whom she finds to be not her intellectual companion?" Her pose was fine, as she uttered these words, and murmurs of appreciation arose among her hearers.

"Few men are women's companions intellectually," I said, having listened to as much as I could without replying "The only men who are the companions of intellectual women are half-baked poets, sophomores, and degenerates. Normal men, nice men, intelligent men, never talk the tomfoolery women want to talk about. They are too busy with things worth while to sit down and ponder over the gyrations of their souls. In fact, they don't have to worry over their souls at all. They are strong and healthy, and live their useful lives without taking time to store their heads with all the nonsense women do."

Those forty women breathed heavily. To them I represented freedom and intellectual advancement, and here I was smashing their ideals unmercifully. I pretended not to notice the effect of my words, and continued:—

"If you expect real men of any nationality to sit down and talk to you about your souls, you will find them disappointing. As for American women, they are as different from you as a dog from a bird. Whatever they do cannot affect you. They are a different stock altogether. Will you tell me what you are working for specifically?"

"Freedom to choose our husbands, and freedom to go about with men as we like," the president answered.

"We want to go about the world unchaperoned and free—to travel all over the world if we choose," another answered.

The last speaker was a girl barely eighteen years old, and beautiful with a beauty the East alone can produce. I laughed openly.

"My dear child," I said, "you could not go alone for half a day without having all sorts of things happening to you."

"But that is just what I want," she retorted. "I am tired of my humdrum life, when such delicious things as one reads of in books might be happening to me."

This girl in her youth and simplicity was really revealing the cause of their malady. They were all fed on French novels.

"Even American women, when they are young, do not go about with men unchaperoned as you think," I said, "nor do they travel alone with men, at any age. Of course there are American women who are compelled to go about alone a good deal, because they are earning their own living; but they only do this because they have to. As to what Zeybah Hanoum said about their divorcing their husbands frequently, I am afraid she is looking at American civilization from the seamy side. I do not deny that there are American women who have parted with decency, and whom one divorce more or less does not affect; but the really nice American women have as much horror of divorce as any well-bred European woman."

Zeybah Hanoum here interrupted me. "I beg your pardon, but I have read in the American papers that a woman may divorce her husband in the morning, and marry again in the afternoon. Also, that no other reason for divorce is required than that she does not wish to continue to live with him. It is called 'incompatibility of temper.' I believe"—here the learned lady threw back her head, and turned to the rest of her audience—"that a nation that has such laws has them not for those who have parted with decency, but for the nice women, in order to help them to rid themselves of undesirable husbands. I hear that the courts proclaim that a woman may not only get rid of her husband, but that the husband shall continue to support her. Can you tell me after that that America does not uphold divorce?"

I was rather staggered by her argument, although I knew that fundamentally she was mistaken.

"What you say is true, in a way," I admitted; "but the fact remains that nice American women do not believe in indiscriminate divorcing."

"Oh, well, there are always backward women in every country. I was told by an American lady, once, that not to be divorced nowadays was the exception. And wait till the women have the power to vote. That is the one thing the American men are afraid to grant women, because they know that then women will make laws to suit themselves."

I did not ask Zeybah Hanoum how much farther women could go, with the ballot, than she thought they already had gone, in the home of the free. I was very sorry for the women who were under her influence, because most of them were young and all of them inexperienced, so I took up another side of the subject.

"Let's leave American women alone then, since you will only believe the yellow journalism, and come to your own affairs. Do you really think that by having six women kill themselves you will accomplish anything?"

"At any rate, we shall teach men a lesson."

"And that is?"

"That we are capable of going to any lengths to get what we want. Woman is a power to-day!"

"But do you think you can bring about what you want by violent methods? There are a great many among your men who believe that women should be free to choose their husbands, and to educate themselves as they like. So far you have been given privileges in studying music and art. Little by little other things will come. But remember, that to one woman who thinks as you do there are a hundred who don't."

"They are blind, and we wish to open their eyes. It is our duty—in the name of humanity. We owe this to the Progress of the World," Zeybah announced oratorically.

"Since you have descended to Duty," I said with some heat, "I suppose you are capable of anything cruel and unkind."

At this point a lady—a visitor, like me—who was an instructress in a girls' seminary, though she was the daughter of a rich man, quietly put in: "Zeybah Hanoum, I should like to hear the lady tell us how she thinks it would be wise to proceed. She knows our ways, what privileges we now have, and our shortcomings."

"Yes, yes," several voices cried.

"Since you do not like your system,—although it seems to me admirable on the whole,—it is only right that you should be allowed to live your lives as you want to. Only you must go about it in a sensible way, and take into consideration the others who are involved in it. For example, I should think that you ought to tear down that banner of 'Down with the Old Ideas!' and put up another, reading: 'Respect for the Old Ideas, Freedom to the New!' Then, instead of closeting yourselves together and behaving like imitation French Anarchists, you ought to have your meetings in the open. Since you all wear your veils, you can invite the men who are sympathetic to your movement, to take an interest in it. Little by little, more men will come, and also more women. Really, your troubles are not so serious as those of European women, because under the laws of the Koran women have many privileges unheard of in other countries. The Mussulman system is very socialistic. What you want is to be free to mingle with men. Since you want it, you had better have it, though you are overrating the privilege. There is a great deal of poetry and a great deal of charm in your system; but if you don't like it, you don't like it. You will all be mothers some day; bring up your sons in the new thought, and thus gradually you will bring about the change."

"But you are spoiling our society," the president cried. "What is the object of it if not to push things along fast?"

"I do not agree with you," the quiet lady said. "I believe in what the foreign Hanoum has just said. We ought to go about this in a rational manner."

"Do I understand that you do not approve of our association?" the president asked, bristling up.

"Not in the least; but I do not believe in the bloody demonstration you proposed."

Thereupon arose a discussion which lasted the whole afternoon. The president was vehemently in favor of her plan for having six of the members kill themselves. Most of the others, however, encouraged by the moral support they received from me and from the quiet lady, finally admitted that they did not wish to die. Yet that they would unhesitatingly have committed suicide, had the club decided on the plan, and had the lot fallen to them, I have not the slightest doubt, knowing the nature of Turkish women as I do.

8.
Zeyneb Hanoum (dates unknown)
ഌ A Turkish Woman's ൠ European Impressions

(ed) Grace Ellison
Seeley, Service and Co, London; J.B. Lippincott Co, Philadelphia,
1913

Zeyneb Hanoum was the pen name of an Ottoman Muslim woman called
Hadidjé Zennour who, with her sister Nouryé-el-Nissa (known as Melek
Hanoum), had collaborated with the French author Pierre Loti (the pseudonym of Louis Marie Julien Vaiud, 1850–1923) on his novel *Les
Désenchantées* (*The Disenchanted*). Born into the Ottoman Muslim upper
class, Zeyneb Hanoum and Melek Hanoum were given a Western-style education by their socially progressive father Noury Bey, a senior bureaucrat in
Sultan Abdülhmamit II's government. The granddaughters of a French aris-
tocrat who had converted to Islam and married a Circassian, the sisters, like
many women of their generation and class, found themselves frustrated
when they were expected to live the life of secluded Ottoman ladies. When
an unwanted marriage was arranged for Zeyneb Hanoum she made contact
with Loti (in 1904) in the hope that the author, already famous for a previous
novel about Turkey, would raise support abroad for the plight of women in
her predicament. Since unauthorised contact with foreigners was forbidden
to Ottoman subjects, in 1906, just before *Les Désenchantées* was published,
the sisters fled their home in Constantinople to avoid imperial reprisals.

Arriving in France, where they were spurned by their grandfather's family, the sisters met the British feminist and Turkophile Grace Ellison.
Already a successful young journalist, Ellison helped them each to publish a
book (going on herself to write several volumes on women in the Ottoman
Empire and Europe, see Extract 10). *A Turkish Woman's European Impressions* is made up of letters exchanged between Zeyneb Hanoum, her sister
and Ellison between 1906 and 1912. Telling the story of their life in Turkey
and their experiences in Europe, the book was edited by Ellison, whose
introduction laid out the sisters' genealogy and confirmed their celebrity status as the *désenchantées*. In this way Ellison validated Zeyneb Hanoum's
status as a 'real' Turkish woman, explicitly endorsing the contents of the
book as more reliable than other harem accounts. Zeyneb Hanoum herself
declared that 'nine out of every ten' books on the harem should be burned,
intending to redress the balance with her own volume.

In her first chapter, extracted here, the account of her arrival in France is
framed by comments from Ellison that illustrate for the reader the nature of

their developing friendship and highlight the interactive character of the book's production. The epistolary form of the book also prompts its contents, such as when Ellison requests more information on particular subjects. These indicate Ellison's grasp of what would be of interest to Western readers, even though her introduction chides them for their often prurient curiosity about harem life. The tension between appealing to a curious Western consumer without being appropriated into Orientalist stereotypes was well known to Zeyneb Hanoum, whose comments about being sought after as a 'living spectacle' by society ladies in France demonstrate the unpleasantness of being commodified as Orientalist exotica. Her illustrations (see Plates 14 and 16) show a similar conflict between presenting the pleasures expected of visual Orientalism and exhibiting the Westernising modernity of contemporary harem life.

Her promised impressions of Europe were not always flattering and provide a comparative analysis of the so-called freedoms of the West. Making clear from the start that Hamidian repression affected men as well as women, Zeyneb Hanoum puts her personal experience of oppression in a national and international context. In this light, it is hardly surprising that she chides Ellison for making a fuss about not having the 'freedom' to choose her mealtimes in her pension – such triviality would hardly register to a woman who endangered herself simply to maintain foreign correspondence. The sometimes frustrating effects of Islamic seclusion are presented as being exacerbated by the hostile political climate: although it was perfectly proper for women to gather in each others' houses, the 'white dinner' women's soirées that Zeyneb Hanoum arranged were dangerous in the context of the endemic restriction of freedoms of association and expression.

Zeyneb Hanoum's provocatively entitled chapter 'Is This Really Freedom?', extracted here, caustically turns the Western Orientalist gaze back on itself, detecting practices of seclusion in Europe. In her relativist critique of the limitations of Western 'liberation,' the London Ladies' Club (an inferior type of harem) and feminist street demonstrations (dangerously degentrifying), as well as her visit to the Ladies' Gallery at the Houses of Parliament (a claustrophobic harem), are found to be an inadequate reward for the dangers of escaping the Ottoman harem. Zeyneb Hanoum's qualms about the aims and methods of Western feminism are in keeping with other commentators who argued that Eastern women should arrive at their own version of liberation, whilst her anxiety about the suffragists' potential loss of class position suggests the ways in which her elite social status was lost in the move to Europe. One indication of her social standing, which she shared with other elite Eastern women such as (the royal) Musbah Haidar (Extract 15), is her scorn for the dubious educational and moral standards of foreign governesses. This in part explains why women like Emmeline Lott (Extract 3), who travelled to the East as governesses, put such an emphasis on markers of rank.

Beginning and ending with reference to the human ramifications of her literary role as a *désenchantée*, Zeyneb Hanoum returned to Turkey where she lived a quiet life, removed from the political activities that engaged others like Halide Edib (Extract 13). Ellison, in a condescending tone characteristic of the period, had signalled the likelihood of this outcome in her introductory comments to Chapter III; but she did have the benefit of hindsight since she was editing the book after Zeyneb Hanoum had returned to Turkey. Though her sister Melek Hanoum married and remained in Europe, for the author of *A Turkish Woman's European Impressions* the advantages were not sufficient to make her stay.

℁   ℂ

CHAPTER I
A DASH FOR FREEDOM

A few days after my visit to the Désenchantées at Fontainebleau, which is described in the Introduction, I received the following letter from Zeyneb:

FONTAINEBLEAU, *Sept.* 1906.

You will never know, my dear and latest friend, the pleasure your visit has given us. It was such a new experience, and all the more to be appreciated, because we were firmly convinced we had come to the end of new experiences.

[...]

Sympathy and interest so rarely go hand in hand—interest engenders curiosity, sympathy produces many chords in the key of affection, but the sympathetic interest you felt for us has given birth on our side to a sincere friendship, which I know will stand the test of time.

We felt a few minutes after you had been with us, how great was your comprehension, not only of our actions, but of all the private reasons, alas! so tragic, which made them necessary. You understood so much without our having to speak, and you guessed a great deal of what could not be put into words. That is what a Turkish woman appreciates more than anything else.

[...]

Since our departure from our own country, and during these few months we have been in France, from all sides we have received kindness. We were ready to face yet once more unjust criticism, blame, scandal even; but instead, ever since we left Belgrade till we arrived here, everything has been quite the opposite. All the European papers have judged us impartially, some have even defended and praised us, but not one censured us for doing with our lives what it pleased us.

But in Turkey what a difference! No Constantinople paper spoke of our flight. They were clever enough to know that by giving vent to any ill-feeling, saying what they really thought of our "disgraceful" conduct, they would draw still more attention to the women's cause; so we were left by the Press of our country severely alone.

The Sultan Hamid, who interested himself a little too much in our welfare, became very anxious about us. Having left no stone unturned to force us to return (he had us arrested in the middle of the night on our arrival at Belgrade on the plea that my sister was a minor, and that both of us had been tricked away by an elderly lady for illicit purposes) he next ordered that all those European papers in which we were mentioned should be sent to him. As our flight drew forth bitter criticism of his autocratic government, he must, had he really taken the trouble to read about us, have found some very uncomfortable truths about himself. But that was no new régime. For years he has fed himself on these indigestible viands, and his mechanism is used to them by now.

I need not tell you that in Constantinople, for weeks, these forbidden papers were sold at a high price. Regardless of the risk they were running, everyone wanted to have news of the two women who had had the audacity to escape from their homes and the tyranny of the Sultan Hamid. In the harems, we were the one topic of conversation. At first no one seemed to grasp the fact that we had actually gone, but when at last the truth slowly dawned upon them, the men naturally had not a kind word to say of us, and we did not expect it would be otherwise. But the women, alas! Many were obliged officially to disapprove of our action. There were a few, however, who had the courage to defend us openly; they have our deepest and sincerest gratitude. But do not think for a moment that we blame or feel unkindly towards the others. Have not we, like them, had all our lives to suffer and fear and pretend as captives always must do? Could they be expected to find in one day the strength of character to defend a cause however just, and not only just, but *their own*—their freedom.

Yes, my friend, we ourselves have lived that life of constant fear and dissimulation, of hopes continually shattered, and revolt we dared not put into words.

Yet never did the thought occur to us that we might adapt ourselves to this existence we were forced to lead. We spent our life in striving for one thing only—the means of changing it.

Could we, like the women of the West, we thought, devote our leisure to working for the poor, that would at least be some amusement to break the monotony. We also arranged to meet and discuss with intelligent women the question of organising charity, but the Sultan came down upon us with a heavy hand. He saw the danger of allowing thinking women to meet and talk together, and the only result of this experiment was that the number of spies set to watch the houses of "dangerous women" was doubled.

[…]

I thought I understood, from the sympathetic interest you showed us the other afternoon, that there was much you would still like to hear. Have I guessed rightly? Then there is nothing you shall not know.—Your affectionate

ZEYNEB.

What a long and interesting letter! and from a Turkish woman too! Several times I read and re-read it, then I felt that I could not give my new friend a better proof of the pleasure that it had given me, than by writing her at once to beg for more. But I waited till the next day, and finally sent a telegram— "Please send another letter."

CHAPTER II
ZEYNEB'S GIRLHOOD

[...]

But I am not really pitying women more than men under the Hamidian régime. A man's life is always in danger. Do you know, the Sultan was informed when your friend Kathleen came to see us? Every time our mother invited guests to the house, she was obliged to send the list to his Majesty, who, by every means, tried to prevent friends from meeting. Two or three Turks meeting together in a café were eyed with suspicion, and reported at head-quarters, so that rather than run risks they spent the evenings in the harems with their wives. One result, however, of this awful tyranny, was that it made the bonds which unite a Turkish family together stronger than anywhere else in the world.

Can you imagine what it is to have detectives watching your house day and night? Can you imagine the exasperation one feels to think that one's life is at the mercy of a wretched individual who has only to invent any story he likes and you are lost? Every calumny, however stupid and impossible, is listened to at head-quarters. The Sultan's life-work (what a glorious record for posterity!) has been to have his poor subjects watched and punished. What his spies tell him he believes. No trial is necessary, he passes sentence according to his temper at the moment—either he has the culprit poisoned, or exiles him to the most unhealthy part of Arabia, or far away into the desert of Tripoli, and often the unfortunate being who is thus punished has no idea why he has been condemned.

[...]

This will perhaps give you some idea of the conditions under which we were living. Constant fear, anguish without hope of compensation, or little chance of ever having anything better.

That we preferred to escape from this life, in spite of the terrible risks we were running, and the most tragic consequences of our action, is surely comprehensible.

If we had been captured it would only have meant death, and was the life we were leading worth while? We had taken loaded revolvers with us, to end our lives if necessary, remembering the example of one of our childhood friends, who tried to escape, but was captured and taken back to her husband, who shut her up till the end of her days in a house on the shores of the Marmora.

You have paid a very pretty compliment to our courage. Yet, after all, does it require very much to risk one's life when life is of so little value? In Turkey our existence is so long, so intolerably long, that the temptation to drop a little deadly poison in our coffee is often too great to withstand. Death cannot be worse than life, let us try death.—Your affectionate

ZEYNEB.

CHAPTER III
BEWILDERING EUROPE

What a curious thing it was I found so much difficulty in answering Zeyneb's letters. To send anything *banal* to my new friend I felt certain was to run the risk of ending the correspondence.

She knew I was in sympathy with her; she knew I could understand, as well as any one, how awful her life must have been, but to have told her so would have offended her. Most of the reasons for her escape, every argument that could justify her action, she had given me, except one; and it was probably that "one" reason that had most influenced her.

In due time probably she would tell me all, but if she did not, nothing I could do or say would make her, for Turkish women will not be cross-examined. One of them, when asked one day in a Western drawing-room "how many wives has your father?" answered, without hesitation, "as many as your husband, Madame."

Zeyneb had once told me that I succeeded in guessing so much the truth of what could not be put into words. She had on one occasion said "we never see our husbands until we are married," and a little later "sometimes the being whose existence we have to share inspires us with a horror that can never be overcome." Putting these two statements together, I was able to draw my own conclusions as to the "one" reason. ... Poor little Zeyneb!

It seemed to me from the end of her letter, that Zeyneb would have been grateful had I said that I approved of her action in leaving her own country. To have told her the contrary would not have helped matters in the least, and sooner or later she was sure to find out her mistake for herself.

And who that noticed her enthusiasm for all she saw would have dreamt of the tragedy that was in her life? The innocent delight she had when riding on the top of a bus, and her jubilation at discovering an Egyptian Princess indulging in the same form of amusement!

Zeyneb told me that *economy* was a word for which there was no equivalent in the Turkish language, so how could she be expected to practise an art which did not exist in her country? It was from her I had learnt the habit of answering her letters by telegram, and the result had been satisfactory. "Eagerly waiting for another letter," I wired her. The following letter arrived:

FONTAINEBLEAU, *Oct.* 1906.

A few days after our arrival began in earnest a new experience for us. The "demands" for interviews from journalists—every post brought a letter. Many reporters, it is true, called without even asking permission; wanted to know our impressions of West Europe after eight days; the reasons why we had left Turkey; and other questions still more ignorant and extraordinary about harem life.

When, however, we had conquered the absurd Oriental habit of being polite, we changed our address, and called ourselves by Servian names.

What an extraordinary lack of intelligence, it seemed, to suppose that in a few phrases could be related the history of the Turkish woman's evolution; and the psychology of a state of mind which forces such and such a decision explained. How would it have been possible to give the one thousand and one private reasons connected with our action! And what would be the use of explaining all this to persons one hoped never to see again—persons by whom you are treated as a spectacle, a living spectacle, whose adventures will be retailed in a certain lady's boudoir to make her "five o'clock" less dull?

"What made you think of running away from Turkey?" asked one of these press detectives. He might as well have been saying to me, "You had on a blue dress the last time I saw you, why are you not wearing it to-day?"

"Weren't you sorry to leave your parents?" asked another. Did he suppose because we were Turks that we had hearts of stone. How could anyone, a complete stranger too, dare to ask such a question? And yet, angry as I was, this indiscretion brought tears to my eyes, as it always does when I think of that good-bye.

"Good night, little girl," said my father, on the eve of our departure. "Don't be so long in coming to dine with us again. Promise that you will come one day next week."

I almost staggered. "I'll try," I answered. Every minute I felt that I must fling myself in his arms and tell him what I intended to do, but when I thought of our years and years of suffering, my mind was made up, and I kept back my tears.

Do you see now, dear Englishwoman, why we appreciated your discreet interest in us, and how we looked forward to a friendship with you who have understood so well, that there can be tears behind eyes that smile, that a daughter's heart is not necessarily hard because she breaks away from the family circle, nor is one's love for the Fatherland any the less great because one has left it forever? All this we feel you have understood, and again and again we thank you.—Your affectionate

ZEYNEB.

[...]

TERRITET, *Jan.* 1907.

Your letter of yesterday annoys me. You are "changing your *pension*," you say, "because you are not free to come in to meals when you like."

What an awful grievance! If only you English women knew how you are to be envied! Come, follow me to Turkey, and I will make you thank Allah for your liberty.

Ever since I can remember, I have had a passion for writing, but this is rather the exception than the rule for a Turkish woman. At one time of my life, I exchanged picture postcards with unknown correspondents, who sent me, to a *poste restante* address, views of places and people I hoped some day to visit.

This correspondence was for us the DREAM SIDE of our existence. In times of unhappiness (extra unhappiness, for we were always unhappy), discouragement, and, above all, revolt, it was in this existence that we tried to find refuge. The idea that friends were thinking of us, however unknown they were, made us look upon life with a little more resignation—and you, my friend, who complain that "you are not free to have your meals when you like," should know that *this correspondence had to be hidden with as much care, as if it had been a plot to kill the Imperial Majesty himself.*

.   .   .   .   .   .

When our correspondence was sent to us direct, it had to pass through the hands of three different persons before we had the pleasure of receiving it ourselves. All the letters we sent out and received were read not only by my father and his secretary, but by the officials of the Ottoman Post.

One day, I remember, the daughter of an ex-American minister sent me a long account of her sister's marriage, and she stopped short at the fourth page. I was just going to write to her for an explanation, when the remaining sheets were sent on to me by the police, whose duty it was to read the letters, and who had simply forgotten to put the sheets in with the others.

You could never imagine the plotting and intriguing necessary to receive the most ordinary letters; not even the simplest action could be done in a straightforward manner; we had to perjure our souls by constantly pretending, in order to enjoy the most innocent pleasures—it mattered little to us, I do assure you, "whether we had our meals at the time we liked" or not.

[…]

CHAPTER VIII
A MISFIT EDUCATION

TERRITET, *Jan.* 1907.

I began to write to you the other day of the influence which Western culture has had on the lives of Turkish women.

If you only knew the disastrous consequences of that learning and the suffering for which it is responsible! From complete ignorance, we were plunged into the most advanced culture; there was no middle course, no preparatory school, and, indeed, what ought to have been accomplished in centuries we have done in three, and sometimes in two generations.

[…]

What I call the disastrous influence was the influence of the Second French Empire.

One day, when I have time, I shall look up the papers which give a description of the Empress Eugénie's visit to the East. No doubt they will treat her journey as a simple exchange of courtesies between two Sovereigns. They may lay particular emphasis on the pageantry of her reception, but few women of that time were aware of the revolution that this visit had on the lives of the Turkish women.

The Empress of the French was incontestably beautiful—but *she was a woman*, and the first impression which engraved itself on the understanding of these poor Turkish captives, was, that their master, Abdul Aziz, was paying homage *to a woman*.

[…]

For a *woman*, had been prepared rose and gold caïques all carpeted with purple velvet. From a magnificent little Arabian kiosk especially built Ottoman troops from all corners of the Empire passed in review before a *woman*; even her bath sandals were all studded with priceless gems; no honour was too high, no luxury too great for *this woman*. The Sultanas could think of nothing else; in the land of Islam great honour had been rendered to a *woman*.

It was after the visit of the Empress Eugénie that the women of the palace and the wives of the high functionaries copied as nearly as they could the appearance of the beautiful Empress. They divided their hair in the middle, and spent hours in making little bunches of curls. High-heeled shoes replaced the coloured *babouches*;* they even adopted the hideous crinolines, and abandoned forever those charming Oriental garments, the *chalvar*† and *enturi*,‡ which they considered symbols of servitude, but which no other fashion has been able to equal in beauty.

As might be supposed, the middle class soon followed the example of the palace ladies and adopted Western costume. Then there was a craze for *everything* French. The most eccentric head-dresses and daring costumes were copied. To these Oriental women were given more jewels than liberty, more sensual love than pure affection, and it mattered little, until they found out from reading the foreign papers that there was something else except the beauty of the body—the beauty of the soul.

The more they read and learnt, the greater was their suffering. They read everything they could lay their hands on—history, religion, philosophy, poetry, and even *risqué* books. They had an indigestion of reading, and no one was there to cure them.

This desire for everything French lasted until our generation. No one seemed to understand how harmful it was to exaggerate the atmosphere of excitement in which we were living.

With the craze for the education of the West, French governesses came to Constantinople in great numbers; for it was soon known what high salaries the Turks paid, and how hospitable they were.

If you had seen the list of books that these unfortunate Turkish girls read to get a knowledge of French literature, I think you would agree with me they must

---

*   Babouche = Turkish slippers without heels.

†   Chalvar = Turkish pantaloons, far more graceful than the hideous harem skirts, which met with such scant success in this country.

‡   Enturi = the tunic, heavily embroidered, which almost covered the pantaloons.

have been endowed with double moral purity for the books not to have done them more harm.

For nearly thirty years this dangerous experiment went on. No parents seemed to see the grave error of having in one's house a woman about whom they knew nothing, and who in a very short time could exert a very disastrous influence over a young life. It was only when catastrophe after catastrophe* had brought this to their notice, they began to take any interest in their daughters' governesses, and occupy themselves a little more seriously about what they read.

When I look back on our girlhood, I do feel bitterly towards these women, who had not the honesty to find out that we had souls. How they might have helped us if only they had cared! How they might have discussed with us certain theories which we were trying to apply disastrously to our Eastern existence! But they said to themselves, no doubt, Let us take advantage of the high salary, for we cannot stand this tedious existence too long. And the Turkish women went on reading anything that came within their reach.

[…]

It was at the beginning of the reign of Abdul Hamid that this craze for Western culture was at its height. The terrible war, and the fall of the two beloved Sultans, woke the women from their dreams. Before the fact that their country was in danger, they understood their duty. From odalisques† they became mothers and wives determined to give their children the education they themselves had so badly needed.

The new monarch then endowed the Ottoman Empire with schools for little girls. The pupils who applied themselves learnt very quickly, and soon they could favourably be compared with their sisters of the West.

This was the first step that Turkish women had made towards their evolution.

[…]

So we Turkish women came to a period of our existence when it was useless to sigh for a mind that could content itself with the embroidery evenings of our grandmothers. These gatherings, too, became less and less frequent, for women were not allowed out after dark, no matter what their age.

Then it was, however, that, in spite of its being forbidden, I inaugurated a series of "white dinner parties"‡ for girls only. This created a scandal throughout the town. Our parents disliked the idea intensely, but we remained firm, and were happy to see our efforts crowned with success. Later, when we were married, we

---

* The Western governesses, in so many cases, took no interest in their pupils' reading, and allowed them to read everything they could lay their hands on. With their capacity for intrigue, they smuggled in principally French novels of the most harmful kind. Physical exercise being impossible to work off the evil effects of this harmful reading, the Turkish woman, discontented with her lot, saw only two ways of ending her unhappy existence— flight or suicide; she generally preferred the latter method.

† Slaves.

‡ They were called "white" because they were originally attended by unmarried women only, and they all wore white dresses.—G. E.

continued those dinners as long as we dared, and then it was we discussed what we could do for the future of women.

And what delightful evenings we spent together! Those *soirées* were moments when we could be ourselves, open our hearts to one another, and try to brighten for a little our lives. The fourteen friends I most loved in Turkey were all of the company of "white diners," and all those fourteen girls have played some special rôle in life.

.   .   .   .   .   .

I am sending you a letter, written by a friend whom I shall never see again.

"Since your departure," she wrote, "we have not been allowed to go a step out of doors, lest we should follow your example. We are living under a régime of terror which is worse than it has ever been before.

"I want to implore you to work for us. Tell the whole world what we are suffering; indeed it would be a consolation, much as it hurts our pride."

[…]

The year that the Belgian anarchist tried to kill the Sultan Hamid, was certainly the worst I have ever spent. Even the Armenian Massacres, which were amongst the most haunting and horrible souvenirs of our youth, could not be compared with what we had then to bear. Arrests went on wholesale! Thousands were "suspect," questioned, tortured perhaps. And when the real culprit had declared his guilt before the whole tribunal and had proved that it was he, and he alone, who had thrown the bomb, the poor prisoners were not released.

It was in the summer. Up till then in the country, a woman could go out in the evening, if she were accompanied, but this was at once prohibited; every Turkish boat which was not a fishing boat was stopped; in the streets all those who could not prove the reason for being out were arrested; no longer were visits to the Embassies possible, no longer could the ladies from the Embassies come to see us; no "white dinners," no meeting of friends. There were police stationed before the doors, and we dared not play the piano for fear of appearing too gay, when our "Sovereign Lord's" life had been in danger.

Of course no letters could be received from our Western friends. The foreign posts were searched through and through, and nearly all the movement of the daily life was at an end. One evening my sister and I went outside to look at the moonlit Bosphorus. Although accompanied by a male relative, three faithful guardians of the safety of our beloved Monarch stepped forward and asked for explanations as to why we were gazing at the sea. Not wishing to reply, we were asked to follow them to the nearest police station. My sister and I went in, leaving our relative to explain matters, and I can assure you that was the last time we dared to study moon effects. Never, I think, more than that evening, was I so decided to leave our country, come what might! Life was just one perpetual nightmare, and for a long time after, even now in security, I still dream of these days of terror.

[…]

How I wish that nine out of every ten of the books written on Turkey could be burned! How unjustly the Turk has been criticised! And what nonsense has been written about the women! I cannot imagine where the writers get their information from, or what class of women they visited. Every book I have read has been in some way unfair to the Turkish woman. Not one woman has really understood us! Not one woman has credited us with the possession of a heart, a mind, or a soul.—Your affectionate friend,

ZEYNEB.

CHAPTER XVII
AND IS THIS REALLY FREEDOM?

[…]

[…] What I do feel, though, is that a *Ladies' Club* is not a big enough reward for having broken away from an Eastern harem and all the suffering that has been the consequence of that action. A club, as I said before, is after all another kind of harem, but it has none of the mystery and charm of the Harem of the East.

[…]

[…] It seems to me that we Orientals are children to whom fairy tales have been told for too long—fairy tales which have every appearance of truth. You hear so much of the *mirage* of the East, but what is that compared to the *mirage* of the West, to which all Orientals are attracted?

They tell you fairy tales, too, you women of the West—fairy tales which, like ours, have all the appearance of truth. I wonder, when the Englishwomen have really won their vote and the right to exercise all the tiring professions of men, what they will have gained? Their faces will be a little sadder, a little more weary, and they will have become wholly disillusioned.

[…]

Since I came here I have seen nothing but "Votes for Women" chalked all over the pavements and walls of the town. These methods of propaganda are all so new to me.

I went to a Suffrage street corner meeting the other night, and I can assure you I never want to go again. The speaker carried her little stool herself, another carried a flag, and yet a third woman a bundle of leaflets and papers to distribute to the crowd. After walking for a little while they placed the stool outside a dirty-looking public-house, and the lady who carried the flag boldly got on to the stool and began to shout, not waiting till the people came to hear her, so anxious was she to begin. Although she did not look nervous in the least she possibly was, for her speech came abruptly to an end, and my heart began to beat in sympathy with her.

When the other lady began to speak quite a big crowd of men and women assembled: degraded-looking ruffians they were, most of them, and a class of man I had not yet seen. All the time they interrupted her, but she went bravely on, returning their rudeness with sarcasm. What an insult to womanhood it seemed to me, to have to bandy words with this vulgar mob. One man told her that "she was ugly." Another asked "if she had done her washing," but the most of their hateful remarks I could not understand, so different was their English from the English I had learned in Turkey.

Yet how I admired the courage of that woman! No physical pain could be more awful to me than not to be taken for a lady, and this speaker of such remarkable eloquence and culture was not taken for a lady by the crowd, seeing she was supposed "to do her own washing" like any woman of the people.

The most pitiful part of it all to me is the blind faith these women have in their cause, and the confidence they have that in explaining their policy to the street ruffians, who cannot even understand that they are ladies, they will further their cause by half an inch.

I was glad when the meeting was over, but sorry that such rhetoric should have been wasted on the half-intoxicated loungers who deigned to come out of the public-house and listen. If this is what the women of your country have to bear in their fight for freedom, all honour to them, but I would rather groan in bondage.

[...]

[Zeyneb is invited to take tea with a Member of Parliament at the House of Commons.] I was conducted through a long, handsome corridor to a lobby where all sorts of men and women were assembled, pushing one another, gesticulating and speaking in loud, disagreeable voices like those outside of the Paris Bourse. Just then, however, a bell rang, and I was conducted back past the policeman to my original seat. What curious behaviour! What did it all mean? I spoke to the friendly policeman, but his explanation that they were "dividing" did not convey much to my mind. As I stood there, a stray member of Parliament came and looked at me. He must have been a great admirer of Mr. Joseph Chamberlain, for he wore a monocle and an orchid in his buttonhole.

"Are these suffragettes?" he asked the policeman, staring at me and the other women.

"No, sir," answered the policeman, "ladies."

It was too late for tea when my host returned to fetch me, but the loss of a cup of tea is no calamity to me, as I only drink it to appear polite. I was next taken up to the Ladies' Gallery, and was sworn in as one of the relations of a member who had given up his ladies' tickets to my host. The funny part of it was, that I could not understand the language my relation spoke, so different was his English from the English I had learnt in Turkey. But what a fuss to get into that Ladies' Gallery! I had no idea of making a noise before it was suggested to my mind by making me sign a book, and I certainly wanted to afterwards. What unnecessary trouble! What do you call it? Red tapeism! One might almost be in Turkey under Hamid and not in Free England.

But, my dear, why have you never told me that the Ladies' Gallery is a harem? A harem with its latticed windows! The harem of the Government! No wonder the women cried through the windows of that harem that they wanted to be free! I felt inclined to shout out too. "Is it in Free England that you dare to have a

harem? How inconsistent are you English! You send your women out unpro-
tected all over the world, and here in the workshop where your laws are made,
you cover them with a symbol of protection."

[…]

CHAPTER XX
THE END OF THE DREAM

MARSEILLES, 5*th March*, 1912.

It is to-morrow that I sail. In a week from to-day, I shall again be away yonder
amongst those whom I have always felt so near, and who I know have not forgotten me.

In just a week from to-day I shall again be one of those unrecognisible figures
who cross and recross the silent streets of our town—some one who no longer
belongs to the same world as you—some one who must not even think as you
do—some one who will have to try and forget she led the existence of a Western
woman for six long, weary years.

What heart-breaking disappointments have I not to take away with me! It
makes me sad to think how England has changed! England with its aristocratic
buildings and kingly architecture—England with its proud and self-respecting
democracy—the England that our great Kemal Bey taught us to know, that splendid people the world admires so much, sailing so dangerously near the rocks.

I do not pretend to understand the suffragettes or their "window-smashing"
policy, but I must say, I am even more surprised at the attitude of your Government. However much these ill-advised women have over-stepped the boundaries
of their sex privileges, however wrong they may be, surely the British Government could have found some other means of dealing with them, given their cause
the attention they demanded, or used some diplomatic way of keeping them
quiet. I cannot tell you the horrible impression it produces on the mind of a Turkish woman to learn that England not only imprisons but tortures women; to me it
is the cataclysm of all my most cherished faiths. Ever since I can remember, England had been to me a kind of Paradise on earth, the land which welcomed to its
big hospitable bosom all Europe's political refugees. It was the land of all lands I
longed to visit, and now I hear a Liberal Government is torturing women. Somehow my mind will not accept this statement.

Write to me often, very often, dear girl. You know exactly where I shall be
away yonder, and exactly what I shall be doing. You know even the day when I
shall again begin my quiet, almost cloistered existence as a Moslem woman, and
how I shall long for news of that Europe which has so interested and so disappointed me.

[…]

[…] *Désenchantée* I left Turkey, *désenchantée* I have left Europe. Is that rôle
to be mine till the end of my days?—Your affectionate friend,

ZEYNEB.

9.

ELIZABETH COOPER (1877–1945)

ᔓ THE WOMEN OF EGYPT ᔕ

F.A. Stokes, New York
1914 (reprinted by Hyperion, 1981)

Elizabeth Cooper was an American, a professional writer who travelled widely to research her books on women. In addition to *The Women of Egypt*, which is excerpted here, she also wrote several books about women in other parts of the world (*My Lady of the Chinese Courtyard*; *The Soul Traders*; *Sayonara*), as well as *The Harim and The Purdah, Studies of Oriental Women*, which was a comparative account of women's lives in Egypt, India, Burma, China and Japan, published in 1915.

In the Preface to *The Women of Egypt* she writes: 'It is my hope that these pages may afford a glimpse into the modern life and problems confronting her [the Egyptian woman] in the present rapid and revolutionary changes which Egypt is now experiencing in common with the entire Eastern world' (p. 10). As a means of establishing her authority as a writer, the Preface also lists some of her experiences in Egypt, such as visiting women of various classes, including the Bedouin, in their homes; visiting schools, missions and hospitals; talking with people involved with social programmes; and keeping house in a Cairo apartment. Cooper's agenda was to discover how Egyptian women, of all classes, were confronting modernity in the early twentieth century, and to report on the changing social institutions emerging in Egypt at this transitional moment. The sociological breadth of Cooper's inquiry is in sharp contrast to the more limited scope available to Sophia Lane Poole (Extract 2), who, writing a half-century earlier with a similar desire to convey as much information as possible about Egyptian women, was confined almost exclusively to descriptions of the elite Cairo harems that were the only destinations considered suitable for a genteel visitor.

Cooper, with the increased personal independence and social mobility won by half a century of American feminism, was able to exercise more choice in how she carried out her investigations. Realising soon after her arrival in Egypt that she would not be able to visit Egyptian women if she stayed in a hotel – since no respectable Egyptian woman would consider visiting her there – she decided to rent a furnished apartment for the few months that she and her husband planned to remain in Cairo. Her account of finding the apartment and setting up housekeeping forms the basis of Chapter IV in her book. Keeping house in the city also allowed her the opportunity to meet women in contexts that would not have been possible otherwise. She recounts her interactions with the variety of women she encountered: the Armenian woman who was their cook; the women and girls working in the vegetable market; the Arab laundry woman; and the itinerant seamstress. These experiences provided her with access to women from a range of classes and ethnic groups and inform her nuanced presentation of Egyptian women in her book.

Cooper's book, arranged in seventeen chapters, covers the subjects typically found in works from this period addressing the 'Woman Question'. Egyptian women are presented in terms of the settings of their lives (city or village); the social institutions that shape their lives (school, harem, marriage, divorce); their social customs; their relationships with their children; their religion(s); and, in the conclusion, the issues confronting the modern Egyptian woman.

Chapter V from *The Women of Egypt* is reprinted here in its entirety. Entitled 'Feminine Characteristics', the chapter sets out to describe the five types of women that Cooper distinguishes among the population of Egypt: the upper-class woman, the middle-class woman, the working woman of the city, the peasant woman and the Bedouin. The chapter is illustrated with nine photographs (not included here) of women from these different groups, in street dress or working clothes, five of which show women doing some kind of work outdoors, mostly carrying water. Cooper's focus in her descriptions of the women is on their dress and the ways in which they spend their time, with some attention given to their homes. Her accounts of dress include information about what they wear indoors as well as their veiling customs and jewellery, demonstrating that she understands the function of both dress and jewellery as critical social markers for women. She is sensitive to change, reporting, for example, that Bedouin women who want to appear modern braid their hair in a fashion different to a few years earlier. Focusing on different social strata, she locates women as part of family and local economies through her discussion of the social role of both their leisure activities and their household and agricultural work.

The format and tone of Cooper's book illustrates how women's writing had shifted from the sometimes disingenuous travel accounts and harem descriptions of the nineteenth century to the more focused investigation of specific subjects characteristic of the twentieth-century authors included in this collection. Unlike earlier authors (Brassey and Poole, for example), who often present their work as an almost accidental result of circumstances, Cooper is explicit about the fact that she set out to write a certain book and travelled to Egypt in order to do so. While somewhat essentialising in her division of Egyptian women into five groups and prone to nostalgia when she describes the 'home of a conservative Egyptian untouched by Western ideas' as 'a thing of beauty', Cooper nonetheless has a very good eye for observing the ways in which the lives of Egyptian women of different classes were changing.

80   03

CHAPTER V
FEMININE CHARACTERISTICS

There are five distinct types of women in Egypt, distinguished from each other to the onlooker chiefly by their costumes: the high-class Egyptian lady, the woman of the middle class, the lower-class labouring woman of the city, the Fellaha or peasant woman, and the Bedouin who dwells in the desert.

Generally the Egyptian women from the age of fourteen to twenty-five are beautiful both in form and face. They have large black eyes with lashes very thick and long; these lashes have no curve and give a peculiar veiled expression to the eyes, making them appear darker and larger than they really are. Their noses are fine and delicate, their lips an exquisite bow shape. Their teeth are white, and their hands and feet, when not deformed by labour, dainty and delicate. The skin is of a light tan, but rarely does one see colour in the cheeks. The hair is of a deep glossy black, rather coarse, but never with the true Egyptian is it woolly.

The lady of Egypt is rarely seen. One catches glimpses of her in carriages or motor-cars, the impression being of a woman dressed in black with a thin veil of white chiffon covering the lower part of her face. This veil, however, much to the disgust of the old-fashioned, conservative Egyptian, is becoming thinner each year; in fact, it is often but an added attraction, making an ugly face pretty and adding an air of mystery and charm to a beautiful one.

In the home the Egyptian lady dresses much like a French woman of the same social standing; even the silk hosiery and high-heeled French slippers are not wanting. This lady also partakes of the Europeanization of Egypt and reveals the influence of Western civilization which is so rapidly and thoroughly working a revolution in this ancient land, but the traditions and customs of her country are still powerful enough to require her to wear the black skirt of silk or satin and a cape-like piece of the same goods turned up at the waist-line for a head-covering, when she appears outside of the harem.

The Egyptian woman of the higher class is becoming Europeanized, as evidenced not only by the motor-cars and carriages with coachmen and chauffeurs in foreign liveries, and her dresses direct from Paris, but also by the furnishings of her home. Instead of the rich Eastern homes of the *Arabian Nights* with their lamps and rugs and elaborate hangings, we now see the drawing-room filled with French furniture, gilt chairs, instead of divans, rich Louis XV. tables in place of the low taborets; electric chandeliers glittering with cut glass have replaced the old elaborate lamps that are now rarely seen except in mosques, museums, and curio shops. The lady also now serves afternoon tea instead of Turkish coffee and the scented drinks that were the favourite beverages in the olden time, while, instead of "visiting" her friends for the day, she now makes fashionable calls.

She travels also, and as soon as the ship leaves the harbour of Alexandria or Port Said, the veil is laid aside and she is to all intents and purposes the cultured, well-educated lady of any country. It would be hard to tell her nationality, as generally her command of the French language is perfect, and she might be considered a woman of Turkey or Greece or even of France. But when again the ship arrives in an Egyptian port she dons the dress of her people and is the veiled Egyptian lady.

Another type also rarely seen in the street, and who are the chief preservers of the ancient customs of Egypt, since they are brought less frequently into touch with European influences, are the women of the great middle class, the wives of the lawyers, doctors, teachers, small officials and professional men of all grades as well as the women belonging to the upper merchant class. Their homes have not been subjected to such a radical change as that seen among the Egyptian aristocracy, although it is evident that the only reason for this difference has been the lack of opportunity.

The middle-class woman, like her sister of the upper class, may be a good judge of what is consistent in the way of decoration of a purely Egyptian home, but when she tries to replace her native furnishings with those of France, the effect is baneful. Instead of the softened colouring of the Eastern carpets and hangings she is likely to substitute the gaudy dyes of Europe's worst manufactures; while she is inclined to mistake gilding, mirrors, and ornate work for cosmopolitanism and culture.

If one is fortunate enough to penetrate the home of a conservative Egyptian untouched by Western ideas, one finds it a thing of beauty and a rest to jaded nerves and tired eyes, with its closely drawn blinds shutting out the fierce tropical light and heat, its court with the fountain sending up its cooling waters, flowers, the comfortable divans covered with soft-toned rugs, shaded lights, exquisite brass trays on which stand the tiny china cups in their small brass or silver holders, from which one drinks the coffee served by white-clad, quiet servants—it is all Eastern and gives the sense of repose and leisure.

The women of this great class dress, when outside of their homes, similarly to those in the highest social scale, but within the house they wear a galabeigh, a sort of glorified empire-gown hanging straight from the shoulder or gathered to a yoke, and having a long train behind. This garment is made of silk or satin, and often is elaborately trimmed. If custom restricts them to black while in the street, they exercise their individual taste in regard to colours within their apartments. I have seen a group of ladies with their pink, blue, and yellow galabeighs, looking like a flock of gaily plumaged birds.

Both the upper and middle class wear an immense amount of jewellery, which lately has taken the shape of pins, ear-rings, and bracelets from the French shops on the Kaiser en Nil, instead of ornaments from the goldsmiths in the bazaars. The long pendant ear-rings covered with fine diamonds, and necklaces of coloured precious stones, are the ornaments now coveted, and quantity not quality is the chief desire of the woman whose husband's purse is large enough to bring her these tokens of his affection. She differs in this respect from the woman of China, who is also peering into the outside world, but who seems to understand that pearls and jade, not diamonds and rubies, are the proper setting for her Eastern beauty.

The third class one sees in the cities of Egypt is the woman of the lower walks of life, the wife of the workman, the small shop-keeper, the servant, and the craftsman. She is dressed in a galabeigh of black or coloured cotton, over which, when in the streets, she draws a piece of black material which entirely covers her body and is held in place beneath the left arm. Her face-veil is black or of cloth inset with pieces of open-work, and often, by the old-fashioned ladies, held down by coins sewed to its lower edges. A nose-piece of yellow wood and gold or brass is sewed to the top of the veil, holding it in place, and is kept firm by a ribbon around the head beneath the shawl. This arrangement effectually conceals the face with the exception of the eyes, and these are difficult to discern, because of the disfiguring nose-piece.

This veil is of remote antiquity, but judging from the sculptures and paintings of the ancient Egyptians, it would seem to have been inaugurated since those early times. It was, however, used by nearly all women of Eastern races, and is spoken of in the Old Testament:

"Rebecca said to the servant, What man is this that walketh in the field to meet us? And the servant said, It is my master. And she took her veil and covered herself." St. Paul also said, "Is it seemly that a woman pray to God unveiled?"

The wife of the poor manual labourer, as her richer sister, has her jewellery. Her ear-rings may be of gold or silver, and her necklace of glass beads or even of brass. Her bracelets and the anklets hanging over her bare feet are often of silver or the cheaper metals. Yet one is surprised often to see a poor woman with gold ear-rings or a necklace worth many piastres. It was the poor man's form of investment of his savings in the olden time when there were no banks in which he could trust his hard-earned money. He bought jewellery, which in the case of gold is practically pure, and can be converted into money with little loss.

A lady in Cairo who employs a woman for rough work in her house, told me a story that illustrates the utilitarian use of jewellery, apart from its beauty. This working woman was extremely poor, having literally but one dress. One day she was given a little lamb, and she raised it until it became the desired weight, when it was taken to the near-by butcher. The money realized was spent, not for clothes nor for food, but for a pair of gold ear-rings. When remonstrated with in regard to the apparent foolishness of her purchase, she said, "I would wear out the clothes and eat the food, but these will last, and when we have no money we can always go to the pawn-shop." Her choice seemed justified because the ear-rings have made many a journey to the man who lends money.

The working-classes of Egypt are little in advance of the wolf that seems to be always following them, and it gives a sense of security to feel that they have at least one thing that will mean bread, if that voracious animal gets too close.

Another reason for the immense amount of jewellery seen on all classes of Egyptian women is the fact that if women are divorced they are entitled to their wearing apparel as well as any part of their dowry which may have been retained by their husbands at the time of betrothal. They may not be able to get the dower, but there can be no question of what they actually have upon their persons.

These reasons for the love of jewellery may be very practical, but these women mainly love jewellery because it is *jewellery*, and all Eastern women, Chinese, Indian, Turkish, and Egyptian, are fond of adorning themselves. As they rely much more upon personal beauty to retain the love of the husband than does the Western woman, they take advantage of all the arts to adorn that beauty, for there is a saying, "A woman without ornaments is like a field without water."

While travelling up the Nile one sees the small villages which seem to be a part of the soil, so neutral is their colour. The houses are made from sun-dried bricks, the only thing to make one really believe they are not a veritable part of the sands of the desert being the whitened cupola of a mosque or the dome of the tomb of some saint or holy man.

Even the dress of the woman is dull and wretched looking. You see her as she comes down the narrow pathway leading to the river or canal, her water-jar balanced sideways upon her head, her blue or black galabeigh hanging in straight lines from her shoulders, her bare feet half covered with the heavy anklets. She has no face-veil, but on meeting you she draws an end of the long black head-covering across her mouth and peers at you curiously from above it. She has a beautiful carriage, and the gesture, superb and supple as she bends to the river and places the filled jar upon her head, cannot be equalled for grace. But her hands are roughened from toil, and she becomes old before her time. Her life is passed in heavy work, and in her simple home are few conveniences.

The house is only a couple of rooms opening upon a small yard, around which is built a wall of the same dun-coloured brick. Within this small enclosure live the family and the animals, the donkey, the camel, and the chickens. The kitchen consists of a bare dark room, with a few baskets or jars along the sides to contain the grain, a couple of stones on which is built the fire to heat the food within the iron cooking-pot. There are no table, no chairs, and no beds; the earth serves for all three. At night a mat is spread upon the beaten ground, and the entire family curl upon it, wrapped in their clothes of the day. The warm sunshine and rainless days and nights make it possible for the Egyptian to live out of doors practically ten months of the year. This fact accounts for their healthfulness, despite their disregard of all sanitary laws.

Their food is simple. Wheaten bread is practically an unknown luxury, millet, maize, and dourha forming a very wholesome substitute. Meat is rarely eaten by the peasant except on great occasions, and then mutton is preferred, but buffalo and goats are also used, as are poultry and pigeons. Beans and lentils, onions and garlic, are the poor man's vegetables, while cucumbers and a large radish are eaten raw and without peeling as a fruit. Sugar-cane at the season of its growth is seen in the hands of old and young, while musk-melons and water-melons are a delight to the peasant. The women make a sweet from the dried and pounded dates, that is used especially at the time of feasts.

All the work of preparing this food falls upon the housewife. She must clean the maize and grind it in the mill, then make the bread, which is a most laborious process. In fact she has no idle life. She spins the wool and cotton for the clothing, often weaves the cloth, carries the water from the river, and gathers the mud and straw to make the round, flat cakes for fuel, which she stores upon the roof or within the courtyard. In the evening she or the children take the camels or the goats and the donkey to the fields and watch them while they eat their allotted portion of bersein or clover.

In moments stolen from household work the women weave baskets from the date-palm leaves or make the sleeping-mats from the reeds, which they themselves must gather. If there is space upon the roof or within the tiny courtyard they keep a few chickens in order to sell the eggs, and add a little to their limited income. The wives of the Fellaheen are true helpmates. At the time of harvest one sees them cutting the ripened grain, or carrying it in great bundles upon their heads to the store-houses within the village. It is a life of toil, with, what seems to Western eyes, little compensation.

In the desert one sees the most interesting type of all, the Bedouin. She is generally a well-formed, tall, strong woman, dressed in the usual black or coloured galabeigh, with the addition of a multi-coloured sash wrapped many times around the waist. Over her head and hanging down her back is a veil or handkerchief, but she does not veil her face unless living in a village. In the life of a true Bedouin, that is a dweller in the tent, the veiling and seclusion of the woman are not practised. But when they move to villages and live in houses they imitate their neighbours the Egyptians and seclude their women.

While the Bedouin does not dress herself in silk or satin, like the city-dweller, she makes up for this lack of richness in goods by her love for native jewellery. She wears gold necklaces with balls as big as hazel-nuts, and elaborate pendants hanging over her chest. Often she has rows upon rows of gold coins attached to chains, the entire body, from the waist up, being covered with the barbaric ornaments. In her ears she wears two great rings, one from the top of the ear and one from the lobe. In her left nostril is an ornament, and her arms are covered with bracelets. When she walks one can hear the tinkle of her anklets. This sound is so common that there is a Bedouin song which begins "The ringing of thine anklets has deprived me of my reason." This jewellery has not changed its shape or form with the passage of time. It is practically the same as worn by the women of Judea in the time of Isaiah:

"In that day the Lord will take away the beauty of their anklets and the cauls and crescents, the pendants, and the bracelets and the mufflers, the head tires and the ankle-chains; the sashes and the perfume boxes and the amulets, the rings and the nose jewels . . . and the turbans and the veils."

The tent Bedouin rarely leaves the camp. Her world is the low tent around the sides of which are folded the rugs and sleeping-mats and blankets which are the work of her hands and the exhibition of her riches. On the part of the tent where the family sit is spread a rug or mat, and in another part on the bare sand are the stones for the fire. Except for the jars or baskets and sacks to hold provisions and extra clothing, there is no furniture. The food is mainly mutton cooked in different ways, and served in a big bowl, around which the family sit, helping themselves from the common dish, using bread as plate and knife and fork. The desert-dweller cares little for vegetables, which fact is, perhaps, accounted for by his inability to raise them in the sands that surround his home.

The Bedouin and many of the lower-class Egyptian women tattoo their faces with three or four dark-blue lines extending from the lower lip over the chin to the neck. Also fancy figures are tattooed on the hands, and the wrists are often marked with bracelets in blue ink. Henna is used to stain the hair, giving it a rich dark-red, that when not used too abundantly is very pretty in the jet-black of the natural colour. Grey hair is considered very ugly and is always dyed.

It is only in the desert and the country that one sees the henna-stained hands and feet, as it is not considered fashionable by city people. The inside of the hands and feet is coloured a deep orange, and the nails of both fingers and toes are touched with the dye, often the fingers showing the stain to the first or second joint, giving a most uncleanly appearance according to Western standards.

Practically all Eastern women wear a covering for the hair both in and out of the house. It is generally a large silk handkerchief or veil of black with a coloured border, but which, at time of festivity, is changed for one elaborately embroidered or sewn with sequins. It is a disgrace to allow the head to be unveiled, the expression "She is a woman without a veil for her hair" is equivalent to saying "She is without shame."

The hair, which hardly shows at all, is braided in two braids hanging down the back, rather like that worn by the school-girls of our country, except that gold coins are braided into the ends, and clink and glisten from under the veil as the wearer moves her head. At present the Bedouin who wishes to be especially progressive makes only one braid, which is a decided change from the fashion of a few years ago, when the hair was parted into fourteen sections, each one tightly braided and woven with gold coins.

The Bedouin woman has much more liberty than the Egyptian woman. She does not impress one as being downtrodden or held in any manner of subjection. She shares in the life of the entire camp, taking a keen and intelligent interest in all that affects her tribe. Because of the Bedouin customs of entertaining the traveller, who may be passing from one part of the desert to another, she gathers the gossip from all parts of the country. At each camp the chief of the tribe has a rest-house where any Bedouin may stop, stable his horse, and receive food so long as he wishes. The traveller may be from Tripoli and bring the latest news of the war or from the Southern Sahara.

At the castle of a chief where I visited there were often as many as thirty strangers within the travellers' courtyard, and I soon learned to consider them far more advanced than their Egyptian neighbour who stays within his village. The blood of the Bedouin is the wanderer's blood. He is a true descendant of Ishmael in that he claims the whole great desert for his home.

10.
Grace Ellison (d.1935)
ॐ An Englishwoman in a Turkish Harem ॐ

Methuen, London
1915

An Englishwoman in a Turkish Harem had previously appeared as articles in the *Daily Telegraph,* published in January and February 1914. Written by the journalist and feminist Grace Ellison, the columns aimed to challenge Western stereotypes about the nature of Turkish female life. Arriving in November 1913 on her third visit to Turkey, Ellison spent some months in Istanbul and travelled into Anatolia. She had previously visited Istanbul in 1908 to report on the new Young Turk constitutional government. It was at this point that Ellison, who had become well connected with prominent Ottoman politicians and public figures, met the senior statesman Kâmil Pasha (at that time Grand Vizier to Sultan Abdülhamit II) and befriended his daughter Makboulé Hanoum, referred to here as 'Fâtima'. When Ellison returned in 1913 she stayed with Fâtima (now married to a supporter of the Young Turks, and facing the exile and subsequent death of her father, who had become a focus for the failed countercoup of March 1913). The prolonged visit gave Ellison the opportunity to observe first hand the life of an elite harem. From the start of her book Ellison was at pains to debunk the ideas cherished in the West of a cruel and sexual containment. Repeatedly she contrasts the protections of the harem system with the harshness faced by Western women trying to earn a living in a modern market economy. But, as someone who was already involved in editing and producing two other volumes of harem literature (see Zeyneb Hanoum, Extract 8), Ellison understood the sales value of even a chapter on the harem. As her provocative title suggests, Ellison's book simultaneously invokes and contests Orientalist fantasies about segregated life. It was her immersion in the presumed to be sexualised space of the harem that gave her report authority, and she, like other writers, explicitly disparaged accounts offered by 'expelled governesses' and the non-Muslim European and Levantine ladies of Istanbul's Pera district.

In contrast, Ellison's investigation is supported by quotations from leading feminists such as Halide Hanoum (later Halide Edib, see Extract 13) and by reports from feminist meetings. In these it becomes clear that the Ottomans rightly understood that the image of the oppressed, indolent harem lady was not just insulting but also informed the ways in which Western nations regarded the Ottoman state. Halide expressly asks Ellison to substitute the word 'home' in the Western imagination and though Ellison continued to use the term harem she did paint a vision of the Ottoman domestic that questioned cherished Western stereotypes. But this was a domestic in which opposing political views vied for primacy. In her friend Fâtima's household, the progressive ideals of her host and her husband are hampered by older women in the family, a generational clash that was felt by many younger women in the period, especially between themselves and their mothers.

It was astounding to Ellison that women in Turkey had male support in their bid for emancipation. Contrasting this with the scorn and hostility that greeted British feminists, Ellison constructs one of the several comparisons in these passages in which the West comes out worst. Though she admitted to feeling frustrated at the apparent lack of activity on the part of Turkish women – who did not instantly throw off their veils – she explains that she can now comprehend how Ottoman women have come to internalise codes of modesty, so that even the radical Edib still veiled as a matter of course. Despite her at-times condescending tone, Ellison realised that concepts of liberty are relative and argued, especially as one who had experienced the hardships of Western 'freedom', that Turkish women should not simply mimic the West. Her account of the charitable activities of the Red Crescent (which provided vocational training for women during the hardships of the Balkan Wars when many women had to support their families) highlights the public service activities of Ottoman women. Women's politicised consumption – renouncing Paris fashions in order to support the Turkish textiles and clothing industries – is presented by Ellison as a stark economic riposte to the vision of luxury and passivity favoured by the West. Though Ellison was careful to distance herself from the excesses of the Young Turks (who would soon go on to side with Germany in the First World War), she had no hesitation in condemning the anti-Turk prejudices that determined British foreign policy. The risks taken by women in their clandestine activities during the Young Turk revolution were rewarded by a government that took female emancipation as one of its aims – unlike the shameful anti-suffrage stance of the British government.

Alongside her emphasis on Ottoman women's political agency, Ellison could not disguise her nostalgic investment in the luxury and ease of the elite Ottoman harem. Giving herself over the calm inactivity of Ottoman domestic life, she was almost reconciled to delays in her writing schedule. She knew that a fully segregated life would not suit her, but the economic protections offered by the harem system, especially to unmarried women such as she, could not be dismissed. Ellison reconfigures the harem as a social space, the obligations and benefits of which extended through charity beyond the elite strata of the householders. In another example of intertextuality, Ellison quotes Zeyneb Hanoum's horror at the lack of charity she witnessed in the West.

Ellison's closing reference to the recent provision of selected university classes for women stresses the contemporaneity of her account, as does her inclusion of photographs. In the short extract here about trying to take photographs Ellison presents herself as a would-be ethnographer, facing the difficulties of superstitious and unwilling subjects. But she did succeed in many instances, also collecting portrait photographs as keepsakes of her respondents, their presence in the book attesting again to her connections with Ottoman society.

೫   ೞ

And now, after five years, here I am back again enjoying once more the calm and peace of an Eastern home, and the interesting society of my dear friend Fâtima (I change the name). To the Western ear, to be staying in a Turkish harem sounds alarming, and not a little—yes, let us confess it—improper. When, before I left my own country, I had the imprudence to tell a newspaper correspondent that I was longing to get back to the quiet harem existence, I was accused of "advocating polygamy," for to the uninitiated the word "harem" means a collection of wives, legitimate or otherwise, and even the initiated prefers to pretend he knows no other meaning.

Worn out with what we in the West call pleasures of society, the fatigue of writing against time, the rush and bustle of our big Western capitals, the hideous and continual noise of the traffic, which, like a great roaring wave, seems gradually to deaden one's understanding; how good it is to be here!

[...]

The diary of my existence as a Turkish woman, which in England I imagined could be written in a very short while, lies day after day in the form of a pencil and exercise book, untouched, on the little mother-of-pearl table in the most comfortable corner of my large bedroom. "To-morrow," I say, like a true Turkish woman, and alas! in Turkey it takes a few to-morrows to beget "some day"; "some day" is soon changed into "never," and who knows whether the best of my Turkish impressions will not be given "their local habitation and name" in a room of some Continental hotel?

Now I understand how weeks and months, years even, may pass without receiving news from Turkish friends; now I understand that lack of what we English call "common courtesy." We have misjudged the Turks. A pen in the harem! The unnecessary intrusion! The reforming fever which has swept over the land of Islam ever since the Constitution has not yet taught the Turkish women the use of a pen as we understand it. When I reproached my friend and hostess with not having written one letter, "Why should I write," she asked; "what have I to say? You know exactly how every moment of my life is being spent. You know my affection for you, and when two friends are really sure of one another's sympathy, each can feel the thoughts the other is thinking ... ." And so we took up the threads of the conversation where we had left them five years ago.

[...]

To be cut off from the society of Pera, however, with few exceptions, is no deprivation for the Turkish woman. She dislikes the women, perhaps, even more than the men, because she knows them better, but she lumps them all, both sexes and all nations, into the somewhat contemptuous term *Perote*. She dislikes the loud voices of the women—she, who is taught as the most elementary form of good breeding to speak in a soft, low voice (the domestics here literally whisper)—she dislikes the Perote's abominable habit of asking questions (for the Turkish woman will not be questioned); she dislikes the inquisitive, staring men, who look as if they would "gimlet" their way through the black face-veil the Turkish women wear. ...

"But why do you Turkish women dislike the Perotes?" I asked one day. "They have the blood of six nations in their veins and the soul of none," replied my friend; "and the vices of the six and the virtues of none," and I have found out recently that it is these Levantines who have told the world the little that is known of Turkish women.

The veiled Turkish woman is always a source of unending interest. A chapter, at least, on harem life will always add to the value of the book; for the word "harem" stirs the imagination, conjures up for the reader visions of houris veiled in the mystery of ages, of Grand Viziers clad in many-coloured robes and wearing turbans the size and shape of pumpkins, and last, but not least, is supplied for the reader's imagination a polygamous master of the harem, and they have made him the subject of their coarsest smoking-room jokes. Poor Turks! How we have humiliated them! The Turk loves his home and he loves his wife. He is an indulgent husband and a kind father. And yet we judge him from the books which are written, not to extend the truth about a people, but only to sell; the West expects to hear unwholesome stories when it reads of the Eastern homes, and all these falsehoods are put into circulation by expelled governesses and Perote ladies, who have given an ugly form and soul to all that passes behind the door through which they are rarely privileged to enter.

[...]

I asked Halidé-Hanoum, perhaps the most active and best known of modern Turkish women, in the name of one of our prominent suffrage societies, how we English women could help the Turkish women in their advancement. "Ask them," she said, "to delete for ever that misunderstood word 'harem,' and speak of us in our Turkish 'homes.' Ask them to try and dispel the nasty atmosphere which a wrong meaning of that word has cast over our lives. Tell them what our existence really is."

[...]

Before I leave this house I hope to get some photos of the interesting persons it contains, but in undertaking to photograph a Turkish household, I had forgotten first that the windows are dimmed by the inevitable lattice-work, which prevents my having a full view of the wonderful landscape which stretches from the foot of our garden to the rising and setting sun, and when the sun shines it shines through the lattices, throwing on to the furniture all around large lozenge-shaped reflections. But there is another and a greater difficulty, and that is, photography is forbidden by the Moslem religion. My friend would certainly let me photograph the house if I asked her. The sacred law of hospitality is part of her religion. She urged me even to eat bacon in the morning, although pork is forbidden in an Eastern house, and no doubt she would have insisted on buying it had I not declared that even in my own country I never eat pork. But Fâtima has to deal with a most fanatical entourage, the women much more than the men, women who for centuries have been taught to interpret the Koran as Mahomet never intended it should be interpreted, women who are purblind to any form of progress, women who still consider that to reproduce the human form created by God involves disobedience to the laws of the Prophet, though the Koran distinctly orders the faithful to march on with the centuries.

It is extraordinary and interesting to watch the working of this household. My host, an exceedingly well-read, intelligent officer, speaking two European languages, and having served three years in the German army, is a man with ideas of feminism and government and social questions quite half a century before his time, and he is surrounded by a household of ignorant fanatics who can neither read nor write. He would give his wife complete liberty this very day if it were possible, and, although she has more liberty than any woman I know, for her sake he cannot too openly defy Islam. The other day one of his brother officers lunched with us in the harem, but we were served by the male servants, as every woman slave refused to appear with bare face before a man who was not a "blood relation" of the lady of the house.

There are some ladies here who blame the Turkish women for not taking their freedom as other women have done; there are times, too, when I feel inclined to sigh for the militant spirit of the Englishwoman, but until one has really been behind the veil one can have no idea of what "fanaticism" really means. Isolated rebellion is of no use—a protest here and there may, or may not, help, but a movement only really counts when women march out in an army, and nothing will ever make them turn back, and there is no fear of death.

[…]

CHAPTER VI
CHAMPIONS OF WOMEN—THE MEN WHO LEAD

I have been to one of the Turkish feminist meetings, which take place every Friday afternoon upon which it is possible to find speakers. This society is not organized according to our Western methods, there being no responsible head and no list of members. It has not even a battle-cry, as, for example, "the vote," nor an official name; it is the society where the different interests of women are discussed, and its best appellation, perhaps, would be "the society for the elevation of womanhood." From articles which have from time to time appeared in our papers I imagined there was in Turkey an organized society for the abolition of the veil, and that "man," the arch-enemy of woman, was the chief obstacle to woman's progress. I believe, however, this idea is prevalent in our Western countries.

Signed always with the name of a Turkish woman, these articles are written by persons who are catering for readers of sensation. The names of the writers are unknown here amongst the feminists, the statements most emphatically denied; it is not to the women's advantage to be described as these articles describe them—beautiful, idle creatures airing their grievances to the women of the West. A Turkish woman never airs her grievances, most certainly not to foreigners, and those who come into intimate contact with her know she resents being asked questions, and she does not ask to be pitied.

I have pointed out in previous chapters that for the present the Turkish woman's aim is not to cast aside the veil, and also the fact which is still almost incomprehensible to me, viz. the encouragement the men are giving to the women in their work. It is they who are trying to give the women courage; they who are urging the women to be a little bolder in their tactics, and who, in their writings and speeches, are imploring them to leave no stone unturned to hasten their enfranchisement. I am told that the men have even written articles for the newly founded woman's paper, and signed them with feminine names, for the number of women writers here is still very limited. The cultured women, it is true, speak Turkish, but as their education has been given by French or English governesses, the study of their own language has been neglected, and at present they can best express themselves in a language not their own.

[…]

The hall in which the feminist meeting was held was the large lecture hall of the university, lent by the men. Men were the stewards, and all four speakers were men. Strange and chivalrous as it seemed to me to see the men conducting the women's meeting, I was, however, disappointed not to hear a woman speak. I had so often heard of Halidé-Hanoum's talent as a speaker, and I particularly wanted to compare her gestures, her delivery, and her subject-matter with the women speakers of my own country. Halidé-Hanoum is the mother of two children. Up till a month ago she taught history, pedagogy, and literature at the Normal School for Girls. She has written five or six volumes of importance, as well as articles on special subjects, and frequently she addresses the Friday afternoon meetings. But in all her work, she tells me, she has been encouraged by the opposite sex, and no one ever questions whether, since she gives so much time to public work, her children and home are neglected, as is generally the case with us.

Long before the meeting began the big hall was crowded with veiled women, a few of whom never raised their face veils during the whole three hours' meeting. The hall, from the entrance, appeared as if it were filled with nuns, for even those who had their veils thrown back carefully covered their hair. […]

[…]

I have discussed with many enlightened Turkish women this question of the veil. Is it a protection or is it not? Halidé-Hanoum considers it creates between the sexes a barrier which is impossible when both sexes should be working for the common cause of humanity. It makes the woman at once "the forbidden fruit," and surrounds her with an atmosphere of mystery which, although fascinating, is neither desirable nor healthy. The thicker the veil the harder the male stares. The more the woman covers her face the more he longs to see the features which, were he to see but once, would interest him no more.

Personally I find the veil no protection. In my hat I thread my way in and out of the cosmopolitan throng at Pera. No one speaks to me, no one notices me, and yet my mirror shows I am no more ugly than the majority of my sex. But when I have walked in the park, a veiled woman, what a different experience. Even the cold Englishman has summed up courage and enough Turkish to pay compliments to our "silhouettes." We have not heeded them, walking as real Turkish women, with stooped backs and bent heads and a rather swinging gait, but these two silent figures only served to excite their curiosity, and no doubt they wondered at my thick veil … .

Another reason for condemning the veil is that it dispenses women from taking the responsibility of their actions. Should they desire to stray away from the path of virtue, who can control the actions of these black-robed, veiled women? During the reign of Abdul Hamid they helped most considerably in bringing about the Revolution, for it was they who went from house to house carrying the letters, as the men never could have dared to do. It was the women who were responsible for nominations being cancelled and for many important appointments, and even I have seen before now veiled women pleading the cause of their mankind at the feet of a Grand Vizier's daughter. Turkish men and women now, however, have both declared that an anonymous power is a danger to the State, and yet who is to be the first woman to leave off her veil?

[…]

The third speaker had been in England, and prefaced his plea of "Turkey for the Turks" by relating some of his experiences in our capital. […] The speaker was not at all enthusiastic about my country; he felt so hurt at being asked the usual questions about the harem life, and how many wives he had, that he finally refused, he said, to converse with such ignorant people. He spoke, too, of the grinding poverty of the East End of our capital. "How dare that nation criticize us," he added, "when within the gates of their own city people are living in a manner unworthy of a civilized nation." He was right, this speaker, much as I wish he could have left unsaid what he had, alas! seen.

[…]

The last speech, however, was the speech which stirred the women most. How I wish it had been possible to read it afterwards in French, for my neighbours, after two and a half hours' constant translating for me, began to grow just a little weary, and I could see they wished to listen to every word. The speaker had no notes, but he spoke with eloquence and a passion I have never yet seen in a man pleading a cause not his own. His subject was "The veil and the subjection of women." He condemned it from a moral point of view, and he condemned it from a physical point of view, and showed how, in spite of the custom which has been accepted now for centuries, veiling is against the teaching of the Koran. "Our Prophet," said he, "considered ignorance a sin. What has been done to help you out of ignorance?"

A woman, according to the Koran, may preach in a mosque, and may exercise any profession she chooses. How have you taken advantage of these privileges? Then he blamed the woman. "Can you not feel your bondage?" he asked. "Who can give you freedom unless you yourselves ask for freedom? What right have the interpreters to bind and fetter and degrade women? I am not against religion; it would be disastrous for Turkey to-day if there were no religion; but what I demand, and what every thinking man and woman should demand to-day, is a reformed religion, a seeking after the truth, the real meaning of the Prophet's teaching." A storm of applause greeted these words. My friend translated. I watched the women with their veils down over their face. Surely, after such a speech they would throw them back.

I, the foreigner, was stirred; it seemed to me that after such a speech I would be capable of any action to be free … there sat the women, a handkerchief occasionally poked behind the thick veil, to wipe away their tears, but never once were their veils lifted. How well he had spoken! How necessary, indeed, in this country is a reformed religion! How extraordinary it is that everywhere the Church is the chief opponent to most reforms! Has the Christian Church given to woman the place that Christ intended her to have? How has the Church helped the women of my country in their fight for freedom? A little mild assistance when the heavy spade work is done, perhaps, is better than no assistance at all. …

[…]

[…] How magnificently he had spoken! After such a speech one would have expected these women to have walked out without their veils … but they are still afraid.

To ask a Turkish woman to go out without her veil is almost like asking an Englishwoman to go out without a blouse. Living in a Turkish household one sees this slavery has become almost part of a woman's existence. […]

[…]

[…] Halidé-Hanoum, who tells me "the veil surrounds the woman with an unhealthy air of mystery"—how does she appear in the street? A thick veil over her face, which she never throws back. I asked her one day the reason why she kept herself so closely veiled. "It is a habit," she answered. […]

[…]

As I have said before, it is not for me to criticize the methods of the women of a civilization so totally different from our own. The men are urging them to take their freedom, and helping them all they can, but if they will be free they themselves must strike the blow. The women of another civilization cannot help them except by giving them the benefit of education whenever they ask for it. […]

[…]

Chapter VII
PASSIONATE WOMEN PATRIOTS—A MASS MEETING

This is the anniversary of the foundation of the Ottoman Empire—a red-letter day for Turkish feminists. To-day for the first time the various women's societies have held a mass meeting, and a member from each society has given an account of the year's work. This meeting, then, marks the end of the old régime for the Turkish woman. She has now given us, as it were, chapter and verse as to the rôle she intends to play in the future. She has cast aside the dangerous rôle she played until quite recently—a powerful part, and all the more powerful since it was anonymous. When anything went wrong with the political pie into which so many of them had put their fingers—it was not a case of "cherchez la femme," for she disappeared behind the veil, and the men least of all suspected how well these women could ruin a cause if only they chose. Turkish women, then, are sacrificing a powerful anonymous rôle for an honest responsible part in the work of the world, and recognizing that only by straightforward, honest methods can they advance the welfare of humanity. And so the Turkish women who declared themselves perfectly satisfied with their bondage, and yet at the same time worked in secret to break those chains, have now come out in the manner of the Western women, openly to demand their rights.

But it is unjust to give all the credit of this meeting to the women. How different would have been their position now had they had a Government against them! I am not going to put halos round the heads of the Young Turks, nor am I going to present them with a pair of angel's wings; such vain flattery would be as useless as it is bad form. The Young Turk, however, has not yet had his opportunity. Youth and inexperience are responsible for many strange blunders—effort is so new a chapter in the life-story of Turkey; effort and blunders beget experience, and experience he must have at all costs. In his political methods he has not been impeccable. I do not defend him. What I do protest against, however, is that an action committed by a Turk should be called "a crime," and yet committed by a Christian neighbour "a diplomatic error." And so in this question of women. "See," says Europe, "how the Turk treats his women." "See," I might answer, "how the British Government treats its women."

[…]

[…] A Turkish Feminist Government! Have the women quite become accustomed to the idea? It is true they never before possessed such privileges. One of the first triumphs of the counter-revolution of April 13 was the total destruction of the woman's club founded by Selma Hanoum, sister of Ahmed Riza Bey, and that lady nearly lost her life as her reward for having espoused the cause of the liberty of her Turkish sisters.

[…]

But there is another side to the question. These men, many of them, were the breadwinners. Who is going to feed the women now? Now is the time to blame the harem system. The idle, protected women, what are they going to do now? In other countries women of this class could cook or sew or clean. I would have been glad of some one to sew for me besides Miss Chocolate, but in all Stamboul, amongst all these starving women, I can find no woman to do plain sewing. It is not when women are actually starving that one can teach them a trade; they must work at once. They can embroider; they can produce embroidery that is worth leaving to one's grandchildren, and yet a European child of ten would be ashamed to make buttonholes as they do.

And this priceless embroidery is less well paid than plain needlework in my country. The Red Crescent Society undertakes to pay one franc a day to these poor women who embroider and weave, and also to find work for the poor refugees who have come back penniless to their native land rather than lose their nationality. It is sad to see these poor creatures arriving. I have been with the women of the Red Crescent Society to meet them at the boats or outside the mosques, where they sit and wait, whilst their husbands try to get work. They look perfectly resigned, these poor women, as they sit huddled up beside the carpets and the cats, kept in bird-cages. Those who have no baby to nurse sit with their elbows on their knees and their heads on their hands. They can only wait their fate. But the Red Crescent ladies are there; they will not starve.

I had no idea before coming here of the splendid self-sacrifice these women are making for these starving souls. They have formed a league and have undertaken to buy only the stuffs of their own country, and have opened a shop in Stamboul where only Turkish goods are sold. No more Paris dresses, no more jewels; not one luxury till these poor, starving women are fed, and if you ask a Turkish woman to-day what is her greatest ambition, she will answer without hesitation, "To save my poor country."

I have no space in this book to write of the other works started by women, but the Red Crescent, which is organized on the lines of the Red Cross Society (and has the embroidery and weaving establishment in addition), and the movement for the education of the women are, to my mind, the most important of all. It is when one sees these women themselves fettered by atavism, crippled for want of education and a misunderstood teaching of the Koran, fighting against the terrible odds of having to find work for women who cannot work, and food for hungry mouths in a country where there is no money, that one understands how bitterly these women resent the manner in which they are introduced by the writer's imagination to the Western world.

I very much doubt whether, in the West, we could have fought this terrible fight against poverty as the Turkish women have done. It is infinitely comforting, however, to think, as I sink at nights into my comfortable cushions, that although the wind is howling and the rain is beating against the windows of this konak, any beggar may come in and find food and shelter in the basement. "Find me one of your Western countries," said one day to me Zeyneb (Pierre Loti's disenchanted heroine, to whom everything Western now is tarnished by a lack of Christian charity), "where the poor are accommodated in the houses of the rich; and if they were," she added, "you would have to employ a detective to watch them."

[...]

Chapter XVIII
ONLOOKERS ONLY

[...]

I came here with perhaps just a little of the "downtrodden woman of the East" fallacy left, but that has now completely vanished. To me, an Englishwoman, there are sides of this life which would irritate me into open rebellion. That the customs of the country should have power to make we wear a veil, whether I wished it or not, that I should be forced to travel in a compartment reserved exclusively for women, that I must always have the hood up when I drive in a carriage, that if I chance to stray into a café of the people, I am served in a superior kind of rabbit-hutch, separated by a grating from the opposite sex, that if I go into a tea-shop where there are men, I will be requested to leave, and last, but not least, that I should have to depend for male society exclusively on my blood relations—Heaven indeed forbid!

A Turkish woman asked me once what it felt like to be able to mix freely with men who are not blood relations. "I cannot *tell*," I answered; "it dates right back to the time when my big brother teased me to tears, and his friend wiped them away. To ask me what it means to mix freely with men is almost like asking what it means to have lungs. I never stopped to think, but I know I should die without them."

But then, after all, is not everything relative? Had I never known the pleasures of male society, had not circumstances forced me to take my life in my own hands and work out my own destiny, I should not perhaps quarrel with what is part of a Turkish woman's existence. If we in the West possess what is known as the "joy of liberty," have not so many of us been denied the blessing of protection? The veiled Turkish woman asks, Can you imagine how distressing it is to be willing to work and for the conventions of the country not to allow it? Many of the poor tired workers of my country might ask, Can you imagine what it is to have to work and not to be able to find work?

All these weeks I have been leading a Turkish existence. I have really tried to put myself in a Turkish woman's place, but I cannot somehow pity her. Is it that I have been too near the suffering heart of my own countrywomen? "Our lives are so empty," pointed out one woman. "Really we do not have enough social distractions." I close my eyes and think of the women of my own country, worn out with a London season and its festivities. In their moments of sincerity they would not tell you they had expended their time and energy only to be bored; but social obligations cannot be taken in moderate doses, you must swallow the whole draught.

[…]

I have called the Turkish woman an "onlooker." She is at present, as it were, only on the margin of the great life; she understands enough of the game, however, to long to take a part. How will she play that part? Is it absolutely necessary for her to come to us for assistance?

This is the question I have asked so many Turkish women. They must think I argue almost like a reactionary. Yet I have not defended the harem system. There is, however, so much in the Turkish home life which is beautiful that I would prefer to see them progressing on the lines of their own civilization, rather than becoming a poor imitation of us. Let them come to us and learn to organize their studies; the rest they can, if they will, manage for themselves.

[…]

And those Turkish women who have come to Europe? How well they have adapted themselves to our civilization. When they were with us who could have supposed they were wearing hats for the first time? Who could suppose, to hear them speaking our language, to see them threading their way in and out of the traffic of our big capitals, that they had not lived with us all their lives? And yet how glad they were to return to their own home life!

[…]

That the Moslem woman has no status, I most emphatically deny. If the Moslem women are "possessions," they are "cherished possessions" and treated as such. Are Moslem women obliged to exercise the most hideous of professions as are their Christian neighbours? Is there anywhere in the East the terrible degradation of our poor Whitechapel women? It is not because he despises her that the Turk has kept his womankind screened from the world. Her rôle is maternity, therefore the cares and temptations of the world must not be known to her, and nothing ought to interfere with this supreme reason of her existence.

Quite recently a decision of the greatest importance and daring was taken by the Ottoman Government. Without their having to ask, the University was thrown open to women, and they are now attending lectures on gynæcology, hygiene, woman's rights, etc.

When I heard the news, much as I rejoiced, I could not help making a comparison between the methods of the East and those of the West. Here are these "unspeakable" Turks giving to women privileges for which they have not asked.

11.
LEYLA SAZ HANIMEFENDI (1852–1936)

ℬ THE IMPERIAL HAREM ℭ
OF THE SULTANS

DAILY LIFE AT THE ÇIRAĞAN PALACE
DURING THE 19TH CENTURY. MEMOIRS
OF LEYLA (SAZ) HANIMEFENDI

(first published in Istanbul in Turkish, 1920/21)
Peva Publications, Istanbul
1994

Leyla Hanımefendi's life spanned a period of dramatic changes in Ottoman society and government. By the time of her birth in 1852, her father had been appointed Royal Surgeon at the palace of Sultan Abdülmecit. Hekim (or doctor) Ismail Paşa's career is indicative of the social and professional mobility that characterised Ottoman society in this period. Of Greek Christian origin, he was sold as a child at the slave market in Izmir to a Jewish doctor who gave him medical training. Subsequently converting to Islam, her father went on to have a successful career in the Ottoman bureaucracy, eventually serving as Governor General of Izmir and later of Crete. Leyla Hanımefendi was taken to Çırağan Palace in Istanbul as a young child to become a lady-in-waiting to Münire Sultane, one of Abdülmecit's eight surviving daughters. She spent most of her time with Münire Sultane and her sister Refia Sultane, and was educated with them at the palace. Very gifted musically, Leyla Hanımefendi played the piano and composed music throughout her life, as well as later giving music lessons to the princesses at the palace. Eventually she married and had four children, maintaining her close ties to the court until the abolition of the sultanate in 1922. Although initially part of the sultanic court, Leyla Hanımefendi went on to participate in the cultural life of the Republic. Her song 'Akdeniz', composed after the proclamation of the Turkish Republic, reportedly became the favourite march of Mustafa Kemal Atatürk, the founder of the Republic.

Leyla Hanımefendi's memoirs focus on her years of close association with the princesses of the Ottoman court, as children in Çırağan Palace and in the separate households they established when married. First published as interviews in the Turkish press in the early 1920s, the original Ottoman text was revised by Leyla Hanımefendi and her son for publication in French in 1925. A Czechoslovakian version appeared later, and in the 1960s a condensed Turkish version. The English version of the book appeared in 1994. Leyla Hanımefendi's memoirs have been several times in print, but her rare insider's account of palace life has never received the widespread attention it merits.

Leyla Hanımefendi's motivation in writing her memoirs stemmed from her realisation that the old customs and traditions of women's lives and of the palace, would be completely forgotten with the passing of time. Aware that few shared her knowledge of this female world, she felt a responsibility to chronicle it. Her 1922 introduction begins:

> The life and customs of the Turkish woman have been profoundly modified over the last quarter of a century. They are still changing daily—particularly in Istanbul. They are so different today than they were only 15 years ago that the young generation is almost completely unaware of the traditions of the Turkish woman ...
>
> If the old customs and traditions of the harem in general begin to fade from our memory, one can be sure that knowledge of the life, customs and organization of the Imperial Harem and the Palace of the princesses will be extremely hazy in the future. (p. 19)

Having introduced her privileged position – '... my sister and I were probably the first and only young ladies of the city who were able to enter and particularly to live in the Serail under the reign of Sultan Abdülmecit (1839–1861)' – she returns to this point a page later when she apologises to the reader for beginning her story by talking about herself, going on to say, '[b]ut I think this must be done in order to dissipate any doubts which might arise as to the spirit of authenticity which surrounds the facts I am going to report' (p. 20).

Her concern to establish authenticity is clearly in response to her awareness of other, less accurate or fabricated accounts of harem life in the Ottoman Empire. But it is also important to acknowledge that her detailed and meticulous recounting of events is overlaid with nostalgia for a happy and long-past period of her own life, and the lives of many of her contemporaries. Much harem literature is tinted with the different nostalgias of Western and Middle Eastern women, but Leyla Hanımefendi's is distinguished by her extreme sensitivity to the lives and conditions of the slave women on whose labour the luxury of the imperial harem was reliant.

While she is comfortable with the concept of slavery as it existed in the late Ottoman context, Leyla Hanımefendi in the first passage extracted here displays an awareness of the horrors of the journey that brought women from Africa to Istanbul that is unusual in Ottoman commentators. She also recognises that enslaved African women had their own community in Istanbul and elaborates the different status and tasks assigned to African and Circassian slaves.

The second passage from her writing discusses the shopping habits of the women of the imperial court, comparing them to those of women from other social strata. While outsiders would likely have been unaware of the subtle distinctions in shopping behaviour among women of different social groups, Leyla Hanımefendi knew exactly what distinguished the shopping habits of women of the court from those of other women, including the non-elite women of the city who patronised local weekly markets or bought from itinerant merchants. Her account emphasises how women's attachment to the different methods of veiling and seclusion used in their shopping procedures was very much to do with signifying and securing class status.

The following three selections describe court ceremony, including religious observance during Ramadan, the return of Sultan Abdülaziz from a trip to Europe (the first peace-time visit of an Ottoman sultan to Europe) and the wedding of two of the royal princesses. Leyla Hanımefendi's account of court celebration remains sensitive to differences in status among the court population.

ഔ   ഌ

THE NEGRESSES

The Negresses formed a class apart among the other slaves. It was necessary, furthermore, to distinguish between real, completely black Negresses from the Sudan and those from Abyssinia who were more of a chocolate colour.

[...]

In the old days the slave merchants of the African countries, or of those countries near to Africa, would encourage Negroes and Arabs who were travelling along the coast and in the interior of the country to steal little Negresses, whom they then would sell to traders for a few coins or for a few valueless trinkets which were so much sought after by African people. Once these little pickaninnys were captured, the slave traders would gag and chain them by their legs and attach them in pairs by handcuffs. They would then be led towards the coast in a long column by paths which were seldom used. There the slave traders secretly put them aboard sailing vessels, hid them in the hold whenever they were near ports and let them up one by one on the deck when they had reached the open sea in orde[r] to let them breathe a little bit. These unfortunate beings, horrified to find themselves in a little shell of wood bobbing on an immense expanse of water and all the time in the company of very unpleasant white men, could only weep and sob throughout the whole journey.

The Circassians who were taken into slavery were also to be pitied but, at the same time, they had a certain knowledge of the world, of life, and, most important, of the fate which was waiting for them and which did not seem to be all that bad in their eyes. Their reactions could not be compared with the horror of these poor Negresses who knew of the world only in the context of their desert and their oasis, having never seen any sort of water except in their wells or in their rare streams. For these beings, so completely ignorant, everything was a source of astonishment and of terror. The question of language was another cause of great difficulty for them because they could never find anybody who could understand their patois. As a consequence, they could never hope to become the consort or the concubine of a great personage and were inevitably condemned to the most difficult and hard tasks of the household. Promptly after their arrival, they were placed in the kitchen in front of the furnace—the laundry was another one of their domains. They were also required to draw the water from the wells, to wash and to scrub the floor. They were never given a moment of leisure but still they did their service without complaining.

[…]

The duration of slavery for Negresses was only seven years. Once liberated, they were given a dowry like the Circassians and married to a Negro, but sometimes to a white person. As long as they were not influenced by other Negresses, they generally behaved themselves well and were clean, punctual and devoted servants.

[…]

May 1st was the day of celebration for the Negresses. On that day almost all the Negresses in Constantinople went to the countryside, riding in carts covered with flowers and drawn by oxen. They had reserved in advance certain fields and around them they placed guards in order to prevent the curious and the indiscreet from looking in on them and, at the center of this place, they set up huge kettles in which they cooked their meals. These meals generally consisted of stuffed ducks, mutton and something called *aside*. *Aside* is a special dish prepared by Negroes. It is made of boiled rice, lightly crushed, and in the middle of it there is a small hollow or a pocket filled with small pieces of meat, pimentos, peppers and okra—all cooked up together.

The day was spent eating, playing the tambourines and indulging in nervous fits. They also sang the old songs of the Negroes, probably full of memories of their African origins.

I never attended one of these parties, but those who had seen them said that it was a most singular spectacle. Innunerable Negresses in *ferace*s and in white *yaşmak*s—we are talking about a time more than fifty years ago—transformed the fields into a vision of poppies and daisies in the middle of which their dark faces and white teeth produced a wonderful and unexpected contrast. These good women, while setting up a circle around their frolics in order to keep away untoward interference, nevertheless offered fruit and food to the women who came to look at them from distance. The costs of the rustic festivals were shared in common; however, to be truthful, it must be said that the *abla*s didn't contribute very much and the *godia*s even less.

At the Imperial Palace, Negro slaves were never used. Neverthess, my readers will recall that during the reign of Sultan Abdül Mecid, there was at the Serail one negress called Zeyneb who played in the orchestra which the Vali of Egypt, Abbas Paşa—the title of Khedive had not been created at that time—had presented to the Sultan. I knew her, she was a very good singer, and a girl with good upbringing and quite agreeable—she often performed before the *sultane*s. There were two other Negresses, cooks who were charged with the duty of preparing certain dishes for the Sultan but who immediately returned to their room as soon as their service was ended.

In the grand *konak*s, there were often one or two Negresses among the slaves; they were given the heavy and dirtier jobs of the household. Particularly in families of moderate means, Negresses were taken into the service because they were much cheaper than Circassians. A Negress could be bought for around 2 Turkish pounds or $600.

My readers will find it perhaps a bit hard to understand, but I cannot deny that I like Negresses quite a bit. Because of their black skin, their white teeth, their kinky hair and their rather clumsy manners, they amuse and please me—very much like an exotic toy. And furthermore I feel very sorry for these poor beings so despised by all the world simply because their skin is black—these poor people should be worthy of pity and sympathy from all of us, particularly since they have been violently torn away from their country and transplanted into an environment completely different from theirs—in a country where even the climate is not particularly suitable for them.

[...]

[...] I find it very unjust to lightly judge other human beings who are only different from us because of the colour of their skins. [...] Can we dare to pretend to ourselves that even given our advanced culture we could so easily assimilate a modicum of education and civilisation if we had passed all of our early life like these Negresses without any contact with the modern world?

[...]

PURCHASES OF THE IMPERIAL HAREM

The Great Bazaar of Istanbul in those days had an importance which it has lost since the opening of the new shops and stores in Pera. These have now become more and more numerous and well stocked.

In those days the main street of the Bazaar was accessible to carriages. The princesses and the ladies of the Imperial Harem were allowed to go there and they did go from time to time, but it was not considered suitable to stop in front of the shops, much less to enter them. They would install themselves in the mosque of Nuruosmaniye, in a part of the building especially reserved for the Sultan and the Imperial Family, just as there is in every one of the Grand Mosques of Constantinople. The shopkeepers, advised by the people of the suite of the princess, would bring their merchandise to them and, in turn, these would be presented to the princesses by the eunuchs. The princess would then make her choice, the material would be cut into the appropriate sizes and other articles desired would be put to one side and then the eunuch would settle accounts with the merchant.

The *kalfa*s had the choice of going shopping in these boutiques, but generally they preferred to make up a small list of articles which they needed and would give it to the eunuch who, in turn, could order a footman to bring it to the purveyors to the Serail in the Bazaar. The material and the other articles requested would be sent back, wrapped up in a square of calico and placed in a box.

The eunuch of the guard would receive these packages at the gate of the Palace and would take them to the *kalfa*s. The material, the lace, the shoes—all carried little price tags.

The *kalfa*s who had asked for these articles would, first of all, make their choice and cut the material into the necessary sizes. Then two girls would take the box or the packet, each holding it at one end, and would make a tour of the Serail; almost always the whole allotment was divided up among the *kalfa*s and the girls of the various services. The payment for the merchandise purchased would be sent to the eunuch of the guard, along with a detailed accounting, and would be given to the merchant who was waiting at the gate of the Serail.

A part of the material just purchased was then immediately sent to the dressmakers who already had all the measurements and quickly made up the dresses and returned them to the Serail.

The dresses were arranged on the shelves of armoires, wrapped up in a double envelope of silk and covered by a piece of calico. The *ferace*s, the *yaşmak*s and the handkerchiefs were all carefully folded and wrapped up. In those days fashion demanded that creases should be very evident; therefore, large tiles of marble were placed on the folded clothes so that they could be carefully pressed while on the shelf.

[…]

The ladies of the great *konak*s also did their shopping in the Bazaar just like the princesses, but out of respect, they would never stop in any of the dependencies of the Mosque in order not to give the impression of imitating the Imperial Harem. Those who lived near the Bazaar would send the eunuch or woman in charge of their household to the Bazaar to pick out samples of material so they could make their choice at home.

In Constantinople there was a class of mobile merchants who would install themselves in great masses in streets and public places on certain days. These were provisory markets and quite temporary. They were held regularly on each day of the week in a different part of the city. The Saturday Market was held right along the wall of our Konak in Beşiktaş and it stretched up to the center of the suburb. We always had material for the winter clothes of our domestic staff brought from this market.

In the summer wandering merchants would get into boats on the Bosphorus and sail up to our *yalı* and bring us simple articles of which we often had need. These mobile and floating merchants, Jews for the most part, knew their good clients and the houses where they could make decent sales extremely well; they would stop in front of the *yalı* in their boats holding a respectful distance and would shout out at the top of their lungs descriptions of their merchandise until they had caught our attention. As soon as they were summoned, they would tie up to the guay [quay,] jump off and it was rare that they left without having made some sales.

The ladies of the small bourgeoisie would generally do their shopping at the weekly markets of their own quarter where they could buy all the things that they needed—from linens, printed cottons to food. The great ladies never went to these markets; when they did go, either by whim or out of curiosity, they would preserve the strictest incognito in their dress and would cover their face with their thickest veils in order not to be recognised.

Many Turkish women would sell their own handwork at these markets. Linen, embroidered napkins and hosiery were sold by people living in Constantinople and its environs, while foodstuff, mutton sausages, smoked meats and patés were all brought there by people from the villages.

In those days, there were strolling merchants who offered their wares from house to house. The Turks would sell linen or cotton, embroidered napkins and muslin handkerchiefs, either dyed or printed; the Greeks would sell needlework. All this merchandise was woven, embroidered and produced by the women of the countryside; it was a little domestic industry which flourished in that period. Polish Jews then began to sell European merchandise—generally taken from the stocks of small stores in liquidation. These wandering merchants, Turks or Jews, were never admitted to the Serail but sometimes they were successful in insinuating themselves into the *konak*s. First of all, they would seek to gain the good graces of the *kalfa*s or the slaves by their persuasiveness and by the very thrill of buying something. When necessary they would offer their wares with credit, quite unknown to the ladies of the house. Often they would even reach the young ladies of the house themselves. They were terrible intriguers and were sometimes involved in the most despicable trades.

This category of merchant has almost completely disappeared today, but the weekly markets are still held in different quarters of Constantinople and its suburbs and are still very much frequented.

[...]

The princesses and the ladies of the Serail having received, since their infancy, good religious instruction and having all the attitudes of piety, closely observed all the demands of religion, notably those concerning the five daily prayers and the fast of Ramazan.

During this month, in the afternoon, the well-known and learned theologians of the *ulema* gave small sermons, the *hafiz*s recited verses of the Koran at the Imperial Palace just as they did in the Great Mosques. At the Palace, this took place in the rooms adjoining the Harem and the *kadın*s and the *sultane*s were able to come and listen to the preachers and to the *hafiz*s from behind gilded screens and grills. Listening to a *hafiz* who was blessed with beautiful and good diction, was a really touching experience.

The *sultane*s and the ladies of the Serail could also go out to the city during Ramazan. They went to visit and to worship at the tombs of the Sultans and the various saints; they would perform their prayers or listen to preachers in the

Great Mosques where they sat in the grilled loges reserved for the Sultan and the Imperial Family.

The 15th day of Ramazan was always reserved for the ceremony of the Hırka-i Serif or Sacred Mantle which took place at the Palace of Topkapı where all the relics of the Prophet and the first *halife* or caliphs were preserved, forming what was called the Sacred Depot. It consisted principally of the Sacred Mantle and of the Sancağı Şerif or the Sacred Standard of the Prophet. The Sacred Mantle and the Sacred Standard were wrapped in rich coverings and were placed separately in a massive, golden coffer which, in turn, was placed in another sort of trunk, also made of gold. [...]

[...]

The ceremony of the Hırka-ı Şerif was presided over by the Sultan in person and it took place in two parts: the first ceremony was for men and to this one was invited the Princes of the Imperial Family, the Ministers, the great dignitaries of the State and functionaries of high rank; the second part was reserved for the Harem. Under the reigns of Sultan Abdül Mecid and Sultan Abdül Aziz, only the *sultane*s, *kadın*s and the daughters of the *sultane*s, accompanied naturally by the *haznedar*s and the Great Kalfas, were invited. No woman who was a stranger to the Serail would ever be invited; it was a ceremony both religious and private.

The day on which the invitation was received, each princess went to the Topkapı Sarayı in a gala state coach, drawn by two horses, and followed by numerous footmen and eunuchs on horseback. At the outer gate of the Serail, the *bey*s of the Enderun and the eunuchs received them with honours. The eunuchs accompanied the carriage right up the interior gate of the Harem, opened it and took the princesses by the arm to aid them while descending.

They were then received by the mistresses of ceremonies who had arrived that very morning and by the elderly *kalfa*s who lived permanently in this old Palace. The princesses were taken to the apartments where everything had been prepared for their reception.

When His Majesty arrived at the Palace, the mistress of ceremonies came immediately to announce this fact to the *sultane*s who then went to the apartments of the Hırka-ı Şerif while passing through two rows of *kalfa*s who held incense in censers.

The coffers containing the holy relics were placed in a silver armoire. His majesty would open the armoire and then the coffer holding the Sacred Mantle. He would take out the sachets with which the Mantle was surrounded and would put them on a high table made of silver placed in a corner of the room. At that point he would fold back partially one of the corners of the first envelope. On a tray placed by his side there were muslin handkerchiefs which were stamped along the edges with verses of the Koran.

[...]

The *sultane*s entered the room of the Hırka-ı Şerif and passed around the right side of the chamber while approaching the platform. They then made a deep reverence before the Sultan who gave each of them one of the muslin handkerchiefs after having brushed it against the cloth envelope which held the Sacred Mantle. The *sultane* took the handkerchief, kissed it respectfully, and withdrew, leaving by the left.

[…]

When the ceremony was over, the Sultan stayed for a few minutes with the princesses and talked to them in a friendly fashion. Then the ladies left the palace and made an excursion into the city, sometimes to Bayazid Square and sometimes to the Şehzade Mosque.

[…]

Those who are more or less aware of Turkish customs will know that during the month of Ramazan everybody, people of modest means as well as the rich, hold an open table for the evening meal—each according to his means. Everyone goes to dinner at other people's houses without invitation; sometimes in the great houses there were people whom nobody knew at all; they were received just like the others. In the great *konak*s there were many tables, all being served at the same time; the principal table was presided over by the head of the house and the others by his sons, his sons-in-law and his intendant.

As for the ladies, usually they were not encouraged to go out to dinner without an invitation unless it was at the house of very close relatives or old and intimate friends.

At the Imperial Harem the *sultane*s had dinner with one another during Ramazan but a stranger was never invited. As for the married *sultane*s, who had their palaces elsewhere, they often invited to dinner various ladies of the city whom they had admitted into their company; but in those days nobody could sit at the table of the members of the Imperial Family; the guests were served separately but always overwhelmed with attention. It was the custom in those days to give silver presents to the guests of the sultanes during Ramazan; with time this custom was abandoned and nowadays presents [a]re only given to old servants who have a real need for them.

[…]

That day, all the princesses and the ladies of the Palace were wearing dresses in green, but all with slightly different shades. I knew very well that green was considered to be the colour of satisfied hopes and wishes as well as joy but it had not occurred to me that I should wear this colour to the Serail upon the occasion of His Majesty's return. By a happy circumstance, my dress was also green and I was rather relieved.

The *sultane*s wore green dresses, quite light, and trimmed with beautiful white lace. They had long trains and they wore big diadems along with rather simple necklaces. The older *kalfa*s also wore green dresses, some plain, some striped and some even with polka dots. The youngest girls wore light green dresses mixed with white and some wore white dresses, trimmed with green, along with small flowered patterns or small green ribbons. At this period, the young ladies and young girls had completely abandoned the old dresses with three tails or trains and the baggy pants underneath; fashion now demanded skirts with a single train which was caught up and attached to the belt—there were now petti-coats instead of *şalvar*s or the baggy pants previously worn. The headdresses had also changed with the times and now usually matched the costumes; there were earrings with jewels, medallions and elaborate hairstyles, garnished with pre-cious stones.

These beautiful young girls, so elegantly dressed, walked around with great grace and they gave the hall of the Serail the appearance of a great green lawn covered with daisies swaying under a gentle breeze. This spectacle ornamented with such beautiful women, gave the impression of Springtime, which is of course nature's beautiful season.

I knew most of these young ladies who had been at the Serail under the reign of Sultan Abdül Mecid. I have already said that the only thing which was ban-ished from the Serail was ugliness. The ladies and girls were beautiful and seductive by themselves; but this day they had a particular charm: their faces were radiant with happiness, their hair was half undone, falling loosely in brown and golden strands over their shoulders and framing their pink cheeks and lily white foreheads. Their shoulders and their arms were beautiful, particularly when seen through the transparent muslin that they wore. Like a charming dream, they offered an enchanting spectacle almost like the rays of the sun which shines from time to time, during a beautiful summer's day through a light mist. The brilliance of this spectacle was such that it almost dazzled the eye.

While I gazed at this charming picture, I suddenly had a vision of days gone by—now so far away, when, on days of grand parties such as this one, rich and heavy costumes covered with golden embroideries, sequins, and huge jewels rivalled in brilliance the lights of the chandeliers in these very same rooms. The large mirrors and windowpanes of the hall reflected the brilliance of the lights and flashes from the jewellery of the ladies' costumes. Just as these old costumes were majestic and imposing, so were those that I now saw, gay and elegant, in their relative simplicity. There was nothing really brilliant in the new costumes except the jewellery which was, by comparison, rather small and simple, although extremely precious. Everything depended on the customs and conven-tions of the times. In the old days one would never have dared to dress oneself in the new costumes and today the old costumes would appear shocking—every-thing is a case of what one becomes accustomed to. For me, both of them were beautiful in their own particular way.

[…]

THE WEDDING OF CEMILE AND MÜNIRE SULTANES

The betrothals of the third daughter of Sultan Abdül Mecid, Cemile Sultane, with Mahmud Celâleddin Paşa, son born of the first wife of Fetih Ahmed Paşa, the Grand Master of Artillery, and that of his fourth daughter, Münire Sultane, with

İbrahim İlhami Paşa, son of the great Abbas Paşa of Egypt, were decided by the Sultan and announced by their mothers.

[…]

I didn't see the engagement presents which were given to Cemile Sultane; but since I was always near Münire Sultane, I was able to see everything that she received and I remember it very well indeed.

Her fiancée sent her, first of all, a ring with a brilliant solitaire which must have been worth many thousands of Turkish pounds, a pair of earrings which were in the form of one brilliant solitaire and another jewel cut in a sort of elongated form called a "briolette" and hung just a little bit below the first. There were also all sorts of perfumes, placed on silver trays, covered with transparent lids—also on the trays were magnificent bowls of musk and mastic; there were crystal carafes containing syrup and porcelain vases from Saxony holding all sorts of preserves; finally, there were both eastern and western candies on plates of Chinese porcelain.

The mother of the Sultane gave some of these perfumes and tasty morsels of food to the other Sultanes; she also distributed them equally to the people in her entourage; I received my share just like the others.

[…]

The Administration of the Civil List was responsible for the preparation of the dresses to be included in the trousseau of the Princesses and their measurements were made available to this office. Their mothers, for their part, were responsible for the rest of the trousseaus.

For the jewellery, the silverware and the golden embroideries, one usually had recourse to the family of Küçükoğlu who were Armenian jewellers in the bazaar. Among them, Agop Ağa was the cleverest and most intelligent. […] Küçükoğlu Agop Ağa would bring to the Serail various samples of jewellery, silverware and similar articles of this sort. Accompanied by some eunuchs he would go up to the little hall of the Sultane's apartments. The Great Kalfa, who was behind the door, would take the samples and bring them in to the mother of the Sultane. Once the choice had been made, the samples were returned and the orders were carefully placed. Agop Ağa then had these orders carried out exactly in the way that he received them.

[…]

The first dressmaker permitted into the Serail was also introduced there by Agop. She was called Meryem and was nicknamed by the girls Kirli Meryem or dirty Meryem because she was always sloppily dressed and had filthy black hands. This woman would take the measurements and do the fittings; eventually she augmented her profits by selling laces, ribbons and then, little by little, rings, earrings and necklaces.

When the trousseau of the Princesses was complete, the sister of Agop Ağa, Miss Sophie, was admitted to pay her respects to the young Princesses and to their mothers.

At this epoch, Armenian ladies of good background would wear, just like Turkish ladies, *ferace*s in all colours but their *yaşmak* was of silk, while ours was made out of gauze. Armenians of an inferior condition, the poor ones, wore black *ferace*s and their faces would be completely veiled with *yaşmak*s, rather like sacks, into which they would stick their heads.

Miss Sophie came to the Palace in the *ferace* and a *yaşmak*. She was a well brought up young lady with beautiful manners; she was really marvellously beautiful to an extent rarely granted by nature to its favourites. [...]

[...]

In recognition of the services rendered by her brother, a present of a magnificent brooch with jewels, along with a rich costume chosen among the garments of a *kadın* were given to Miss Sophie—the clothes that were worn by a princess were considered to be far more precious than anything brand new. [...]

12.
HUDA SHAARAWI (1879–1947)

℘ HAREM YEARS ❧

THE MEMOIRS OF AN EGYPTIAN FEMINIST
(1879–1924)

Translated, edited and introduced by Margot Badran
The Feminist Press, New York
1987

Huda Shaarawi dictated *Mudhakirrati* (*My Memoirs*) in Arabic to her secretary, Abd al-Hamid Fahmi Mursi, in the 1940s. The manuscript lay in a cabinet in a Cairo apartment for twenty years following Shaarawi's death until her cousin, Hawa Idris, shared them with an American scholar, Margot Badran. Badran, who has produced groundbreaking research concerning the feminist history of Egypt, realised the significance of the memoirs and received permission from Hawa Idris to publish them. The project involved careful collaboration with Hawa Idris, as well as extensive research interviewing women who had been younger contemporaries of Shaarawi, and, of course, translation from Arabic to English. The result is a document that provides insight into a period of dramatic social and political upheaval, a way of life that has long since disappeared, and the life of one of the most important women in Egyptian history.

Shaarawi was a member of a wealthy, elite Cairo family. Brought up in the harem system and unhappily married in 1892 to an older cousin when she was thirteen, she was an articulate observer of the traditional lifestyle of the Cairo Muslim elite, a lifestyle that would completely change in her own lifetime. However, the importance of Shaarawi's memoirs extends far beyond a fascinating glimpse into a vanishing harem system. Refusing always to accept the status quo, Shaarawi set herself apart at an early age with her desire for education, as the first passage from her memoirs demonstrates. Her intelligence, independent thinking, family connections and wealth led her to become a leader in social reform, the movement for Egyptian nationalism, and the struggle for women's equality.

Shaarawi's account of her education, excerpted here, provides a good example of the kind of instruction available to girls of elite families in the late nineteenth century; a traditional system that, as Woodsmall discusses, was subsequently replaced by the widespread public education for girls established in the first decades of the Turkish Republic (Extract 14). Shaarawi was educated by tutors who came to the house to teach her what her family considered appropriate. In her case, this included reading, but not writing Arabic, memorising the Qur'an, Turkish (including grammar and calligraphy), French and music. Shaarawi pursued her passion for poetry on her own, and strayed into other areas that were not considered suitable for girls. Her experience demonstrates the extent to which a girl's access to education and to intellectual life was controlled by the status and opinions of her family (generally her father or other male relatives).

Like the writing of some of the other women included here, particularly Ellison (Extract 10) and Woodsmall (Extract 14), Shaarawi's memoirs document the shifts in women's consumption practices that took place during her early life. Living in her mother's house as a young girl, she encountered the women pedlars who came to the house, selling a variety of goods. Later, she writes about her first trip to a modern department store, heavily veiled and accompanied by several members of her household. Despite her initial opposition to Shaarawi's shopping trips, her mother was eventually won over to the advantages of doing her own personal shopping. The same kind of gradual acceptance of shopping in person would have been taking place among other elite Cairo families in this period. Shopping practices were clearly class specific (as Leyla Saz Hanımefendi also notes, Extract 11), and this transition would have played out in different ways among women of different classes. However, the new ability for women to make their own decisions regarding what to buy and from whom represents a significant shift in their level of empowerment and engagement in the everyday economy. Women of Shaarawi's class may have previously owned significant investments and property, but generally these would have been managed for them by their male relatives, distancing women's economic engagement.

As a young woman, Shaarawi played an important role in the newly emerging public, intellectual life of elite Egyptian women, working with other prominent women in the formation of the Intellectual Association for Egyptian Women in 1914. She was also active in various philanthropic projects, as would have been expected of a woman of her class. Her memoirs provide fascinating detail of how Egyptian women went about organising themselves. The example described by Shaarawi concerns the establishment of a medical clinic and school to serve some of Cairo's poor. Shaarawi was very clear about the fact that she wished to be involved with projects organised by Egyptian rather than English women – a clear indication of her strong nationalism well before the nationalist movement took hold. Her account also reveals the extent to which the support of the Egyptian royal family (both men and women) was essential for the success of a new endeavour of any scale. Elite society in Cairo was not monolithic; the intellectual elite, political leaders and the court moved in overlapping, interconnected circles as Shaarawi's account demonstrates.

The last section of Shaarawi's memoirs recounts her increasing involvement with the Egyptian nationalist movement in the late 1910s and early 1920s. As Egyptian women of different classes and religious faiths became politicised, this was in some cases a time of unusually close contact between husbands and wives. Certainly this was true for Shaarawi and her husband, Ali Pasha Shaarawi (d. 1923). However, Shaarawi's writings also illuminate the divide that opened up between men who led the nationalist movement and women who were also involved in the movement. Frustrated by the lack of acknowledgement of their views and opinions, Shaarawi eventually withdrew from national politics and devoted her full attention to advancing the cause of women's freedom, founding the Egyptian Feminist Union in 1923, the same year that she attracted international attention by publicly removing her face veil at the Cairo train station upon her return from an international women's suffrage congress in Rome.

[LESSONS AND LEARNING]

[...] The next day, when he [the tutor] arrived carrying an Arabic grammar under his arm, Said Agha demanded arrogantly, 'What is that?' to which he responded, 'The book Mistress Nur al-Huda has requested in order to learn grammar.' The eunuch contemptuously ordered, 'Take back your book *Sayyidna Shaikh*. The young lady has no need of grammar as she will not become a judge!' I became depressed and began to neglect my studies; hating being a girl because it kept me from the education I sought. Later, being a female became a barrier between me and the freedom for which I yearned. The memory and anguish of this remain sharp to this day.

When I was nine years old, and had finished memorizing the Koran, my mother celebrated the event with a party, during which I recited verses from the Koran in the presence of my teacher. I was happy on that occasion and later boasted to my friends of my success. It was the first day of joy in our house since the death of my father.

[...]

Some people thought I had mastered the Arabic language because I had memorized the Koran but that was not the case. I could read the Koran because the vowels are marked but, unfortunately, I could not read anything else. I went on to study Turkish with eminent teachers like Anwar Afandi, Hasan Afandi Sirri, the famous calligrapher, and Hafiz Afandi, accomplished in elocution and widely celebrated for his recitations of Turkish and Persian poetry. They taught me grammar and calligraphy. I learned to write Ottoman Turkish in two scripts, *riqaa* and *naskh*, which helped me in writing Arabic, as the alphabet was nearly the same. About the same time, an Italian woman began to teach me French and the piano; however, she excelled more in music than language.

[...]

I had a natural love for poetry and bought every book of poems I came across. My passion increased all the more because of the itinerant poet, Sayyida Khadija al-Maghribiyya, who often visited our house, where she stayed several days at a time in a room set aside especially for her. In the morning I usually found her composing verse while seated on the bed under the mosquito netting. She always obliged my requests for a recitation, but once when I asked her to teach me to compose verse, she answered, 'It is impossible because it requires a knowledge of grammar, morphology, and prosody.' My ignorance pained me and I blamed Said Agha for it.

Sayyida Khadija impressed me because she used to sit with the men and discuss literary and cultural matters. Meanwhile, I observed how women without learning would tremble with embarrassment and fright if called upon to speak a few words to a man from behind a screen. Observing Sayyida Khadija convinced me that, with learning, women could be the equals of men if not surpass them. My admiration for her continued to grow and I yearned to be like her, in spite of her ugly face.

[…]

WOMEN PEDLARS

Numerous women pedlars—not at all like 'The Flower Water Lady'—came periodically to the house. These women, Coptic, Jewish and Armenian, were assisted by young girls carrying wares wrapped in great bundles which they deftly undid in the middle of the hall. Displaying their goods to the members of the household, they urged them to buy various items, claiming that the wife of a certain pasha or bey had purchased a particular article. If anyone inquired about the health of these ladies the pedlars disclosed bits of gossip and were quick to elaborate if their listener appeared eager for more. I didn't like most of these pedlars—although some were quite witty—because they often damaged prominent families through their indiscretions and lies. They also charged exorbitant prices. As a young girl I was cautioned about the pedlars and told of the trouble they could cause. With the unfolding of the years I saw this borne out.

[…]

[SOJOURNS IN ALEXANDRIA]

[…] I also enjoyed going into Alexandria to call on friends or make excursions to the new modern department stores, despite the continual grumbling and fussing I had to endure from Said Agha. I remember the first shopping trip to Chalon. The mere prospect of it threw the entire household into an uproar and provided the main topic of discussion and heated debate for days. They looked upon me as if I were about to violate the religious law or commit some other crime. After considerable persuasion on my part, however, my mother gave in to my wishes and, along with everyone else around me, issued endless orders and instructions for my correct behaviour. They insisted it was not proper for me to go alone, but I must be accompanied by Said Agha and my maids. The day of the outing, Said Agha made doubly sure I was completely hidden with wraps and veil.

When I entered Chalon, the staff and clientele were visibly taken aback by this veiled apparition and her retinue. In the lead Said Agha stared into the surrounding faces, silently warning them to look the other way, while the maids followed in the rear. The eunuch proceeded straight to the store manager and brusquely demanded the place for the harem. We were led to the department for women's apparel, behind a pair of screens hastily erected to obscure me from view. A saleswoman was assigned to wait on me and to bring whatever I wished. One of her young assistants—amazed by the proceedings—asked about me and my family. Said Agha attacked her with ferocious looks and immediately complained about her impertinence to the manager. She trembled in fear while the other assistants covered their smiles with their hands. The manager was about to dismiss the young assistant then and there. I intervened, however, and asked him not to. I was thoroughly ashamed of the whole scene. Whenever I went shopping the procedure would be repeated all over again until one day I finally persuaded my mother to accompany me. She was then quick to see the advantages of shopping in person. Not only was there a wide range of goods to choose from but there was money to be saved through wise spending. From then on she resolved to do her own shopping and permitted me to do my own as well.

[...]

THE FIRST 'PUBLIC' LECTURES FOR WOMEN

One evening, as my guest at the Opera House, she [Marguerite Clement] talked about her travels and the lectures she gave and asked if Egyptian women were in the habit of giving and attending lectures. We were not, I had to admit, but I invited her to give one. I suggested she compare the lives of oriental women and western women and talk about social practices such as veiling. She asked me to find an older woman to sponsor the event, as I was too young at the time. I was not optimistic about finding anyone. I was certain my mother would not be persuaded to do it. However, that very evening, as we were leaving the box, we met Princess Ain al-Hayat, with whom I had been on cordial terms for a long time. I presented Mlle Clement to her, mentioning the proposed lecture. Would she give her patronage to a general meeting? She accepted without a moment's hesitation.

Next I had to find a suitable place for the talk. My husband suggested a lecture hall at the new university or the offices of the recently founded paper, *al-Jarida*. I preferred the university and requested permission from Alwi Pasha, who proposed holding the lecture on a Friday, when the faculty and students would be in recess. The Egyptian university was, at the time of its foundation, under the patronage of His Highness, Prince Ahmad Fuad, later King Fuad.

The lecture drew a good audience. Mlle Clement had begun to speak when Princess Ain al-Hayat made her entrance. I had reserved chairs in the front row for the princess and her entourage but when they failed to appear after an appropriate interval I ushered some of my relatives into them. As soon as they saw the royal entourage they rose to offer them the chairs. When the others in the audience saw it they stood up as well, whereupon the speaker paused. The princess apologized for the disturbance. Later, I heard that some of the European women present had criticized the episode, remarking that in their countries a speaker would not stop no matter what the status of the latecomer. However, the speaker, herself, was not familiar with our customs. In any case, the lecture was an unprecedented event.

The talk met with such enthusiasm that I invited Mlle Clement to return to give a whole series of lectures for women. His Highness, Prince Ahmad Fuad, supported the women's lectures and ordered a hall to be reserved at the university on Fridays. Soon, Egyptian women began to speak. The best known was Malak Hifni Nasif who wrote under the name, Bahithat al-Badiyya (Seeker in the Desert).

THE *MABARAT* MUHAMMAD ALI

Shortly after Mlle Clement's lecture, Princess Ain al-Hayat invited me to a tea given for the new Lady Cromer, who wished to thank the women who had supported the dispensary established in memory of the late Lady Cromer. I replied that I had not participated in the work of the dispensary and it was not fitting for me to attend. My mother had supported the charity, however. A few days later, the princess sent for me. When I arrived she received me in bed. 'I understood your reason for not attending the reception for Lady Cromer. It is, indeed, shameful that we in Egypt do not undertake such projects, ourselves. It is our duty to be at the head of charitable works in Egypt. I intend to sponsor a dispensary.' I praised her plan and confessed I had declined to take part in the enterprise headed by an Englishwoman, however much I appreciated the charitable works of Europeans, and notwithstanding the participation of other Egyptian women.

I proposed the establishment of a school, providing classes in infant care, family hygiene, home management, and the like to help spread the benefits of modern health-care. The school could function as an adjunct of the dispensary. The princess promised to give the project serious consideration. However, largely for practical reasons, she decided to concentrate exclusively on the dispensary in the beginning. Before I left she confided, 'I am anxious to encourage the princesses of the royal family and Egyptian women to cooperate in works that will serve the nation and humanity.' She insisted I help her achieve that goal and I pledged my support.

The following week I received an invitation from Princess Ain al-Hayat to come to her palace on Shariah al-Dawawin for the first meeting about the dispensary. Many princesses and Egyptian women attended and, after talk over tea, they elected a committee headed by Princess Nazli Halim, with Princess Ain al-Hayat as treasurer and other princesses as secretaries, as well as Mme Fouquet. We each pledged at least fifty pounds to launch the project. Princess Ain al-Hayat announced that Her Highness, the *Walda* Hanim (the mother of Khedive Abbas Hilmi) would make a generous bequest and would give one hundred and twenty pounds each succeeding year, and that Their Highnesses, the Khedive Abbas Hilmi, and the Wife of the Khedive, likewise, would give their support. Princess Ain al-Hayat distributed stamps with the image of a woman embracing a poor girl, to be sold for a piaster each. To increase sales, it was decided to distribute stamps to the various ministries and provincial governorates. The revenue, added to the initial donations, would form the working capital of the society that was to oversee the running of the dispensary.

When summer came, however, Princess Ain al-Hayat went to Europe for medical treatment, and there she died before reaching the age of fifty. I had been very fond of her and admired her intelligence, generosity, and delicate manner. One night, in a dream, she entered my study dressed all in black followed by her daughter, Princess Kazima, who was carrying a closed book placed upon a pillow. I approached the princess to greet her. After returning my greeting, she nodded to her daughter, who gave me the book. I interpreted the dream as a sign that the princess was entrusting me to carry out her plans for the dispensary and I resolved to do everything in my power to fulfil her wishes.

After her death, the other princesses ran into difficulties over the treasury. When they approached her son, Prince Kamal al-Din Husain, about the committee's funds, he asked for the records of their money. But they did not have any receipts for the donations or stamp sales and they began to despair. I suggested that the records of the committee's accounts would surely be found among the late princess's papers. The others said that it would be necessary to search the papers of the late princess's estate, and wished to know who would be competent to examine the accounts once found. I mentioned that a French friend of mine familiar with bookkeeping might assist us, whereupon I was delegated to handle the matter. My friend, the widow of Monsieur Baccus who had taught French at the Taufiqiyya School, volunteered her services. After getting permission from the prince to search, we found the papers and receipts of the committee and proved that its assets amounted to three thousand Egyptian pounds. The prince arranged for prompt payment of the money and thus we were able to move ahead with the dispensary.

We rented a modest building on Shariah Baramuni in the populous Muhammad Ali section of Cairo. We commissioned the architect, Mahmud Pasha Fahmi, to convert the building into a place to house the dispensary and later, a school. Members of the committee took charge of furnishing the new building: Princess Nazli Halim provided forty bolts of white muslin for sheets and bed covers; I donated the beds; my brother gave the desks; and various others took care of additional needs.

On the day of the inauguration ceremonies, Her Highness, the Wife of the Khedive, honoured us by her presence in that small house where Princess Nazli

Halim, the head of the committee, and the other members received her. After touring the rooms of the dispensary, she was ushered into the reception hall where the rest of us had gathered. Princess Nazli Halim delivered a short address in Arabic, welcoming Her Highness and thanking her for supporting the new project which she hoped would render worthy services to humanity under the patronage and guidance of His Highness, the Khedive. The dispensary opened under the name, *Mabarat* Muhammad Ali.

When the work of the *Mabarat* Muhammad Ali expanded I was honoured to become head of the new executive committee. Princess Nazli Halim, head of the original committee was a member along with Princesses Sivekiar, Aziza Hasan, Bahiga Tusun, Zina Hasan and Irfat Hasan; the Egyptian women included *Haram* Takla Pasha, *Haram* Rushdi Pasha, and *Haram* Shafiq Pasha. A French-woman, Mme Carleton de Fière, served as treasurer. The dispensary was administered by an Irish woman, Miss Crouser, a specialist in childcare, who was assisted by a number of Egyptian women. Several Egyptian and European doctors volunteered their services, including Alwi Bey, Sayyid Bey Rifaat, Sami Kamil, Abd al-Hamid Waafa, and Rodier, a French ear, nose, and throat specialist. Sayyida Tumshush assisted with eye examinations. We later requested His Highness, the Khedive, to confer the title of Pasha on Alwi Bey and to decorate Dr Rodier for his services. The operations of the *Mabarat* Muhammad Ali were supervised by the women of the executive committee, who took turns at the headquarters. The valuable humanitarian services of the *Mabarat* continue to this day.

To raise money, the committee of the *Mabarat* Muhammad Ali began holding annual charity fêtes in royal and aristocratic palaces, of a splendour that evoked the days of Harun al-Rashid (the famous Abbassid Caliph of Baghdad). I remember the very first one, at Prince Umar Tusun's palace in Shubra, the likes of which Egypt had not seen since the days of Khedive Ismail. The princesses and princes, rivalling each other to make it a success, sent their most precious possessions for display. The khedive loaned his enormous collection of antique, jewel-encrusted arms. Prince Tusun exhibited a priceless set of Saxe china, a gift of King Louis Philippe of France, and my brother Umar loaned some Pharaonic antiquities that still remain in the house of our late father.

Rooms in the Tusun Palace were transformed to mirror the motif of the extravaganza, the *zifaf*, wedding celebrations of old, as known in the palaces of rulers and princes. A bridal chamber was fitted out with gilded furniture inset with diamonds, pearls and other precious gems. In the banquet hall, a gigantic tray of solid gold stood at the center of the room, in the ancient manner, upon which were placed golden spoons inlaid with pearls and coral, and a magnificent golden ewer and basin. Surrounding tables held an immense collection of gold plate embellished with diamonds, emeralds and rubies. The great hall where the principal entertainments were held was ornamented with masses of trees and shrubs festooned with coloured lamps. At the center of the hall stood a *mashrabiyya* cage with cashmere shawls swagged round the wooden grille. It was amusing to see the singers and musicians being ushered blindfolded by eunuchs into the cage to prevent them from seeing the women. Scattered around the enclosure were heaps of cushions for the women to sit upon while they enjoyed the music and singing of Egyptian and Turkish performers, including Shaikh Yusif al-Minyawi, much acclaimed in Egypt at the time.

Everyone was splendidly attired. Princesses, decked out in heirloom jewels, appeared in gowns their grandmothers had worn, while young girls stood nearby fanning them with ostrich and peacock feathers studded with precious stones. The Egyptian women also dressed in the sumptuous styles of old. Among the special guests were the wife of the heir to the German throne and princesses of the British royal family. His Highness, the Khedive, honoured the large gathering of royalty and aristocracy with his presence. There was no mingling of women and men, but a special place was set aside for the men, many of whom paid hundreds of pounds for a brief glimpse of the festivities in the main rooms.

In the years to come, the Zaafaran Palace and others were the scenes of receptions no less magnificent. In this way we raised substantial sums for the work of the *Mabarat* Muhammad Ali.

THE INTELLECTUAL ASSOCIATION OF EGYPTIAN WOMEN

The intellectual awakening of upper-class women that had been underway over the past years, stimulated and shaped in part by the women's salon and the lecture series, convinced me of the need for an association to bring women together for further intellectual, social and recreational pursuits. I mentioned the idea to some of the princesses and asked for support, which they willingly agreed to give. We met in my house to conclude plans. Princess Amina Halim presided over the gathering of princesses, Egyptians and foreign women. Thus in April 1914 the Intellectual Association of Egyptian Women was born. Among the members were Mai Ziyada, the gifted writer, then at the beginning of her literary career, and Labiba Hashim, the founder and editor of the magazine, *Fatat al-Sharq* (*The Young Woman of the East*, established in 1906), who also served as the Arabic secretary.

In my correspondence with Marguerite Clement, continuing since her visit to Egypt, I had revealed my hopes for creating an intellectual society for women. She promised, if it happened, she would come to Egypt to take part in our programme and offered to give lectures on themes of our choice. I wrote a formal request for her to present to officials in France to facilitate her travel. She came to Cairo and delivered a series of lectures held in my house and at the Egyptian university. She also became a corresponding member of the society.

Before long, I began to search for a headquarters for our society which we had dared not call a club (*nadi*), as our traditions would not allow it. At that time it was still not acceptable for women to have a place of their own outside private houses. […]

[FROM THE EPILOGUE]

The women continued to support the Wafd and at the same time gave encouragement to the people. We consoled relatives of students and others injured by British bullets, visited the wounded, and did what we could to assist the poor and needy among them. In the working class quarters women went to their windows and balconies to applaud their men in displays of national solidarity. Sometimes soldiers fired at the houses, killing and wounding women. Some were hit by bullets that pierced the walls of their houses. The death of Shafiqa bint Muhammad, the first woman killed by a British bullet, caused widespread grief. Egyptians of all classes followed her funeral procession. It became the focus of intense national mourning. Events like these, coming one after the other, did not please the British. They disregarded the solemnity of funeral processions, often scattering the mourners and precipitating bloody confrontations. We women began to compile a list of the dead and wounded. Among the women I remember Shafiqa bint Muhammad, Aisha bint Umar, Fahima Riyad, Hamida bint Khalil, and Najiyya Said Ismail—all from the working classes.

[…]

Exceptional women appear at certain moments in history and are moved by special forces. Men view these women as supernatural beings and their deeds as miracles. Indeed, women are bright stars whose light penetrates dark clouds. They rise in times trouble when the wills of men are tried. In moments of danger, when women emerge by their side, men utter no protest. Yet women's great acts and endless sacrifices do not change men's views of women. Through their arrogance, men refuse to see the capabilities of women. Faced with contradiction, they prefer to raise women above the ordinary human plane instead of placing them on a level equal to their own. Men have singled out women of outstanding merit and put them on a pedestal to avoid recognizing the capabilities of all women. Women have felt this in their souls. Their dignity and self-esteem have been deeply touched. Women reflected on how they might elevate their status and worth in the eyes of men. They decided that the path lay in participating with men in public affairs. When they saw the way blocked, women rose up to demand their liberation, claiming their social, economic, and political rights. Their leap forward was greeted with ridicule and blame, but that did not weaken their will. Their resolve led to a struggle that would have ended in war, if men had not come to acknowledge the rights of women.

13.
HALIDE EDIB (ADIVAR) (C.1883–1964)
✌ MEMOIRS OF HALIDÉ EDIB ᘓ

The Century Co., New York and London
1926

Halide Edib (her married name was Halide Edib Adıvar) was a writer, a politician, an educator and a feminist who came of age at a critical period in Turkey's history. Born in the 1880s (her birth date is quoted variously as 1882–5), she grew up in a wealthy Istanbul household in the last years of the Ottoman Empire. Her father, a prominent social progressive and upper-level bureaucrat in the household of Sultan Abdülhamit, provided an entrée into politics and social welfare work for Edib that, along with her own interests and convictions, positioned her to play a critical role in shaping Turkish women's involvement in the political issues of the day. Her period of greatest political activism spanned the turbulent years leading up to the First World War, through the Turkish War of Independence, and the first decade or so of the new republic. She had a particularly significant impact on the reformation of the Turkish education system, especially concerning the education of girls and women.

Despite her considerable achievements in the areas of politics and public education, Edib always identified herself primarily as a writer, and in fact spent the bulk of her career as the head of the English Language and Literature Department of Istanbul University. The book excerpted here, *Memoirs of Halidé Edib*, is the second of the numerous books she published over the course of her life. Her first book, *The Shirt of Flame* (1924), was an autobiographical novel drawing on her own experiences as a political activist, nurse and, finally, interpreter and press secretary to Atatürk. Following the establishment of the Turkish Republic, and as a consequence of serious political differences with Atatürk, Edib and her second husband, Adnan Adıvar, a former deputy speaker of the nationalist parliament, lived in England for about a decade. This is where Edib wrote her *Memoirs*, the first of two volumes of life writing.

Edib's *Memoirs* is valuable because of her vantage point as a member of an elite political family in Istanbul and because of her own close association with the crucial political events surrounding the formation of the republic. She recounts her traditional upbringing in the home of her grandmother, as well as her education at the American College for Girls in Üsküdar, where in 1901 she was the first Muslim woman to graduate. Edib's writing is a rich source for social and political history. The selections here focus on only two of many subjects that recur throughout the book – female education and polygyny (or polygamy, as it was known at the time).

Unlike most Western authors, Edib could write about polygyny based on her own experiences. Her mother having died when Edib was very young, her father eventually remarried twice. Watching the consequences for the entire household of her father's decision to take a second wife, Edib described the ensuing emotional upheaval and tension. Years later, she was to court unwelcome notoriety herself by insisting that her (first) husband grant her a divorce when he took a second wife. Her accounts reveal the personal cost of divorce (she suffered a long period of serious illness) and the ways in which gossip could police women's behaviour. Edib presents her views on polygynous harem life in sharp and specific contrast to the writing of others, particularly Demetra Vaka Brown, whose book *Haremlik* (see Extract 7) she mentions by name. Edib criticises romanticisations of polygyny, but demonstrates her familiarity with Western ideals of romantic love, by exposing the evils of infidelity that often accompanied so-called monogamy.

In writing about polygyny, Edib presents both her recollections as an informed participant in that social system, and her feminist critique of the system. The extensive passages in *Memoirs* concerning education reveal a similar duality; in this case nostalgic recollections of her own education combined with accounts of her professional involvement with the creation of a public education system for girls. Nevertheless, she provides a very good idea of the rapidity and range of transformations in education, especially the changing place of religious education, and how class featured in the old and new systems.

The education of girls and women was a specific focus of the government in this period, and the subject of intense public debate. Writing here in the pre-Republican period, from the vantage point of one who was deeply involved, Edib identifies the large numbers of women from diverse ethnic backgrounds and classes who contributed to the ambitious project of creating a new education system for women. Her careful account also details the manner in which aspects of traditional religious education were brought into the new system. Her book provides a fascinating counterpoint to that of Woodsmall, published a decade or so later about the same subject from the perspective of an outside observer.

Edib's social activism, as well as her commitment to education for girls and women, led her to become involved with one of the first women's clubs in Istanbul, the Taali-Nisvan Club. The club provided classes for a small number of women to learn about housekeeping and childcare, organised public lectures and became involved in nursing Turkish soldiers. This club and others like it were an important means of providing continuing education for women and helping to prepare women to work, at a time when many were seeking work outside the home for the first time.

Following the end of the First World War, when the British occupied Istanbul, Edib was completely caught up in the Turkish War of Independence. For her, nationalism was by far the most important project, with female emancipation part of it, and essential for the advancement of nationalist objectives.

ॐ   ﻼ

[WHEN THE STORY BECOMES MINE]

Little children in Turkey started to school in those days with a pretty ceremony. A little girl was dressed in silk covered with jewels, and a gold-embroidered bag, with an alphabet inside, was hung round her neck with a gold-tasseled cord. She sat in an open carriage, with a damask silk cushion at her feet. All the little pupils of the school walked in procession after the carriage, forming two long tails on either side. The older ones were the hymn-singers, usually singing the very popular hymn "The rivers of paradise, as they flow, murmur, 'Allah, Allah.' The angels in paradise, as they walk, sing, 'Allah, Allah.'" At the end of each stanza hundreds of little throats shouted, "*Amin, amin!*"

They went through several streets in this way, drawing into the procession the children and waifs from the quarters they passed through until they reached the school. In the school the new pupil knelt on her damask cushion before a square table, facing the teacher. Kissing the hand of the instructor, she repeated the alphabet after her. Some sweet dish would then be served to the children, and each child received a bright new coin given by the parents of the pupil to be. After this sort of consecration, the little one went every day to school, fetched by the *kalfa*, an attendant who went from one house to another collecting the children from the different houses.

The ceremony was as important as a wedding, and fond parents spent large sums in the effort to have a grander ceremony than their neighbors. Each family who could afford a costly *bashlanmak* would arrange for a few poor children of the quarter to share the ceremony and would thenceforward pay their schooling, as well as that of their own child. The old systematic philanthropy of the Ottomans, although fast disappearing, was not entirely dead yet.

[...]

Father had arranged that I was not to begin by going to school, but a hodja was to come and give me lessons at home. The *bashlanmak* too in my case was not to be the usual one. There was to be a big dinner at home for the men, and the ceremony was to take place at home after the night prayers.

Granny had her own way about my dress for once. She could not bear to have me begin my reading of the holy Koran in a blue serge dress. I remember well the champagne-colored silk frock with lovely patterns on it, and the soft silk veil of the same color, that she got for me instead.

A large number of guests arrived, both from our own neighborhood and also from the palace.

Some one held a mirror in front of me after I was dressed, and I looked strange with the veil over my hair and bedecked with the really beautiful jewels of the palace lady. Fikriyar was moved to tears. "Thou shalt wear a bride's dress and I will hold thy train one day," she said. She was wishing me the one possible felicity for a Turkish woman.

Then hand in hand with Mahmouré Abla, who was unusually subdued, I walked to the large hall where every one had assembled for the ceremony. A young boy chanted the Koran while our hodja sat by the low table swaying himself to its rhythm. Mahmouré Abla had already been to school, and so she only knelt, while I had at the same time to kneel and to repeat the first letters of the alphabet, frightened to death at the sound of my own voice. As I rose I forgot to kiss the hand of the hodja, but some tender voice whispered behind me, "Kiss the hodja's hand." All ceremonies in Turkey, even marriages and Bairams, tend to take on a sad and solemn tone; always the women with wet eyes and the men in softened silent mood. What makes other people rejoice makes the Turk sad.

My lessons took place in the same room in the selamlik, before the same table and in the same kneeling attitude as at the *bashlanmak*. My teacher, who was a regular schoolmaster and busy with his own school in the daytime, could only come to our house in the evenings. Two candles therefore were placed on the table and burned under green shades, while I struggled with the Arabic writing of the holy book.* Of course it was difficult to go on without understanding the meaning of the words one read, but the musical sound of it all was some compensation.

[…]

[OUR VARIOUS HOMES IN SCUTARI]

If there is an ecstasy and excitement in times of success, there is a deeper feeling of being singled out for importance when a great and recognized misfortune overtakes one. When a woman suffers because of her husband's secret love-affairs, the pain may be keen, but its quality is different. When a second wife enters her home and usurps half her power, she is a public martyr and feels herself an object of curiosity and pity. However humiliating this may be, the position gives a woman in this case an unquestioned prominence and isolation. So must Abla have felt now. The entire household was excited at her return. As she walked up-stairs and entered the sitting-room, she found only Teïzé standing in the middle of it. But the rest must have been somewhere in the corridors, for every one witnessed the simple scene of their encounter. Teïzé was the more miserable of the two. She was crying. Abla, who had somehow learned what awaited her home-coming while she was still away, walked up to her and kissed her, saying, "Never mind; it was Kismet."

[…]

---

* All Moslem children used to learn to read from the Arabic Koran, of which not a word would naturally be understood by a Turkish child. In the higher classes they would go on applying their alphabetic knowledge to the reading of their own language.

Although this dramatic introduction to polygamy may seem to promise the sugared life of harems pictured in the "Haremlik"* of Mrs. Kenneth Brown, it was not so in the least. I have heard polygamy discussed as a future possibility in Europe in recent years by sincere and intellectual people of both sexes. "As there is informal polygamy and man is polygamous by nature, why not have the sanction of the law?" they say.

Whatever theories people may hold as to what should or should not be the ideal tendencies as regards the family constitution, there remains one irrefutable fact about the human heart, to whichever sex it may belong. It is almost organic in us to suffer when we have to share the object of our love, whether that love be sexual or otherwise. I believe indeed that there are as many degrees and forms of jealousy as there are degrees and forms of human affection. But even supposing that time and education are able to tone down this very elemental feeling, the family problem will still not be solved; for the family is the primary unit of human society, and it is the integrity of this smallest division which is, as a matter of fact, in question. The nature and consequences of the suffering of a wife, who in the same house shares a husband lawfully with a second and equal partner, differs both in kind and in degree from that of the woman who shares him with a temporary mistress. In the former case, it must also be borne in mind, the suffering extends to two very often considerable groups of people—children, servants, and relations—two whole groups whose interests are from the very nature of the case more or less antagonistic, and who are living in a destructive atmosphere of mutual distrust and a struggle for supremacy.

On my own childhood, polygamy and its results produced a very ugly and distressing impression. The constant tension in our home made every simple family ceremony seem like a physical pain, and the consciousness of it hardly ever left me.

The rooms of the wives were opposite each other, and my father visited them by turns. When it was Teïzé's turn every one in the house showed a tender sympathy to Abla, while when it was her turn no one heeded the obvious grief of Teïzé. It was she indeed who could conceal her suffering least. She would leave the table with eyes full of tears, and one could be sure of finding her in her room either crying or fainting. Very soon I noticed that father left her alone with her grief.

---

* The word haremlik does not exist in Turkish. It is an invented form, no doubt due to a mistaken idea that "selamlik" (literally, the place for salutations or greeting, i.e., the reception-room, and therefore, among Moslems, the men's apartments) could have a corresponding feminine form, which would be "haremlik." The word is, however, a verbal monstrosity. "Harem" is an Arabic word with the original sense of a shrine, a secluded place (cf. Harem sherif, the Holy of Holies in the Kaaba at Mecca). Hence it came to be identified with the seclusion of women, either by means of the veil or by confinement in separate apartments; and hence again it came to be used for those apartments themselves.

And father too was suffering in more than one way. As a man of liberal and modern ideas, his marriage was very unfavorably regarded by his friends, especially by Hakky Bey, to whose opinion he attached the greatest importance.

He suffered again from the consciousness of having deceived Abla. He had married her when she was a mere girl, and it now looked as if he had taken advantage of her youth and inexperience. One saw as time went on how patiently and penitently he was trying to make up to her for what he had done.

Among the household too he felt that he had fallen in general esteem, and he cast about for some justification of his conduct which would reinstate him. "It was of Halidé that I married her," he used to say. "If Teïzé had married another man Halidé would have died." And, "It is for the child's sake I have married her father," Teïzé used to say. "She would have died if I had married any one else." Granny took the sensible view. "They wanted to marry each other. What has a little girl to do with their marriage?"

[…]

The wives never quarreled, and they were always externally polite, but one felt a deep and mutual hatred accumulating in their hearts, to which they gave vent only when each was alone with father. He wore the look of a man who was getting more than his just punishment now. Finally he took to having a separate room, where he usually sat alone. But he could not escape the gathering storm in his new life. Hava Hanum not inaptly likened his marriage to that of Nassireddin Hodja. She told it to us as if she was glad to see father unhappy. The hodja also wanted to taste the blessed state of polygamy, and took to himself a young second wife. Before many months were out his friends found the hodja completely bald, and asked him the reason. "My old wife pulls out all my black hairs so that I may look as old as she; my young wife pulls out my white hairs so that I may look as young as she. Between them I am bald."

The final storm, kept in check for some time by the good-mannered self-control of the ladies, broke out in the servants' quarter. Fikriyar and Jemilé were always running down each other's mistresses. Fikriyar called Abla common and ignorant, and Jemilé called Teïzé old and ugly. "Besides, she is a thief of other women's husbands," she added. One day the quarrel grew so distracting that the ladies had to interfere, and for the first time they exchanged bitter words. That evening father went up to Abla's room first, and he did not come down to dinner. The next morning it was announced that father was going with Abla and her little girls to Beshiktash to the wisteria-covered house, and we, the rest of the composite family, were to take a house near the college, and my education was to begin seriously.

It was in 1893 and 1894 that I went to the college for the first time. I was perhaps the youngest student, and my age had to be considerably padded in order to get me in; and no amount of persuasion was available to have me taken as a boarder, so that father's plan to remove me from the influence of "that woman" as he now called Teïzé had to be postponed.

[…]

[SOME PUBLIC AND PERSONAL EVENTS, 1909–1912]

I visited and studied the school with Nakie Hanum. She was an old graduate of the normal school and had been for some time a teacher in the American College, where she had assimilated during her training there all that was best and most applicable to school management in Turkey. Endowed with intelligence, character, and constructive ability, she developed into one of our best organizers. Her natural understanding and knowledge of the students and of the teachers of the time fitted her especially for the task. She was appointed director of the normal school, and it was with her that we carried out the reform which the ministry of education accepted in my report.

At first the school was in Ak-Serai, an old dilapidated building, and its dominant teaching features were Arabic, Persian[,] domestic science, and a thorough instruction in religion. It needed a curriculum with a newer and more scientific spirit, a living language, and a more modern atmosphere and equipment. The most vital change was to be the development of a new spirit in the Turkish student. A new sense of responsibility and of coöperation, a new self-respect in the child, as well as a more earnest and open-minded and less autocratic attitude in the teacher were necessary before the new education in Turkey could take shape.

[...]

Nakie Hanum's teaching corps showed real self-abnegation and made very serious efforts, conscious as they were of the importance of their part as pioneers in a new realm of education for women. I entered the school as a teacher of the principles of education, and my first contact with the teaching and student classes in Turkey began at that time.

It was a year of liveliest interest. In two years the educational department saw the necessity of a girls' college, and as the normal school had shown real progress it was turned into a college, and a new normal boarding-school was opened in another part of Istamboul.

For five long years I was a teacher in the girls' college, teaching the history and principles of education and ethics to the young and some other things which one teaches behind the lines, things which are necessary if one means to build new country. If I taught I also learned, and in the give and take my students formed and molded me as much as I did them. It was with the help of some of the students of those years that we were able to modernize and organize the mosque schools some years later with Nakie Hanum, and it was with the aid of the same element that I organized the schools and the orphanage in Syria, of which I shall speak in coming chapters.

Before I pass on to another subject I must say that Saïd Bey—the counselor of the ministry of education, several times minister of public instruction, and a well known professor in the University of Istamboul—must have the honor of being the pioneer advocate of the modernization of women's education in New Turkey.

[...]

In 1910 I was having serious domestic trouble. I felt that I was obliged to make a great change in my life, a change which I could not easily force myself to face. Salih Zeki Bey's relation with and attachment to a teacher looked serious enough to make it seem conceivable that he contemplated marriage. A believer in monogamy, in the inviolability of name and home, I felt it to be my duty to retire from what I had believed would be my home to the end of my life. But knowing Salih Zeki Bey's passing caprices of heart and temperament I wanted to be absolutely sure, before breaking up my home, of the stability of his latest attachment. I therefore took the little boys with me and went to Yanina near my father with the intention of waiting there for a few months.

At my return Salih Zeki Bey told me that he had married the lady, but to my great surprise he added that polygamy was necessary in some cases, and he asked me to continue as his first wife. There was a long and painful struggle between us, but at last he consented to a divorce, and I left what for nine years had been my home.

It was a cold April night when I drove with the boys to Fatih, to the big old-fashioned house of Nakie Hanum, where I stayed till I found a suitable house. What now seems an almost ordinary incident in a woman's life was then of supreme importance and the cause of great suffering to me. My foolish heart nearly broke. I think the women of Turkey must be more used to divorce nowadays, for one hears little of broken hearts in the many divorce cases that now take place there.

[…]

Salih Zeki Bey's second marriage had aroused such personal curiosity that every eye probed me hard to see how I bore my own trouble after having written so much about other people's. I remember one fat woman in particular among my acquaintances who used to come with stories about the love-making of the new couple and watch my face with obvious curiosity. I neither questioned nor commented; I had a strange feeling of wonder at her apparent desire to see me suffer. I passed the test of vivisection rather successfully I believe, for my calmness and apparent lack of interest made her after a time drop the subject. Still it was a great pity that every one spoke of me as having consumption at this moment of my life, for consumption is ridiculously associated in the public mind with disappointed love.

I allowed myself no sentimental self-analysis or morbid philosophizing at this time, such as I had occasionally indulged in during the other serious illnesses I had gone through. I meant to conquer all physical ills, and I meant to make a home for my sons equal to the one they had had to leave, and to surround them with a happy and normal home atmosphere. I was determined to live, and not to leave them to the sort of life which children have when their mother is dead or crushed in spirit.

As I write these lines I feel as if I were writing of the life of a young woman who has passed away. I see her lying on a simple bed of high pillows; I see her struggling to write her daily articles or short stories; and I hear her cough continually. Then the evening lights blaze over the waters, the little boys come back, and she makes painful efforts to conquer her wild desire to kiss and hug them. They chatter about the American school they attend, and finally they go down to dine with granny, while she is left alone in the twilight room, with the utter mysterious loveliness and strange longings of the evening. She looks at pain with a quizzical smile, while she listens to the voices of the evening in the streets. The sellers of yogurt, cadaif, the chanting of beggars, the footsteps of workers who pass down to Koum-Kapou, and at last the call of the childish voices and the patter of small feet scampering in the dusk in those large, lonely streets.

[...]

In the autumn of 1910 I was once more going on with my lectures and lessons, and the cough and fever had gone. Besides my lessons and writings I had become a busy public speaker.

[...]

[MY EDUCATIONAL ACTIVITIES, 1913–1914]

Nakie Hanum resigned a few months after me. She had created a girls' college which was notable from every point of view and had proved herself to be a serious educator. Before she had had time to rest, she received an offer from the education department of the ministry of *evkaff* (pious foundations), to which all the mosque schools belonged.

Hairi Effendi, the great sheik-ul-Islam of the Unionist régime, had began a series of interesting and serious reforms in *evkaff*, which was under his control. The department had in its charge a large number of theological schools (*medresses*) of an extremely scholastic and reactionary kind as well as all the primary mosque schools, mixed or unmixed. A great deal of money was spent on these institutions. Hairi Effendi began an able and drastic reform in all of them. The *medresses* for the first time were to have modern science taught by modern teachers instead of the old scholastic curriculum and the old teachers. The mosque schools, which so far taught only the Koran and which were housed in little holes, were to be modernized, and a dozen schools were amalgamated in one big and up-to-date building in an important center. Each was to have a modern staff with a modern curriculum. The boys' schools were organized by Ali Bey, a very capable and progressive section chief in *evkaff*. The girls' schools as well as the small mixed ones were to be organized by Nakie Hanum as the general director. I became their inspector-general and adviser.

Nakie Hanum soon succeeded in creating a hardworking, sincere, and capable body of teachers. She was greatly helped by the young graduates of the college whom we had ourselves trained. Her schools immediately became the best primary schools in Istamboul. The best specialists on educational subjects offered to train her teachers, and her own central school in Sultan Ahmed acquired an atmosphere of learning and happy camaraderie among the old and young elements of *evkaff*. [...]

[...]

None of the old teachers of *evkaff* lost their place when Nakie Hanum undertook to modernize the mosque schools. She trained them, giving them only Koran, domestic science, and sometimes history courses to teach. They made a great effort to accustom themselves to the new atmosphere, for material reasons at first, but later on because the warm fraternity of the organization attracted them genuinely. In some ways the older ones seemed more familiar with the peculiar needs of the children and their families than did the younger ones, and some of them had the charm of old-fashioned Turkish manners, which one rarely found in the new generation of teachers, although the younger ones had better and more up-to-date training.

There was one little school in Jihanghir with a woman at the head who came from an old family and had gone into teaching for financial reasons. She had the old Arabic and Persian culture and was well trained in Oriental history. Her name was Fikrie Hanum, and I can never forget the clear pious expression of her face, so mild and so serious and tolerant.

Her school was always full of flowers, and the old bare boards were always scrubbed and clean, while her white curtains were always gleaming. Her little ones had acquired something of her personal charm of manners; they were individual little women and little men instead of only students. They took care of the flowers in the garden, felt proud of their happy little place, and talked to one with unconscious grace and freedom. Their garden was like an eagle's nest, perched over the wonderful beauty of the Bosphorus, with countless ledges of brightly colored earth and here and there plantations between the garden and the foaming blue waters of the narrow winding Bosphorus. The garden was full of geraniums and carnations, lovely bright reds; and the place had wooden stools made by the little boy students, where one could sit and watch the children play.

Nakie Hanum gave her a young assistant who introduced more scientific teaching, while she went on with the general care and religious teaching. Youth and change had appeared to her harsh and ugly at first, but in time she became one of Nakie Hanum's most loyal and loving hands. The little schools with three grades had usually these older ladies with young assistants; but the six-graded ones, which were being newly opened in larger centers with modern buildings, were run with completely young staffs. It was good to see them grapple with their problems and meet their successes and failures.

[...]

[THE BALKAN WAR]

[...] I stayed in Fatih at Nakie Hanum's house and worked with the women of the Taali-Nisvan Club for relief and nursing.

We, with some teachers and some educated Turkish women, had formed that first women's club. Its ultimate object was the cultivation of its members. It had a small center where the members took lessons in French and English. It also opened classes for a limited number of Turkish women to study Turkish, domestic science, and the bringing up of children. We had Mrs. Marden, of Guedik Pasha school, and Mrs. Bowen, who helped us in the teaching of English, as well as in lending us the Hall of Guedik Pasha school, where we opened a series of lectures for women. There was a feministic tendency in the club, but as a whole it kept within the bounds of usefulness and philanthropy, and we tried to maintain a quiet tone, avoiding propaganda, which becomes so ugly and loud and offers such an easy way to fame for any one who can make sufficient noise.

The club organized and opened a small hospital with thirty beds in Istamboul. A young surgeon and a chemist, both husbands of club members, volunteered to help; the beds and equipment were provided by the members; and one member lent a house. We took only privates. As the Balkan war saw Turkish women nursing men for the first time, any little human incident became a tremendous scandal.

[...]

In the meantime an organization of a semi-official character was trying to raise money to help the refugees and the hospitals. The Taali-Nisvan organized a meeting of women in the University Hall in Istamboul, both to help the refugees and to send a protest to the queens in Europe asking them to use their influence to stop the massacre of the non-combatant Turks and Moslems in Macedonia.

There were about six women speakers, and the hall was more than crammed. Before the meeting was over women were throwing their jewelry to the pulpit, tearing their furs off to be given to the refugees and the sick. The meeting chose two women delegates to go to the embassies in Pera, to ask them to convey the protests to the queens.

14.
RUTH FRANCES WOODSMALL (1883–1963)
ᔓ MOSLEM WOMEN ENTER ᘰ A NEW WORLD

Round Table Press, Inc., New York
1936

Ruth Frances Woodsmall's 1936 book, *Moslem Women Enter a New World*, is presented as the product of research undertaken specifically to investigate the changing status of Muslim women in the region. Woodsmall was not writing a travelogue or a memoir, but a research study, one of three that she produced over the course of her professional career. From 1921 to 1928 Woodsmall was living in Istanbul, serving as the executive secretary of the YWCA (Young Women's Christian Association) in the Near East. In 1928 the Laura Spelman Rockefeller Foundation awarded her a fellowship to undertake the study, co-sponsored by the American University of Beirut, which was later incorporated into her book. She was interested in many of the same kinds of subjects that Julia Pardoe (Extract 1) wrote about a century earlier (dress, social custom, education, religion). In some ways Woodsmall's book can be understood as a twentieth-century version of the accounts written by Pardoe and others, constructed in a differently directed and focused manner and presented with almost none of the explicit personal references that shaped nineteenth-century writing. Woodsmall's research in the Middle East was one aspect of her long career in international women's work, which took her also to India, Japan, China, Indonesia, France and Germany. Over the course of her working life, from 1917 until shortly before her death, she shifted back and forth between serving in senior administrative positions for international organisations and conducting sponsored research in the social science arena, always focusing on women's needs and issues.

Moslem Women Enter a New World is a wide-ranging examination of different aspects of women's lives in the Middle East of the 1920s and 1930s, when Woodsmall conducted her research (her 1928 study was updated for the book, published in 1936). Divided into six parts of uneven length, the book addresses change in the areas of education, employment and health, with shorter sections devoted to social change more generally, the relationship between women and Islam, and the broadening interests of Muslim women. In some parts of the book, the author breaks down a specific topic according to region (India, Iran, Turkey, Egypt, Syria, Palestine and Trans-Jordan), but at other times, she is less specific. The book is illustrated with a series of nineteen photographs taken by Woodsmall (four of which are reproduced in the Photo Essay above).

Like other authors in this collection, Woodsmall is attentive to the impact that changes in fashion and consumption patterns have had on other aspects of women's lives. She mentions repeatedly how the adoption of Western goods produces social changes; for example, that Western-style furniture and eating make Eastern-style hospitality impossible. She notes also that the diversity of store-bought goods required by Western fashion (as opposed to the hand-produced accessories of traditional costume) has led to changes in shopping patterns, with more women shopping in public places, and a consequent shift in the gendering of public spaces. This change in women's consumption practices has been noted by other authors: Grace Ellison on her visit to Istanbul in 1908 (Extract 10) and Huda Sharawi in Alexandria when she recalls her first excursion to a new department store (Extract 12).

The first passage excerpted here concerns a different aspect of fashion, the transformation in women's appearance that resulted from the adoption of the style for bobbed (or short) hair, which reached the Middle East at about the same time as it did Europe and North America. Just as in the West, bobbed hair was a daring innovation, both from a fashion and a social point of view, only slightly less controversial than trousers for women. This was not the first example of Western-styled coiffure for elite women – previously Edwardian bouffants had been popular – and it indicates the continued close attention many elite women in the region paid to the fashion trends of Europe. However, especially in Turkey where discouraging the veil (in favour of hats) was part of republican policy, bobbed hair was an extremely visible marker of modernisation.

Woodsmall's chapter on education for girls and women in Turkey, a subject on which she was particularly well informed, provides a detailed account of the government's approach to educating women in the early years of the Turkish Republic. Acknowledging the important roles of Halide Edib (Extract 13) and Nakiye Elgün in establishing schools for girls, Woodsmall goes on to detail the reasons behind the government's decision to pursue co-educational schools, especially at the elementary level. She highlights the fact that the government realised that the disparity in education for girls and boys could only be successfully addressed by giving girls priority in the state-run system, an extraordinary policy that had an immediate and dramatic impact on the rate of education among girls in Turkey.

The author touches on some of the issues faced in the building of the new public, state education system, for example, the difficulties in training new teachers and the challenges of distinguishing new teaching modes, distinct from the religious education of the past. Physical education became an essential part of the new school system, as did vocational education, which for women primarily involved home economic and secretarial studies. Millinery classes were particularly useful, since Turkish women now needed hats.

Women had equal access to higher education in Turkey from the early 1920s and began entering the legal and medical professions immediately. Woodsmall details their participation in university life, as well as investigating other avenues of adult education available to women. She is clearly aware of the wide-ranging impact that Turkish women's access to education was having on Turkish society in the 1920s and 1930s. Woodsmall also provides a surprisingly cogent analysis of the relationship between the Turkish educational policy and the European models from which Turkish bureaucrats chose selectively to create an education system suited to their own needs.

ℬ   ℭ

Along with the complete modernization of costume underneath the outside garment and veil, has come the imitation of the West in adopting bobbed hair, which is often a record of real achievement. Just as other changes have come slowly in different stages, bobbed hair has not always been accomplished by one snip of the scissors. I was intrigued and amused by the rather interesting and unique semi-long and semi-short style which I noticed first in a harem in Kadhimain and afterwards in various harems in Iran and the Near East. The explanation was that it was not a matter of having chosen this as a special style, but that it represented the half-way stage. The daughter or wife, ambitious for a bob, finds the father or husband very reactionary on the subject, so tries it out by degrees, cuts the sides first, then as he gradually becomes accustomed to that much, she tries a little more, until she is entirely bobbed. But to-day the number of only semi-bobbed is steadily decreasing. A great number of Moslem women, whether veiled or unveiled who have adopted European styles in clothes, have also bobbed their hair.

At the beginning, I learned, Moslem women often act as coiffeur for each other; then perhaps later after the first fatal act, the husband may serve as the barber. In the few places where there are women barbers in the East, they have become quite affluent. An Armenian woman in Baghdad, who was enterprising enough to take a course in Paris, has flourished. At first she had all the trade, but now some of the less conservative and especially the *élite* patronize Mustapha, *the* barber of Baghdad, who knows all about his clients, chats very freely *with* them and *about* them later on.

[...]

Perhaps there may be some relationship between the freedom of bobbed hair and the growth in photographs of Moslem women, for freedom to have a photograph taken is another of the cherished new measures of advance. I found that carrying a camera when visiting harems and *zenanas* was an interesting method by which to test conservatism. Where the veil still persists, Moslem women are as yet for the most part conservative about having their photographs taken. Usually younger Moslem women are very eager for a photograph but inhibited by the fear of some male member of the family. Therefore the consent of the father or husband was required. Sometimes with the ultra-conservative, if I promised to give them the film afterwards, I could meet their opposition, as that eliminated the idea of having the film developed and seen by a strange man. A woman photographer a few years ago had a very good field for work in Moslem countries and still would in places where photographs of women are as yet taboo. But in certain places, for some time past, women have patronized men photographers. A clever Baghdad photographer confided to me five years ago that his best clients were Moslem women who of course were all veiled. He seemed surprised that "for some reason or other" as he said, "they understand the art of posing."

Until recently it has been difficult and practically impossible to take photographs in girls' schools. Some of the group illustrations in this book required much persuasion and most meticulous care in securing the parental consent even of the girls behind the veil. To have a photograph of a group in the girls' Normal School in Baghdad the principal said she must get the sanction of the Minister of Education and the permission of the parents. But out of a class of thirty-two only five refused consent in 1934 whereas a few years ago probably not five would have given consent. Among the uneducated, middle or lower class of Moslems, there is a very strong prejudice against photographs of women, because of a complex of tradition and religious scruples.

[…]

CHAPTER XIV
TURKEY ACHIEVES MODERN EDUCATION FOR GIRLS

[…]

It would be a fallacy, however, to believe that education for girls in Turkey was the sudden product of the new régime. The almost passionate drive to educate the masses is the distinct result of the new republic, but a period of preparation came before. A few Turkish women of the upper class began to receive the private cultural education of the home soon after Turkish men came under the influence of French ideas, even as far back as Mahmud the Great (1809–39). Later, during the period of the *Tanzimal* reforms (1839–79) foreign governesses were introduced into the harem for the privileged few. Even the severity of Abdul Hamid could not stop the flow of Western influence, although it dammed up the outlet and made the open acceptance of Western ideas and attendance at Western schools difficult, especially for girls. But the few pioneers, like Halidé Edib, persisted secretly and oftentimes at real personal danger.

For the great majority of Turkish women, however, aside from the Koran schools and a girls' normal school for training elementary teachers, attended primarily by orphans and poorer girls, there was no real educational provision for girls, until after the Constitution in 1909. The first serious efforts at more than mere elementary education for girls came in 1913 with the establishment of a co-educational or secondary school for girls by Bayan Nakiye Elgün, for over thirty years the outstanding educational leader of Turkey, now a Deputy in the Grand National Assembly. The extension of primary education followed, and also the reorganization of the *Evkaff* (Mosque Foundation) schools was undertaken and effectively carried out by Halidé Edib and Bayan Nakiye. These schools were consolidated in 1916 under the Ministry of Public Instruction.

[…]

[…] The decade between 1913 and 1923 shows a gradual development and improvement of girls' education but with no distinctive change in direction.[*] The next decade between 1923 and 1933 reflects not only the strenuous drive for increasing girls' education, but also the introduction of co-education. Most of the elementary education for Turkish girls is now provided through mixed schools.

The increase of girls in schools in the decade from 1923 to 1933 is remarkable,[†] as is also the fact that the rate of increase of girls in the elementary schools has been greater than the rate of increase of boys; and, in the secondary stage, the growth in the number of boys and girls has been practically equal. The increase in school attendance, as marked as it has been, does not, however, represent adequate school provision; for a school population of at least one and a half million, there are only school facilities for a little over half a million.

Furthermore, the fact that the rate of increase of the girls' enrolment has compared favourably with that of boys does not mean that the education of girls and boys has been equalized.[‡] In 1933–34 there were two boys for each girl in the elementary schools; three boys for each girl in the intermediate schools, and five boys for each girl in the *lycées*. Because of this disparity between boys and girls' education in Turkey as elsewhere in the East, although in Turkey the disparity is much less—the real task of education is not merely to provide equal facilities for boys and girls but more for girls. This fact has been clearly recognized. As the former Minister of Public Instruction, Husni Bey, said in discussing this

---

[*]   1913 to 1923 shows an increase of one-third in girls' elementary schools; and one-third in enrolment of girls in elementary schools; the addition of a girls' *lycié* and a normal school for women; and a small increse in women teachers. Information from a member of the Council of Education, Ankara.

[†]   The first decade of the New Republic shows a marked growth in the education of girls from the primary grade through the university.

	Girls attending schools	
	1923–24	*1933–34*
Primary	62,954	205,922
Secondary	2,072	11,376
Lycées	612 (1924–25)	2,321
University	285	933
Vocational Schools	592	990
Normal School for Primary Teachers	782	2,537

Information from Basvekalet Istatistik Umum, Mudurlugu-Maarif Istatikleri, 1933–34, Ankara, Devlet Matbaasi, Istanbul.

[‡]   Information from the Ministry of Education, Ankara.

problem: "It cannot be a question as in the past of providing for girls *after* the needs of boys have been met. If there is any question of *after* in Turkey to-day, it must be the boys after the girls."

As a primary means of solving this tremendous problem of the disparity in the education of girls and boys, Turkey adopted co-education in 1925, beginning with the elementary schools, later introducing it to a certain extent in other stages. The success of co-education, as a national programme is shown by the rapid increase of girls in primary schools, an achievement which would have been obviously impossible under the system of separate schools because of the double expense as well as the lack of teachers. In the adoption of co-education Turkey differs from all other Eastern countries, which have not yet cut the Gordian knot of their difficulty in promoting general education and especially education of girls. [...]

Strangely enough or perhaps naturally enough, co-education has been introduced especially in the Interior rather than is Istanbul. The primary reason is doubtless economic. The only possibility of extending education has been through the economy of mixed schools. Hence, not only primary but also some middle schools and *lycées* in the Interior are co-educational; whereas in Istanbul there are separate girls' middle schools and *lycées*, and co-education has not replaced the already well-established system. But if new schools are built in Istanbul as elsewhere they will doubtless be co-educational.

[...]

In order, however, that the best social as well as educational values may be safeguarded in the co-education system, certain wise precautions are being taken. [...] that teachers shall not present extremes in modern social customs. Rouge and lipstick and lurid finger-nails are frowned upon, and a frown often equals an order. Teachers, moreover, are not allowed to enter the Turkish beauty contest. [...]

In the extension of schools in rural areas, one of the major problems in Turkey obviously is the provision of trained teachers. To allocate an individual teacher to rural schools is always difficult, because of the social adjustment to an isolated village life. This problem is being met in some places in Turkey by the appointment of a married couple to a village. The married couple conducts the school on modern lines, creates a modern home, which invites imitation, and adds greatly to the general community life. As a further effective use of teachers in rural areas, to facilitate the spread of rural education, the idea is being developed of establishing a school with a number of teachers and a boarding home for students in a central village, perhaps also a clinic and small hospital, the whole unit thus serving the needs of the surrounding area. The boarding school is required as a modification of the usual consolidated school because of the lack of bus lines and the great distances between the villages.

[...]

The promotion of education in the new Turkey has meant the modernization of the whole educational programme. Of central importance in this process of building Turkish education on a modern basis is the policy of secularization of schools. The starting-point for all of the reforms in education was the elimination of the power of the ecclesiastic authorities. For example, co-education, which has increased especially the education of girls, could scarcely have been accomplished under the old régime, when schools were dominated by religion. One of the modern Turkish leaders, in an interview with me in Ankara some years ago, said: "Other attempts at social reform in Turkey have failed because they did not assert complete independence over religion. Lay education is the only basis of success."

Following out this policy, the schools have been completely secularized. The Turkish girls of to-day, therefore, have no formal religious instruction in the school. The chanting of the Koran, the teaching of the Islamic formula, the proper ritual and prayers, as far as the schools are concerned, are all things of the past, since definite religious instruction is regarded as the function of the home, not the school. Religion as such is not repudiated, but is regarded as an entirely individual matter. Whether the home will assume the responsibility is a question for the individual home to answer. The State no longer fulfils this function. What will finally result from the elimination of religion from the school only time will tell. Such questions as these are sometimes raised in the Press: "Is it necessary to give importance to moral and spiritual education in view of the need of strength and power in times of misfortune?" or "Can moral strength be imparted to children entirely within the circle of secularism?"[*]

Not only in reference to religious teaching but in general there is a distinct trend in education away from the old traditional ideas. One of the most important developments is the introduction of physical education on modern lines, given by well-trained teachers. Observing a crowd of Turkish girls playing on the school playground, which is now a vital part of every school, or watching a basket-ball game of a Turkish girls' *lycée* at recess, which, incidentally in Turkey is given between every class, I was impressed with the contrast in the vitality of the present-day physical education programme with the anaemic type of physical exercise given in the schools a few years ago. [...]

[...]

[...] Another significant emphasis in the education of Turkish girls is the promotion of vocational education. A number of excellent vocational schools have been established to teach practical arts, as their name *Sanat* schools signifies. The Ismet Paşa Institute in Ankara serves as a model for the rest of Turkey for schools of this type, with its fine modernistic building, its excellent class-rooms and laboratories, its splendid equipment, adequate dormitory facilities, and well-trained staff.

In addition to regular middle school subjects—a primary certificate is required for entrance—two main courses are offered, household economics and a clerical course. The Household Economics Course is very complete, including home arts,

* *Hizenet*, November 28, 1930.

sewing, tailoring, embroidery, cooking, laundry and millinery, which has a rather special interest in Turkey, because of the discarding of the veil. As the veil was less expensive than the hat, there is a distinct economic value in having Turkish girls learn millinery. Also, this offers a very good commercial opening for Turkish girls, as one of the students explained to me. Two enterprising graduates of the school have set up hat shops in Ankara and are doing a flourishing business. The Clerical Course also meets a timely need in view of the recent entrance of Turkish girls into business life. In addition to one of these two special courses, Home Economics or Clerical Training, all of the students have a simple course in Home-making and Child Care, taught by a well-known young Turkish woman doctor, a specialist in child welfare. A further special feature of the Ismet Paşa Institute is the night school for married women. Between two and three hundred women come every evening for practical courses in home subjects, home hygiene and child care and the simple education courses.

This Institute offers an interesting illustration of the consistent year-by-year growth of education in Turkey. In a five-year period it has become established in its very spacious new building. The French Directress has been replaced by a Turkish Director, with a Turkish woman assistant, both of whom have studied in Europe. Turkish teachers, several trained abroad, have replaced all of the foreign teachers except one, the French specialist in millinery.

In addition to the clerical course at the Ismet Paşa Institute, training along commercial lines is offered for girls in the very up-to-date Ankara Commercial School, a co-educational institution under a Russian Principal. This school has a number of modern emphases in education; such as student co-operatives, student savings department, a student shop and the student management of the library.

In the development of Turkish education along modern lines, the problem of the training of women teachers is receiving serious consideration. Training for primary teachers is provided in a number of normal schools throughout Turkey; training for secondary teachers is given in the Higher Normal School in Istanbul, connected with Istanbul University. The requirements for teaching have been advanced: to teach in a *lycée*, a diploma from the university is necessary; for the primary or secondary grade, a normal school certificate.

The relationship of the teacher to the community is for Turkey to-day a vital question. The young normal-school graduates from Istanbul, fully emancipated young Turkish women wearing hats, fond of dancing and a normal social life, face a difficult problem of social adjustment when they find themselves planted in backward communities, where perhaps some of the women are still veiled and old social customs are still observed. Moreover these young teachers in the Interior have the responsibility of interpreting by their own example the meaning of social freedom. For all this they must be adequately prepared. Hence, the task of the normal schools is not merely to give academic training in methods of teaching, but to socialize education and interpret the career of teaching on a very high moral level. Some of the directors of the normal schools and teachers have grasped the significance of the problem, and are working creatively to develop in every way possible the social values in education. The young graduates, on their part, eagerly take advantage of all opportunities, especially extra-curriculum activities, such as folk-dances and games for recreation, in order to prepare themselves for the varied demands of teaching service in the Interior.

[...]

Higher education in all lines in Turkey is open to women on a basis of full equality with men. Women were admitted to the university in 1915 during the World War, but attended at first as quite a separate section; the men's classes were held in the morning, the women's classes in the afternoon. This involved a duplication of time and effort on the part of the Faculty, and hence a double expense. In the summer season of 1921 accordingly mixed classes were begun, with men and women students on different sides of the room and with no contact outside of classes. The women students entered the classes veiled, raised their veils during the class, and lowered them when leaving. The fact that this first group of pioneer women students was in a conspicuous and difficult position, was shown by their extreme care in the details of veiling. These early days of co-education in Turkey are typical of the present situation in some countries in the Moslem East, where co-education is regarded as a doubtful social experiment.

After 1923 all distinctions between men and women students in the classroom were discontinued, and the sense of segregation of women soon ceased. Visiting the University of Istanbul recently, and seeing men and women studying together and freely associating with each other, inside and outside of the classroom, in the same atmosphere of unconscious freedom that is characteristic of any co-educational university in Europe or America, I had difficulty in imagining the restraint and separation of university co-education in the earlier days. Turkish women students now participate very freely in all student activities, hold offices in the Student Union, are prominent in class organizations and assume responsibility in university student publications. In all of their university relationships women have taken their place naturally and in this short period have become intimately related to university life.

Since 1922, when the Medical Faculty was opened for women, there has been a continuous increase in the number of Turkish women in the University of Istanbul, studying law, science, letters, medicine, dentistry, pharmacy, and even engineering. In 1934 the total number of women students was over one-fourth the number of men students.[*] An interesting evidence of the increasing response

---

[*]   The following statistics of Istanbul University are of interest:

1928.   Total enrolment 2,500; women students 230
1934.   Total enrolment 3,148; women students 934
1934.   Women students were divided as follows;

Faculty of Letters	209	Pharmacy	28
Science	288	Midwifery	62
Medicine	66	Engineering	6
Dentistry	44	Commerce	50
Law	181		

of Turkish girls to the opportunity of a higher education is the number of out-of-town students now attending Istanbul University. It is a distinctly new development for a hundred or more Turkish women students to come from the Interior to Istanbul for higher education. Many of these non-resident women students live with relatives or friends, but soon a regular dormitory provision for them will doubtless be needed.

The question as to whether women students are fitted for higher education, would scarcely be raised in Turkey to-day. The presence now on the university faculty of several young Turkish women assistant professors is certainly one answer to the question. The scholarship of the women students is another. In the Ankara law school graduating class of 110 students in 1929, a woman student took first honours. "Women are on the average more conscientious than men and regard their opportunity for higher education as a personal responsibility to excel" was the interesting opinion expressed by Adil Bey, formerly a professor in the Law Faculty. A German professor, Dr. Freundlich, a noted astronomer formerly associated with Einstein, now on the faculty of Istanbul University, expressed his appreciation of the quality of Turkish women students. "They have a certain finesse in their manner and can always be depended upon for thoughtful effort. Their presence adds greatly to the university classroom."

An interesting counterpart to this opinion about women students is the expression of a woman medical student, on the general position of women in the university. "We are considered not merely as individuals, good, bad, or indifferent, like men, but as representing women as a whole. We cannot afford to fail; it would be considered that higher education for women is a failure. If we succeed it means that we have advanced the whole idea of women's ability."

[…]

In addition to promoting regular education in all its phases, Turkey has vigorously attacked the problem of general adult education. The illiteracy of Turkey some years ago was estimated at eighty-five per cent; the general illiteracy of women was higher than men, as is usually the case. The adoption of the new Turkish script in 1928 presented the opportunity and drastic necessity for a nationwide drive for literacy. The change from the old to the new letters meant for the time being that the whole nation was reduced to the level of illiteracy. It was immediately necessary for all—the learned and the unlearned—to go to school. Consequently, a campaign for literacy, unparalleled perhaps in world history, was launched. In October 1928 the nation's schooling began, including Kamal Ataturk, Cabinet ministers, officials, teachers, peasants, men, women, and children of all classes.

1924. First graduates in law   3
1927. First graduates in medicine   6
From the Ministry of Education, Ankara.

Attendance at these National Schools the first year was compulsory for everyone between the ages of sixteen and forty. As soon as the student learned to read and write and could pass an examination, a certificate was issued which served as exemption from further study. Enforcement of the law was vigorously prosecuted by the Turkish police. The course was taught by regular teachers, who received a small supplementary salary for this extra teaching. School buildings and other public buildings were utilized. The courses were held outside of regular school hours, classes for women for the most part in the daytime; for men, at night. Over 800,000 received certificates.* The courses during the second year were of two types: the simple course for literacy, and a more advanced course including geography, higher arithmetic, additional reading, letter-writing and civics.

Women constituted over half of the million students in the National Adult Schools, which were established in September 1928, when the new language was officially adopted, and continued during two years. According to reports, women made equal progress with men. Women of all classes took advantage of the opportunity to learn to read, even mothers attending classes with babies in their arms. The upper class of women, highly educated in the old Turkish language, entered into this pursuit of literacy in new Turkish with zest as in a game, studied at home or in one of the national schools, passed their public examinations along with the masses, and proudly received their diplomas with their pictures attached as on a passport. The women of the people especially have profited by this drive for learning the new letters. Illiterate before, with little thought of ever learning to read and write, they have suddenly, through the national schools, been awakened to an idea of their ability, hitherto unknown. The number of women reading newspapers on the trams and boats is a visible proof of their new literacy.

Adult Education along other lines also has been promoted by the Government and semi-official agencies. The *Halk Evi*, Peoples' House, is one of the main agencies for adult education, offering various courses to all of which women are eligible. A marked trend is the emphasis on foreign languages, English, German and French. The present promotion of the study of foreign languages not for a select intelligentsia but for the general public is one of many indications that Turkey has turned Westward in her thought. The increasing stress on English and German, furthermore, indicates a distinct cultural shift, as French hitherto has always been promoted as the second language.

In Turkey as in other countries of the East, foreign influence has permeated the life and thought of the country. We have already mentioned the French and English governesses in the home of wealthy pashas. Through these isolated individuals, the West first entered the Turkish woman's life. It is difficult to estimate what was the full measure of this foreign influence silently pervading the Turkish harem, and bringing glimpses of a different world, for such subtle influences are not summed up in statistics. [...]

* *Statistical Annuaire*, 1930.

[...]

But modern Turkey to-day does her own shopping for education and culture and for scientific progress—it may be in Berlin, or Paris, Moscow, London, or New York. It has been of special significance to the education of girls that this process of selecting foreign values has indicated a definite interest in Anglo-Saxon and perhaps especially in American methods. In speaking of European culture and education, a former Minister of Public Instruction said in a personal conversation that "the culture of Europe was more suited to old régime than the new. Turkish girls have come out of the harem and need now an education of practical emphasis and social value, so that they may be better fitted for civic and national responsibility."

It is important, however, that one should remember that the choice of foreign values is only a means to an end. The primary basis of Turkish education and culture is not foreign but Turkish. The sense of direction in Turkish education as in Turkish life is singularly clear. A vibrant spirit of nationalism is the force motivating all social reform and progress. Woman's education has definitely benefited by being regarded as a necessity for building a strong nation. The passion for nation-building has been followed with a swiftness and sureness of aim which has counted no sacrifice too great, no reform too drastic. Secularization of schools, co-education, equality of opportunity for boys and girls from the primary school through the university, emphasis on vocational courses for girls, equality of salaries for men and women teachers, a new language, education of the masses, the use of foreign experts, a deepening of the Turkish consciousness are all steps in the general educational process which has definitely raised the intellectual level of Turkish women.

15.
MUSBAH HAIDAR (1908–77)
ჱᲘ ARABESQUE ᲓᲘ

Hutchinson & Co., London: New York: Melbourne: Sydney
1944

Musbah Haidar was the daughter of Amir Ali Haidar, a Sherif of Mecca who held a number of high-ranking positions in the Ottoman government, and also served briefly as the Amir of Mecca. While many of the women whose writing is presented here were members of the political elite of the Ottoman Empire or Egypt, Musbah Haidar, or Sherifa Musbah Hanım, as she was also known, was of truly royal birth. The honorific title Sherif (Sherifa in the case of women) is hereditary, and indicates direct descent from the Prophet Muhammad. Haidar's mother, Isabelle Dunn, was the daughter of a British Brigadier General in Turkish service, who converted to Islam upon her marriage, changing her name to Fatima Hanım. Haidar and her siblings were regarded as princes and princesses, raised in Istanbul, Syria and Beirut, as her father negotiated the treacherous political intrigues and shifting alliances of the region in the first decades of the twentieth century. Her childhood home was a gathering place for high-ranking members of the political and religious elites, men whose conversations Musbah Haidar considered carefully. Haidar eventually settled in England where she married a British officer, and where she wrote *Arabesque*.

In the brief Foreword to her book, Haidar describes her work as 'not only the story of my childhood and girlhood; but also a chronicle of an epoch that is already History'. Obviously she is aware of the unique vantage point from which she can recount the events of her lifetime. She writes that she wishes to tell the world 'the point of view of an Eastern woman', but also describes herself as a fusion of East and West. Haidar's sense of her status and of her multiple identities is evident throughout the book, and features prominently in several of the passages excerpted here.

One indication of the privileged life into which Musbah Haidar was born appears in her description of her early education, which involved at least six different women, of different nationalities and ages, and one old gentleman, all of whom came to the house to teach English, French, drawing, piano, dancing and Turkish to Haidar and her sister. This was the traditional means of educating the daughters of the elite (described also by Huda Shaarawi), which was gradually replaced in the early years of the Turkish Republic by the public education system developed by Halide Edib and others (see Extract 13). As she grew older, Haidar worked hard to convince her father to allow her to attend school with other children, and was eventually successful. Haidar's education, at both home and school, as well as the daily gatherings which took place at her home, created an international, cosmopolitan environment for Haidar and her siblings.

Her deep knowledge of contemporary politics and overriding interest in current events is evident throughout the book, for example, in her assessment of the political difficulties confronting the Arabs excerpted here. This discussion grows out of her account of the way in which Syrians identified themselves on the basis of religious difference as opposed to ethnicity or nationality. Her family's move to Syria sharpened her own Arab identity and awareness of her family's royal status, but also brought her into closer contact with the issues facing the Arab, as opposed to the Turkish, world. She is profoundly critical of the British handling of the issue of Palestine and of Jewish influence in the region.

Haidar's political description is combined with perceptive social commentary. She is an accurate observer of the details that were a part of the far-reaching social changes taking place in the period about which she is writing. Her account of the entry of the Allies into Istanbul at the end of the First World War shifts from relating the varied responses of different groups within the city to the presence of foreign troops and ships to an analysis of concurrent changes in the status of women and in the relationship between men and women. Defending the traditional harem structure, with its clearly defined codes of behaviour for both men and women, she is scornful of the harem literature produced by 'globe-trotting journalists' relying on 'some ninth-rate Levantine' or 'self-styled and much advertised *Hanoum*' for their information. A few pages later, she describes a visit made by an American woman to their home. Haidar's awareness of the fact that Mrs Bristol was not prepared for their sophistication or cosmopolitan conversation ('What did these people imagine they would find or see? ... Women in gauzy trousers sitting on the floor?') is indicative of the extent to which many elite women were fully aware of the stereotypes perpetuated about them in Western art and literature. However, while Haidar sometimes defended the traditional ways in her writing, in her life she often pushed against the limits set by her family for her and her sisters, for example in her desire to attend school, and later when she was the first female member of her family to perform in a music recital. Her shifting stance towards tradition surely reflects the tensions that characterised aspects of Turkish society in the period in which she grew up and about which she wrote.

Haidar's book ends with the establishment of the Turkish Republic and the abolition of the caliphate by the new government. The Ottoman imperial family is sent into exile, including some members of her own family, a momentous event that she describes in detail. Raised in Istanbul in the milieu of the Ottoman elite, but also fiercely loyal to the idealised Britain of her mother's memories and her royal Arab heritage, Haidar has a unique and extremely well-informed window onto the political and social events unfolding around her.

ഉ   ര

CHAPTER VII
EVENTS MOVE FASTER

[...]

I
POLYGLOT TEACHERS

Life became very complicated for Musbah. She had now very few hours to sit and twirl on a swing or watch the chickens. Lessons had begun in real earnest. Miss Petela still came and walked with her round the garden holding her tightly by the hand, or listened to Musbah reading from the "Royal Primer". In addition, she had now Omar Pasha's daughter, Alice Novotny, to give her English lessons. Alice was so different from old Miss Petela. Tall and slim, smartly dressed, of English, Italian and Hungarian descent, Alice spoke several languages; could dance, could play, and in fact could do most things well. Musbah liked her. Then she had an Armenian, called Asnif, for drawing. Though Asnif had great talent, she—like all her race—gave herself airs. Having studied painting in Paris, she felt far too superior for daily life. Dressed *à la* Bohemian, she used to pose herself in attitudes which she presumably considered artistic!

Mlle Boutan, her French teacher, was sensible and quiet, and for her Musbah had a great respect. Mademoiselle was her favourite teacher, especially when she came on Thursday accompanied by a Hungarian girl called Eva. Eva was a pretty girl who danced like a fairy, and taught it also. Dancing was the best of all the lessons, when all the tables and chairs in the large *salon* were pushed back. Mademoiselle would play the piano, whilst Eva taught both Sfyné and Musbah. The former was always the cavalier, Musbah the lady. The first dance they learnt was the gavotte, in the last figure of which Sfyné, as the gallant cavalier, had to kneel and kiss Musbah's hand. This seemed terrible to the Aunts, the elder kissing her younger sister's hand! Musbah would pretend to make eyes and flirt with her fan at Sfyné—the latter could never stand this kind of play.

"Don't be silly. Don't make faces at me," she would hiss, at the same time trying to kick the would-be Pompadour's ankle.

A Jewess, Mlle Goldenburg, came for piano lessons. These would have been delightful, as Musbah adored music, but the Goldenburg seemed to think that as she was the youngest she should be kept back and not allowed to play anything her sister was learning at the same time. For weeks in succession she had to repeat the same lesson. How she hated that hand with the many gold bangles, as it marked the same page, time after time!

"Can I not have a new lesson?" Musbah would plead.

"No."

"But I know my lesson."

"You will play what I tell you." The thin lips would be pulled tighter.

Both Sfyné and Musbah went every morning to the Sherif for their Koran lessons. They also listened to Fatma reading the Bible to them, and had to learn the psalms and hymns by heart. The Sherif had said:

"One could acquire no harm from any religion, but only good."

Turkish was taught by a venerable white-bearded Baghdadi gentleman, Amin Effendi, who had been Amir Abdul Muttalib's secretary.

And so this group, an odd and varied collection of nationalities, worked at the education of the two young Arab Princesses.

These days were enlivened by the weddings of Princess Adela and Princess Attiya, the two younger sisters of Sultān Yenga. The festivities were on the same lines as that of the elder sister, but were made gayer with music. The Sultan's band played outside, and within the Palace oriental music, oude and tambour, was provided. The old Kadin Effendi was satisfied and happy; for at both these marriages the *Koltuk* was celebrated.

The two children were now great favourites in the Palace.

[…]

CLASH OF WESTERN CULTURE WITH EASTERN TRADITIONS

Ever since her arrival in Aley [in Syria], Musbah heard constantly of Druses, Maronites, Protestants, Armenians, Catholics, Muslims, Alouites, Greek Ortho-dox and Greek Catholic! It seemed so extraordinary to her, who up to now had always heard people in Stamboul referred to by their race or nationality: Bulgari-ans, Greeks, French, Armenians, Montenegrins and Levantines,* certainly as varied in nationality as the others were in religion.

In Syria, people were called after their respective creeds—and what an end-less array of them! Thus the Maronite maid, Marie, was at daggers drawn with the Druse washerwoman. Hereditary enemies, just because one was born a Druse, the other a Maronite!

The same was just as true of the other sects. It was not just a question of, say, Christian *v.* Muslim—the ramifications were far deeper than that, and were too tangled for any outsider to grasp all at once.

And this did not end just there!

Three distinct cultures played their part in making these differences still more acute, and the division between the people ever wider. French and American schools, and in a lesser degree English, had vied with each other for years in col-ouring the mental and political outlook of the people.

The French perhaps preponderated. Their *lycées* and Jesuit schools were scat-tered all over the country. The Maronites appeared to be their most faithful followers, together with a sprinkling of Orthodox.

The Americans with their University at Beyrouth, and an excellent hospital attached, with mission schools in many parts of the country, were increasing their influences. They could already boast of quite a strong body of Protestant con-

---

* Levantine was the term used for one of mixed blood, i.e. Greek-French, Maltese-English, Italian-Greek. Levantines were not held in high repute in Turkey, and the term had a somewhat derogatory meaning.

verts—and, as usual, the Armenians, their especial *protégés* in whichever country they happened to be.

The Druses had a great admiration for the English and very little love for the French. The Quaker school at Brumana could be justly proud of the excellent work which it did amongst those mountaineers, especially in character-building.

The Muslims had somewhat naturally supported the Turks, but they had their Nationalists amongst them who had begun to preach a Free Syria. The Muslim Arabs had their own Universities in Beyrouth and Damascus, and were highly suspicious of the other sects, held back as they were from real progress by narrow-minded fanatical *softas* (Muslim religious teachers) and Imams.

The Alouites, or the "Assassins", were the most ignorant and uneducated, but were hard manual workers.

The men provided the *hamals* (porters) of Beyrouth, whilst the women were the scavengers of the city. The latter wore bright-coloured voluminous skirts, with long frilled tight pantaloons reaching down to the ankle, orange-coloured turbans on their heads, over a long muslin veil, which hung down the back. They were strong, fair, handsome creatures, with free manners and impudent tongues. Cornelians appeared to have a special charm for them; great beads of these stones hung round the necks of all these women. Carrying a tray on their heads and accompanied by a man with a bell, they would go from house to house collecting the refuse, which would be dumped into a cart—later a lorry.

The Alouites live around Baalbek and Tripoli, and are the followers of the Agha Khan, their religion being as mysterious as that of the Druses.

Syrians and Lebanese are as a race healthy and intelligent, but are handicapped by the diversity of their many creeds and cultures—and still further handicapped by the influence, education and propaganda of certain Powers working for their own interests against each other in this small country. Thus an even greater division of natural antagonism is created, causing friction between the different communities, where there should be only one aim, one thought, one determination—AN ARAB NATION.

The result of these conflicting cultures and influences is a country whose inhabitants speak several languages easily but none perfectly, not even their own native Arabic. A lack of ideals, a scorning of old traditions, ties and customs. A discarding of religion, manners and morals, with no substitute to take their place, except those learnt from the cinema, the cabaret and dance-halls.

The new wisdom which they have learnt from Europeans has shaken their home ties, has broken down their own traditions and ideals—but has given nothing to put back in those empty niches. The West may have taught some lessons in the way of hygiene and science, but has left the people weak, unguided, unsupported in their spiritual and moral needs.

Until the Arabs can organize their own educational and cultural systems, they can never hope to become a United Nation. For the results of this polyglot education of today are either men who are at home in other countries and out of touch with their own—or perhaps, still worse, despise their own countrymen, and pretend to be Frenchmen or Americans and so on. Anything but an Arab! Others instead have become extreme Nationalists, and refuse to have dealings with those who do not share the same views as themselves; who believe that no benefits or knowledge can be acquired from other races of mankind, and distrust all those who are not of their own faith and nationality.

Division, the curse of the Arab race, has broken them and reduced them from having once been a great Empire, cultured and civilized, tolerant and wise, to small, ignorant, fanatic states for ever jealous and suspicious of each other.

An Arab Federation! The desire and dream of all Arabs who wish to see their race again occupy its former great position. Yet how is this to be done? When every Iraqi considers a Syrian inferior! When a Syrian, in turn, thinks an Iraqi uneducated! When a Hedjazi, or a Bedouin, tribesman thinks all others no true Arab because they live as Europeans, and eat and dress in a different way from himself, and have no ancestry, and they too in turn are considered to be savages by a Palestinian or an Egyptian! And so this tragic misunderstanding continues in addition to all the other handicaps.

The British are the only European Power with whom the Arabs should have any dealings. Many Arabs live and have their being within that Empire, or within its spheres of influence. With the tragic exception of Palestine, the British have understood the Arabs better than have any other European race. It is therefore unfortunate that the other Powers have been allowed to make their voice heard in Arab affairs. France has her own interests, and these have often conflicted with those of her ally. America too must have her say; and Jewry, backed up by influential and wealthy co-religionists across the Atlantic, rattles the money-bags and must be satisfied.

Yet if England could but be wise and honest over this question of the Arabs in Palestine, scrap the Balfour Declaration as she did the MacMahon promises, start once more with a clean slate, she would find that the apparently insoluble and thorny problem of that minute country could be quickly solved. In return, Britain would enjoy the unstinted loyalty and affection of all Arabs. This might prove to be in the long run a wiser policy, and even a more profitable one, than backing Zionism so blindly. On the one hand, there is a continent, a vast sub-continent, stretching from the Kurdish Mountains in the north to the coasts of the Hahdramaut in the south, from the Mediterranean to the Persian Gulf—a continent to unite and open up! On the other hand—what?

But Britain can only be of help to the Arabs when she has proved herself to be unbiased and loyal to her promises.

Through bloodshed and tears, through suffering and fighting, the Arabs will rise again. So long as they follow their own traditions and remember their own glorious history, they will surmount all obstacles.

[...]

"THE OLD ORDER CHANGES"

Everyone went to see the official entry of the Allies into Stamboul. The Princess, as a British woman, naturally rejoiced at the victory of her own people, but what of her husband's position and future?

She took the children with her to Pera to watch the march past. Musbah could feel the tense excitement of the crowds that lined the streets. Allied flags hung everywhere, from every window and balcony. How had they managed to produce them and from where?

The Greeks were in an ecstasy of excitement; always volatile and quickly roused, they saw in the defeat of the Turks a great future for their own country. In their heated imagination the Byzantine Empire was a reality again. Was there not a prophecy that said: "When a Constantine and Sophia were King and Queen again, they would be crowned in Saint Sophia"? So they waved and cheered the Allies, who could make their visions a reality.

The Levantine population, always following the current of popular emotion, also made merry. But the Turk looked on dazed, hardly realizing that foreign soldiers were now flooding their streets; the Dardanelles in Allied hands; their Empire broken, with its provinces being formed into separate states.

Musbah held on to her Mother's hand as the crowd round them cheered, waved and threw confetti at the troops who marched by. This was the first time that Musbah saw soldiers, other than German, Austrian and Turk.

Detachments of British, French, Italian, American and Greek troops marched past. Fatma clapped when the British came into view. It was a proud day for her as an Englishwoman.

The entry of the Allied Fleet was even more dramatic. On November 13, 1918, the Allied Navies were to sail into the Bosphorus.

The balcony of the konak afforded an unrivalled view. The group watching from it saw away in the distance over the waters of the Marmora small grey dots which grew larger and larger as they approached. A magnificent sight of sea-power, as the ships came steaming up the Bosphorus and dropped anchor in stately procession. British, American, Italian, and even Greek, the *Avaroff*.

Musbah, with a pair of binoculars glued to her eyes, gazed at this new sight. Her elders around her seemed to be in odd moods. Her Mother exalted, but had tact enough not to show it too much. The Amir, with his usual breeding and reserve, said nothing. He, who had a love and admiration for the Navy, especially the British, had now a wonderful opportunity of seeing a fine display. He could now satisfy his interest in ships by the sight afforded him.

Were his desires and ambitions always to be gratified—at a price? and at what a price!

But all he said was, "Look, my daughter!" to Musbah. "See how trim and clean the British ships are in comparison with the others. No other Navy in the world can beat her on the seas; all others are amateurs compared with hers."

Uncle snorted and went inside. He was having trouble as a member of the Committee of Union and Progress, of which many members had already been rounded up, and who were to be sent to Malta. Uncle was in a bad temper these days. His outspokenness and frankness with his own party at the end had caused much ill-feeling towards him.

The *Avaroff* turned and anchored off Dolma Bagtche Palace. That was the last straw to many Turks who watched this triumphal entry. But those in charge of the Armies of Occupation were to show an amazing lack of tact, and a complete ignorance of psychology and ingrained hates and prejudices of the many races they had come to patronize or to control.

One of the outstanding features of the occupation was to be the complete absence of confidence and co-operation between the Allies themselves. Those who watched and waited marvelled at it.

One of the most noticeable developments in Stamboul was the slow but sure emancipation of the women. The change was more apparent in the upper and middle classes than the lower. The *pelerine* of the *hanoums* grew shorter, the veil thinner, and even, in some cases, the face was actually left uncovered! The veil merely becoming a decoration to float behind gracefully.

There was, naturally, great excitement and discussion in the Palaces and Harems at these innovations. The amount of liberty permitted the fair ones varied in accordance with the feelings of their respective menfolk. Some of the young Beys, for example, even accompanied their wives out of doors and allowed them to receive gentlemen in their homes, other than members of the family—an unheard-of event!

A few fast ladies began to frequent the Pera Palace and Tokatlian Hotels.

There was much horror and indignation expressed by the older *hanoums* and the "diehards".

"Such behaviour was scandalous," they cried. "It means, in fact, that the husbands of these women no longer love them and, therefore, they can feel no jealousy! It means the breaking-up of homes, of purity, of chastity! When strange men's eyes have taken the bloom off their unveiled faces, what man worth his salt would want to marry any of them? The good old times," they sighed, "these Giaourized Beys wanted to marry the girls they had seen … !—instead of accepting the virgin their fond mothers had chosen for them. Worse still, the girls also wished to know the men before becoming betrothed; and even desired to go to Giaour schools! They actually asked to be educated!"

"What did a woman want with education?" cried the mothers. "All that a girl needed was looks, and the ability to hold and charm her man's senses, and to present him with sons! Of what use was it to be able to speak outlandish languages; to be able to hit a ball hard in some stupid kind of Giaour's game; and yet be unable to satisfy their husbands in their beds, and manage him as they themselves had done with silken, honeyed words and tender caresses? Had they not been happy? Had they ever lacked jewels, silks and a devoted man? What taste and allure could there remain in a woman for the male, when he had complete licence given him to go from woman to woman, and she from man to man? Allah! What a world it was!"

With the rapid decline of the old courtesies, breeding and old customs, all that the women got in their place was the doubtful liberty of being able to go out when and where they liked; instead of being guarded and protected as they always had been, always attended and back in their homes by sunset.

The days of the Great Hanoum Effendis were dying, and nothing that the younger modern set could produce would ever take their place in grace and charm.

The Westerner's mind runs riot when it thinks of Eastern Harem life! These people would certainly have been amazed if they had ever been privileged to visit a Harem. They would then have seen for themselves how false and exaggerated their ideas were of the "Life behind the Veil"!

Scandalmongers and sensation writers who could NEVER penetrate into that well-bred and exclusive circle have written highly-coloured versions of Harem life, which could have only existed in their fevered imaginations.

In all the years which Musbah spent in Turkey, never did she see Europeans being either allowed or accepted into the Imperial circle, or those of other great houses. Great Eastern ladies were not in the habit of receiving inquisitive and curious foreigners. If occasionally an Ambassador's wife or that of a Consul-General was permitted to visit the Harem, it was done most ceremoniously, and no lady present ever relaxed her polite and formal hospitality into intimate friendship.

So these so-called intrepid travellers and globe-trotting journalists could only pick up their impressions and ideas from some ninth-rate Levantine, or from some self-styled and much advertised *Hanoum*! And then rush their false knowledge into articles and books, as far from the truth as the writers were from ever entering those well-guarded, exclusive and dignified homes—THE HAREMS.

A high degree of love and loyalty existed between husband and wife. Contrary to popular belief, a Muslim man could not run amok in his Harem at his own sweet will. There were certain clearly defined rules of conduct and obligations which had to be observed; and a high degree of morality and faithfulness was the rule. There were exceptions, as in every community and race, but these were few and far between; amongst these could be numbered some of the older members of the House of Osman.

With the Armistice and the subsequent influx of many foreigners of all nationalities and types, new ways and ideas began to permeate society. The young Beys, in their ignorance, thought that they could imitate the European. They started to do so by frequenting the numerous cabarets, music-halls and night clubs the Westerner seems to find indispensable to his well-being and pleasure, and which spring up wherever he goes!

What is it? A drug—a stimulant?—for his emotional and physical well-being ... !

From the great number of Russian refugees who poured into Stamboul, the cabarets were well supplied with *soi-disant* Princesses and Countesses. Gallant

British officers and young Beys would chivalrously rescue these "aristocrats" by marrying them! To rescue them—from what ... their profession?

Gradually the old order changed—the new one, aping European morals and manners, came to take its place. A tinsel synthetic substitute for what had once been genuine and precious.

[...]

One day, Medjid asked the Princess to receive Mrs. Bristol, wife of Admiral Bristol, the United States representative, who wished to call. Fatma consented; the children grumbled.

"They only come to gape and stare," was Sfyné's opinion.

A few days later the lady came with her husband, who remained in the *Selamlik* with the Amir, whilst Medjid brought in Mrs. Bristol to the Harem.

A gay, vivacious woman, who asked innumerable questions. When tea arrived, carried in by two black slaves on the great round gold tray, chased and enamelled in red, on which rested the exquisite Sèvres tea service, she could no longer restrain herself.

"What a gorgeous tray! Oh, my! What a museum-piece! And those cups and saucers, and these dear little gold knives and forks! You know, I can hardly believe my eyes. The appointments of the house and your dresses! My!!"

What did these people imagine they would find or see? thought Musbah. Women in gauzy trousers sitting on the floor?

In their abysmal ignorance these foreigners did not realize that many of the veiled ladies of the Harems were better born, better read, spoke several languages, and dressed with a greater chic than some of their own most famous society women.

Mrs. Bristol was, with difficulty, persuaded to talk of other subjects. She had never been in such a cosmopolitan and elegant circle as she found herself to be in in Stamboul, and she confessed that she enjoyed every moment of it.

When she had left, Hatija and Little Marie came to clear the tea-things. A few moments later there was a great crash from the stairs, and the sound of china breaking. Everyone rushed out to the landing. Disaster met the eye.

Hatija stood in the centre of a circle of broken cups and plates, while the great tray continued to roll down the stairs till it came to rest in the hall below. No one broke the silence. Every single cup, plate and saucer of the beautiful Sèvres set was lying in pieces.

A door shut. The Princess, without a word, had gone back into her room. To make up for her forbearance, everyone now began to scold and shout at Hatija and Little Marie.

Big Marie had seized her niece and was banging her head against the stairs.

"Wooden head!"—bang. "Great bullock!"—thump. "I will break every bone in thy miserable body." Little Marie burst out howling.

Fayrial Baji came to the fore.

"Oh, thou great ape, the daughter of a she-ape, the grand-daughter of an ape. Dost think that thou art playing at ball with the treasures of the Great Sitti?"

"It was not my fault," wailed Hatija, "the *Giaour Hanoum* with the pot on her head gave it the Evil Eye!"

[…]

Chapter XXVIII
THE CALIPHATE ABOLISHED

[…]

I

SO ENDS THE OCCUPATION

On July 24, 1923, the Treaty of Lausanne was signed, thereby sealing the Turkish victory and independence. All foreign control ceased, and the Capitulations, always a source of irritation to the Turks, were abrogated. Turkey had no more use for the Arabs or their land. It was now Turkey for the Turks. The control of the Straights returned to Turkey; and the repatriation of Greek and Turk minorities to their respective mother countries was immediately put in hand. Though at the time the scheme was considered by many to be cruel and unjust, and also difficult of attainment, in the end it proved to be a wise and long-sighted policy.

Turkey received back many countrymen who were industrious workers, skilled in carpet-weaving and tobacco cultivation. Once and for always the question of Minorities in both countries was finally settled.

Foreign intrigue suppressed, points at issue between the two countries settled, Greeks and Turks soon forgot their former animosity and have behaved towards each other ever since with neighbourly friendliness.

Of all the countries who had entered the Great War against the Allies, Turkey was the only one to emerge victorious and strong. She was no longer an Empire, but in losing that cumbersome, unmanageable framework which she had borne so long, she discarded that which had grown alien and uncontrollable and was at last free to concentrate on herself, to show her mettle, to follow modern trends and innovations, and to break with age-old traditions that had, in some ways, stifled all initiative and progress.

Turkey broke with old ties and constraints, and prepared herself to meet Western nations on an equal footing as a modern, progressive and free nation.

Turkey, in her newly awakened eagerness to embrace modern ways of life, may have pushed aside and crushed many old traditions and graces that would have aided and beautified her own growth; but such mistakes are inevitable in a social and cultural revolution.

Turkey, in the brave step which she took, has been the pioneer for other Eastern countries. Turkey was ripe for emancipation; but to follow blindly and hastily in her path would be but to court disaster—as Amanullah did in Afghanistan to his cost.

Arabs and Turks are widely dissimilar in character and outlook, yet the example of Turkey should encourage and stimulate the Arabs in their efforts for freedom and progress.

*   *   *   *   *

In October the last of the British troops who remained in Turkey were to leave. On the day of their departure the three Sherifas, attended by Emina, went to town, ostensibly to shop, but secretly hoping to get a last glimpse of the British Army.

On crossing over to Beshiktash they found large, happy crowds thronging the streets, which had been gaily decorated. At some distance from the shore a large transport ship lay at anchor, waiting for the last of the senior British officers who were to embark from near Dolma Bagtche Palace.

The carriage into which the three girls had got could not take them further than the Palace, as the immense crowds made all traffic impossible. They descended and were immediately caught in the surging, pressing, pushing crush of people. Emina became frantic with anxiety over her charges. Nemat and Sfyné began to question the wisdom of their action. Musbah was thrilled; a great crowd always interested her, and to become one with its feelings and excitement gave her a delicious sensation of adventure and curiosity.

Emina moaned as they were inexorably pushed along. "May Allah protect us. Why did you listen to your young Sister and come here, instead of going to the Bridge (Galata)?" she scolded Nemat and Sfyné. "Shopping! What shopping? How am I to protect you from this scum—the common people who are so close to you? Eh?"

She elbowed her way along, cursing and grumbling.

"Oh, my mother, dost think that thy elbow is as soft as thine breasts, which are of such a desirable size?" cried a man into whose stomach she had pushed an extremely sharp elbow, in her elephantine advance ahead of the Sherifas to make a path for them.

"Hold thy tongue, thou wizened bastard," she retorted sharply, "thou shrivelled excretion of a shameless goat."

"Eh, thy tongue is like that of the bulbul, O breaker of hearts!" the man replied glibly.

Musbah spied a small hole in the wire behind the iron railings of the outer gardens of the Palace, up to which they had been swept by the crowd.

"Come, follow me," she called to her sisters, and before they could stop her she had wormed her way in on all fours through the wire and was flitting over the lawns towards the guarded, walled and sacred precincts of the Imperial Palace. A cry of anger and threats from her sisters did not stop her. She only laughed and told them to follow, as she disappeared from view behind a large tree.

Nemat and Sfyné were distinctly angry. To crawl in their elegant silk manteaux and white gloves through a hole no more than a foot wide, close to the ground, was certainly not easy—and decidedly undignified.

"We had better not leave that little monkey alone," muttered Sfyné. Emina wailed her protests. She was told to stay where she was. After some difficulty the two managed to crawl through, practically on all fours, and emerged on the other side none the worse. They dusted themselves and straightened their clothes. Having once started they began to enjoy the adventure. They found Musbah waiting for them at the end of the path.

"Now what are we to do?" asked Nemat. "Of all the wicked——"

"Look, look, we can watch everything from here," cried Musbah.

They found themselves only a few yards from the Imperial landing-stage, on which the Caliph with his attendants stood talking to General Sir Charles Harrington and some other officers.

The Caliph's keen eyes, on seeing the *samade* and *aighal*, glanced at the unusual spectacle of two ladies and a young girl in the *Selamlik* gardens of the Palace. He recognized who it was at once; only Musbah and his own daughter wore that head-dress. His Majesty sent an equerry to show the Princesses to a convenient place from which to view the proceedings. Chairs were brought and the officer took up his position behind them.

Musbah chuckled with glee. Her sisters, behind their chiffon veils, which they had at once lowered when they entered the gardens, frowned at her.

"You don't need to be so superior," she jeered at them. "I saw the way you two crawled through the railings. You did look a sight. Anyway, this is more suitable for us than the crowd, you must admit."

After some moments more of conversation between the Caliph and the British General, a launch drew alongside, and the British, after saluting the Caliph and his entourage, embarked and were quickly borne to the waiting transport.

And so that Occupation, which had begun in such difficult circumstances in 1918, came to an end. The last remaining elements of those Forces were soon out of sight.

That regime had ended!

Salaaming the Caliph, who stood talking to his visitors and suite, the Sherifas turned to go. Their exit was certainly quite different from their entry.

Escorted by the equerry, they were led through the gardens with great ceremony and respect to the Ceremonial Entrance Gates, where a carriage had been summoned and was waiting for them. With great dignity the three returned the salutes of their attendants and mounted the carriage.

"If you dare do such a thing again," Nemat and Sfyné threatened, "we'll——"

Musbah giggled.

That night she regaled her Father and Mother with a ludicrous description of their adventures, which made them both laugh.

"But I still don't see how you managed to be there, child. I thought you were going shopping in Pera," said the Amir.

A pause followed. Sfyné glanced at her sister.

"We—we thought—we lost the boat to the Bridge, and took the one to Beshiktash, and there we were," explained Musbah.

"I see," said the Prince; there was an amused twinkle in his eyes. "I see ... !"

On October 30, 1923, soon after the departure of the Allies, Mustapha Kemal was proclaimed President of the Turkish Republic.

To many the days of the Imperial Family seemed numbered. But they themselves continued to be oblivious of that which threatened them.

Ankara did not like them? Well, why worry about Ankara? Ignore Ankara!

16.
EMINE FOAT TUGAY (B.1897)
THREE CENTURIES
FAMILY CHRONICLES OF TURKEY AND EGYPT

Greenwood Press, Westport, Connecticut
1963

Emine Fuat Tugay, born in the closing years of the nineteenth century, is, in some ways, emblematic of the Ottoman Empire as it faced the political and social challenges that were looming just ahead. On her father's side, she was the descendant of a distinguished Turkish family whose members had played important parts in the military and court life of Istanbul. Her mother was a princess in the Egyptian royal family. Tugay grew up speaking Turkish, German, and English, often living abroad with her parents as a child. As was the case for other privileged women of the period, her family brought together the political and social elite of both Turkey and Egypt, and, because of their political prominence, were deeply entrenched in the intellectual and political elite of Europe as well. Firmly linked to the Ottoman past, they were nonetheless intimately involved in the events that were shaping the future of the empire.

Her book is divided into two sections, the first a detailed account of both sides of her family's history, and the second her own childhood through the first years of the twentieth century until the eve of the First World War. Like other women extracted here (Musbah Haidar, for example), Tugay grew up in a political family and was keenly aware of the tumultuous events in which her father, Mahmud Muhtar Paşa, and grandfather were embroiled. The first extract from of her book presents the story of her father's role in the revolution of 1908 and the counter-revolution of 1909, as well as his subsequent political appointments and diplomatic missions. Hearing of the 1908 revolution from Europe, Tugay's father immediately returned to Istanbul, where he became commander of the First Army of Istanbul. Following the counter-revolution, he fled Istanbul, with the assistance of German and British allies (the European powers were obviously closely involved in local politics). Upon his return to Istanbul, within a period of four years he held a series of high-level government posts and was eventually appointed as the ambassador to Berlin, from which post he opposed Turkey's entry into the First World War on the side of Germany. Tugay's recounting of her father's role in Ottoman political life conveys a good sense of the climate of fear that existed around the government spies of the Hamidian government, as well as the way high-ranking officials fell in and out of favour, and the impact of that political instability on their families. Here and throughout the book her writing is intertextual, quoting both Western and Ottoman historians, private correspondence and women's writing.

Tugay was related, closely or more distantly, to many members of the Egyptian royal family, and she details aspects of their lives in subsequent chapters of her book. While her male relatives were involved in matters of state, her aunts and female cousins were otherwise occupied. Although their primary duties would have been the care of their husbands and children, they had a great deal of wealth and time at their disposal, as well as a religious obligation to undertake charitable acts. In earlier centuries such responsibilities would have been fulfilled, for example, by making monetary donations to shrines, or even paying for the construction of charitable institutions such as soup kitchens or primary schools. As Tugay's descriptions of the activities of her female relatives indicate, they became much more directly involved in philanthropy, founding or serving as the officers of organisations that targeted specific social needs, such as medical care or job training for women. This extension in elite women's philanthropy, through both increased personal participation and a range of new venues, marked a modernisation of previous practices, akin to the recently developed professionalisation of women's charity in Europe and North America, where middle- and upper-class women first began entering the world of work through voluntary social services. Moreover, the idea of training women to earn a living was a departure from earlier models that concentrated on traditional charitable structures in the Islamic context (hospitals, soup kitchens, baths, schools, hostels) but no job training for either sex, and shows royal women involving themselves in recognisably feminist enterprises. In a related passage, the elaborate social life in which women of the elite participated is described, providing a counterpoint to similar descriptions by other authors in this collection.

The last passage from Tugay's book included here presents the romanticised family myth of her maternal grandmother's life, beginning with her childhood as Circassian slave, continuing through her life as favoured companion of the Khedive Ismail, then her role as the object of dramatic harem rivalries and her eventual death in Nice. Although nostalgic, the story nonetheless illustrates the way slavery worked in this context, as well as providing insight into the functioning of the elaborate and complex polygynous household of the Egyptian court. Tugay's grandmother experienced polygyny in a royal household, with different expectations and spatial arrangements that allowed for a more complete separation of the households. Her account has a very different tone to that of Halide Edib, writing of a polygynous household one generation later, with none of the nostalgia for a romantic and luxurious past evident in the earlier accounts. Moreover, expectations were very different for Tugay's grandmother, who entered the royal household as a slave, to those of the women of Edib's family, who were not necessarily expecting to participate in a polygynous marriage. In the one generation that separated Tugay's grandmother and Edib's mother, and even more for Edib's own generation, far-reaching changes had taken place in household structures and living patterns.

ഔ   ര

[MY FATHER]

After the Constitution had been declared on June 24th, my father was promoted to the rank of general and appointed Commander of the First Army in
Istanbul. Without being actually a member of Union and Progress, he sympa-
thized with the aims of the Young Turks and was a fervent partisan of
constitutional government. On account of his complete integrity, the choice was
approved by all parties, but an important factor had been ignored. Mahmud
Şevket Pasha, Commander-in-Chief of the Third Army in Salonika, a senior general and an influential member of Union and Progress, had coveted this post for
himself. Thwarted in his ambition when it fell to my father, he became his bitter
enemy. One year later fate played into his hands and offered him his revenge.

[…]

Meantime the ferment which was to set in motion the tragic events of the 13th
of April 1909 was secretly affecting the soldiers under my father's command.
Although he was aware of this underground movement and, as far as lay in his
power, had tried to counteract its effects and had warned those in authority about
the gravity of the situation, he had no precise knowledge of the imminence of the
outbreak. On the fateful day he had risen early as usual and was about to leave
the house when news reached him that certain regiments had mutinied. […]

[…]

Ibrahim Alaeddin, the Turkish historian, in his encyclopedia, *Meşur Adamlar*
(Famous People), gives the following description of what then took place.

> On the 31st of March [Julian Calendar, i.e. 13th April], being personally at the
> head of his troops, Mahmud Muhtar Pasha again gave proof of great courage
> when he and his men attacked the mutineers in Bayezid Square. But the Coun-
> cil of Ministers having prohibited fighting in the city at all costs, this young and
> valorous commander himself worked in the square, exposing himself to the
> bullets of the rebels. He was finally forced to retire to his own home, and later,
> when it was attacked, to seek concealment.

The 'work' mentioned by Ibrahim Alaeddin meant literally going out alone
amongst the insurgents, and urging them to observe law and order and return to
their barracks. Fearing for the lives of his officers, the General had left strict
orders that he should not be followed by any one of them. Cries of 'Kill him,
don't let him talk', punctuated by shots which fortunately missed their mark,
continually interrupted the General's speech. Although friend and foe were unan-
imous in praising his courage, he has since been criticized for obeying orders
received from the Minister of War, Ali Riza Pasha. Had it been feasible to reach
the scene of action before the Minister, my father might have acted differently
and on his own initiative. As he lived in Moda, on the Asian coast, the distance to

be travelled made his earlier arrival impossible. Once the orders had been issued, his sense of military discipline precluded any other course than obedience.

My father came home after nightfall. Friends who were waiting for him brought news that his life had been declared forfeit, and urged him to flee. Bands of mutineers had already crossed the sea and were roaming the streets in a manner which threatened danger. The General finally consented to escape. As it was impossible to leave his property by the gates, he jumped over the wall into an adjoining garden. The level of the next-door property was about thirty feet lower than our own, but his fall was happily broken by some shrubs. The owner, a Frenchman with whom my father was acquainted, gave him permission to cross his grounds and helped him to enter the neighbouring park, which belonged to Sir William Whittall, my father's friend. When informed of his predicament, Sir William and Lady Whittall courageously insisted on his spending the night in their house, where he remained till the next day. Meantime, with the help of some of my father's foreign friends, my mother had been making arrangements for him to leave the country. At midday on the 14th, the German Embassy launch conveyed him from the Whittalls' private landing stage to a British steamer bound for the Piraeus, which had been detailed by the British Embassy to await him off the Islands of the Marmara.

[…]

I no longer remember the exact date of my father's return to Istanbul. Sultan Abd-ul-Hamid was dethroned and succeeded by his brother Sultan Mehmed V. Mahmud Şevket Pasha virtually ruled supreme and the Young Turks were all-powerful. The hour had struck for settling old scores between political and personal enemies. In May a law was passed reducing the ranks of army officers who had not attended the Staff College in Turkey. Although actually still valid according to an agreement which continued in force between Turkey and Germany, my father's diploma from the Berlin Staff College was now deemed invalid, and his rank reduced to that of colonel. After having been a pasha for eleven years, he was again a bey.

But Mahmud Şevket had gone too far. The injustice of the decree soon caused a reaction. My father was appointed Governor-General (Vali), of the province of Aydin, Izmir being its principal city. In those days that province was almost as large as Belgium, and my father's post was equivalent to that of commander-in-chief of an army. He took up his duties in June 1909, and with his customary energy set to work to reorganize the province. [...]

Appointed Minister of Marine in Hakki Pasha's Cabinet, he left for Istanbul at the beginning of January 1911, and the family followed shortly afterwards. It was an unfortunate year for Turkey. War broke out with Italy, which ended with the loss of the province of Tripolitania, the prelude to greater misfortunes which were soon to follow.

In January 1912, Sultan Mehmed V nominated my father chief of a mission to convey his greetings to Tsar Nicholas II of Russia, who was then passing the winter at Yalta in the Crimea. This act of courtesy was always observed whenever the Tsar, in his travels in times of peace, approached the Turkish frontier. With the other members of the mission, my father went to Yalta by cruiser and remained there three days as the guest of the Tsar. Before his departure he was decorated with the order of the White Eagle with diamonds. From the conversations which he had with the Tsar and his suite, my father concluded that closer relations between Turkey and the Entente, that is, Britain, France, and Russia, might be possible to arrange. He was already convinced that they were necessary, and on his return he urged on his colleagues the need for a *rapprochement*. But at that time circumstances were unfavourable and nothing came of his representations.

My father resigned after the fall of Hakki Pasha's Cabinet in 1912, but he was reappointed to the office a few months later when in July his father, Gazi Ahmed Muhtar Pasha, became Grand Vezir. During his two terms of office as Minister of Marine he exhibited his usual energy in improving the condition of the navy, which under the former régime had been neglected even more than the army. He went on tours of inspection, notably to the Naval College at Heybeli Ada, and did everything to raise the standard of training and discipline. Two large battleships were ordered in England, and paid for. This latter fact was to have far-reaching consequences for my father when for political reasons they were retained by the British Government in 1914. As the responsible minister, many years later, he was accused of having paid out national funds before the delivery of the goods, and was obliged to restore the amount to the state from his own private means.

When the Balkan War broke out in the same year, my father was Minister of Marine, but he resigned from this post and asked for active service in the army. With the rank of major-general, he first commanded the Third Army Corps of the Thracian Army's right wing, and then was placed in command of the Second Army Corps. After the initial defeat at Kirkkilise, where the invading Bulgarian forces overwhelmed the Turkish troops, he rallied the soldiers and succeeded in checking the enemy advance between Vize and Pinarhisar. After this he took over the command of the Terkos-Chataldja line of defence, which barred the way to Istanbul. On November 17th 1912, when the Bulgarian onslaught had been broken, Mahmud Muhtar Pasha began a counter-attack. While leading his men at the front, he fell badly wounded in the thigh and knee-cap. The soldiers did not know of this and continued their advance, trampling over his prostrate form, until one of them recognized the General and saw that he was still living. Under continuous enemy gunfire this youth of twenty half-carried and half-dragged him back to safety. He was an Anatolian peasant, and was later rewarded by my father for his courageous act with the means to buy a farm of his own.

A Bulgarian military attaché whom I met in Istanbul in 1924 said that at that time, my father's strategy during the Balkan War was the subject of lectures in Bulgarian military academies.

In February 1913, after a short convalescence, my father was given the choice of being Ambassador either in St. Petersburg or in Berlin. He refused the former, feeling that the political atmosphere in Turkey at the time was unfavourable to his opinions, and went to Berlin at the end of the month. When he was joined by the family in April, he was able to walk without a stick and had resumed daily rides, keeping three horses in Berlin for this purpose. During week-ends in the season he went shooting, until the outbreak of war. The Embassy was run with military discipline and he expected the same attitude from his staff, though out of office hours he was on congenial terms with those who worked under him.

In this last year of pre-war Berlin, social life was brilliant. The court balls, receptions, and dinners were attended by society people and the diplomatic corps. While the season lasted my parents were rarely free to sit down to a meal with the family. My father, who liked to keep open house, entertained lavishly.

The outbreak of war in August 1914 marked the end of an era. Germany brought pressure to bear on Turkey to enter the war on her side. In the Turkish Cabinet opinions were divided. When it became known that Russia's claim to Istanbul had been approved by her allies, and also that Germany, as an inducement to join her, had made Turkey a gift of the warships *Goeben* and *Breslau*, the pro-German party won, and Turkey entered the war on the side of Germany and Austria. This is common knowledge, but less well known is the fact that my father had strongly advised his government to remain neutral. As his views were not palatable to the majority of the Cabinet, it was decided to recall him from Berlin. Informed of this decision, my father replied that he was willing to resign, should he be allowed to make arrangements with the Auswärtiges Amt regarding his successor, and received the Grand Vezir's promise to that effect. However, since the Emperor, who liked my father, was opposed to his removal, the matter was temporarily dropped. Shortly before Turkey entered the war my father again, and more forcibly, warned his superiors against this decision. By order of the Grand Vezir, Prince Said Halim Pasha, his confidential report was sent to the Auswärtiges Amt, to be submitted to Kaiser Wilhelm, who immediately withdrew his objections to my father's removal. Prince Said Halim Pasha, who for personal reasons disliked my father, summarily dismissed him.

[…]

[MOHAMED ALI PASHA'S DESCENDANTS]

Ahmed Rifat had two sons, Ibrahim Fehmi and Ahmed, and a daughter, Ayn-el-Hayat. The eldest, Prince Ibrahim Fehmi Pasha, married his first cousin, Princess Zeyneb, a daughter of the Khedive Ismail, who died a year after the wedding. Several years later he became engaged to the youngest sister of his wife, my mother, when she was fifteen. Her father, who did not believe in girls marrying too young, had consented on condition that the wedding was postponed until she was eighteen. […] The wedding, however, never took place, as the bridegroom died of heart failure a month before the date fixed.

Slight, with blue eyes and fair hair and beard, Prince Ibrahim Fehmi Pasha was known for his kindness and integrity. He had three children by a previous union with a Circassian, the eldest a daughter, Şivekiar, and two sons, Mohamed Ibrahim and Ahmed Seyfeddin. [...]

Princess Şivekiar first married her cousin Prince Fouad, who later became King of Egypt. They had a daughter, Fawkieh, and a son, Ismail, who died in infancy. Prince Fouad was deeply attached to his wife, but three years after their marriage the princess obliged him to divorce her and embarked on a series of matrimonial ventures which resulted in her having five successive husbands and four divorces. Towards the end of her life she devoted herself to the furtherance of social welfare and, as president of the Mohamed Ali Benevolent Society, and of the 'Mar' al Guedida (New Woman), a society which trained young girls for various professions, notably nursing and dress-making, rendered great service to her country. During her last years she was renowned both for the splendour of her entertainments and for her unfailing charity.

[...]

Ahmed Rifat Pasha's second son, Prince Ahmed Pasha, was a man greatly esteemed for his love of justice and the austerity of his life. He loved horses and had a stud of magnificent Arab thoroughbreds, and the finest carriage-horses in Egypt. None the less he enjoyed driving in a hired cab, stopping at small cafés and talking with humble folk. One of the greatest landowners in the country, he lived very simply in a small villa at Matarieh to the east of Cairo, not far from the site of the ancient sycamore which is said to have afforded shade to the Holy Family after the flight to Egypt. [...]

[...]

Ahmed Rifat Pasha's daughter, Ayn-el-Hayat, was a child when her father met his tragic end. Dark, *petite*, and vivacious, she had great charm. Her uncle, the Khedive Ismail, was very fond of her and took a personal interest in her education. In order to induce her to study he used to say: 'If you really try to learn your lessons and all your teachers are satisfied, I shall marry you to my son Huseyn.' The child was so delighted with the idea that once when she was twelve she ran out to meet her uncle, who had come to see her, saying: 'Today all my teachers are pleased. Now may I marry Huseyn Ağabey?' The marriage took place in due course, four children were born, and Prince Huseyn was devoted to his wife, who at first appeared to be happy. Then quite suddenly she insisted on a divorce and obtained her freedom.

Princess Ayn-el-Hayat never remarried. She is remembered as the founder—in 1909—and first president of the Mohamed Ali Benevolent Society. The members of its committee were all women, something till then unheard of in the annals of the Middle East. Medical and financial advisers were the only men consulted. The society began by opening a dispensary for women and children in the populous quarter behind the Abdin Palace. The funds were chiefly supplied from the Princess's own resources and by donations from the Khedivial family, as it then existed. According to the original rules of the society, the president was always to be a princess of the ruling family. The seed planted by Princess Ayn-el-Hayat has grown into a large tree, with branches spreading over most of Egypt's provinces. In 1952, Cairo alone boasted of two hospitals, three dispensaries, and eleven flying units with temporary quarters in the poorest parts of the city and suburbs. Controlled by the Cairo Committee and supervised by local ladies' committees, hospitals and dispensaries were doing excellent work everywhere. In 1910, a year after the opening of the Abdin dispensary, the number of patients was 28,605. At the end of 1952, the annual total of persons treated at all branches had risen to 1,583,964.

(The foundation at this time of numerous welfare societies run entirely by women, though of minor importance, was characteristic of the emancipation of Moslem womanhood. In 1910 Hoda Hanem Sharawy, the wife of Sharawy Pasha, formed the Mar' al-Guedida (New Woman), which opened a school where young girls were taught every kind of domestic work, dress-making, embroidery, and the weaving of rugs and carpets. Hoda Hanem also founded the Feminist Union, which aimed to raise the standards of women of the uneducated classes and to protect their rights. These societies opened the way for many others, which gradually came into being in the following years.)

[…]

[MOHAMED ALI PASHA'S WIFE AND DAUGHTERS]

Yusuf Kamil Pasha's subsequent career in Istanbul was brilliant. After having held several other high offices he twice became Grand Vezir. In 1861, during Said Pasha's rule, he and his wife again visited Egypt. Said Pasha warmly welcomed his sister and brother-in-law, insisting on their remaining several months, and all three went together on pilgrimage to Mecca. This visit was followed by many others.

Yusuf Kamil Pasha was of medium height, with dark eyes and hair grown prematurely white. He became stout as he grew older. Besides his native tongue, Turkish, he could speak, read, and write Arabic, Persian, and French, the latter less fluently than the Oriental languages. A translation of Fénélon's *Télémaque*, into Turkish, as well as books of prose and verse, remain to his credit. He had a sense of humour which found expression in his letters and some of his poems. The Pasha, who was a scholar, had collected a large library, containing rare and valuable books and manuscripts in the four languages with which he was familiar. Although he had spoken of bequeathing them to a public library, he died before he could put this wish into effect. Yusuf Kamil, like his father-in-law, was opposed to the construction of the Suez Canal, as he foresaw that international complications might follow the execution of the enterprise. With Mohamed Ali he also felt the urgent necessity of educating the people. His wife and he endowed, repaired, and built schools and hospitals in many parts of Turkey. Irrigation works in barren districts, as well as the construction of two main roads, are due to their public spirit. In Üsküdar, the old Chrysopolis, where the Bosphorus meets the Marmara, Zeyneb Hanimefendi and her husband built a hospital with a lunatic asylum near by. New buildings and modern equipment make this one of the best hospitals in the land. It was and still is called the Zeyneb Kamil Hospital, and the donors' tombs lie side by side in its garden.

Besides her charitable activities, Zeyneb Hanimefendi was a born hostess. Her receptions and the variety of her entertainments were still a topic of conversation in my youth. Since she lived at a time when the segregation of the sexes was strictly observed, all her many friends and acquaintances were women. These ladies, like herself, all dressed and lived in the old Turkish style. As in all great houses of the period, Zeyneb Hanimefendi had her own private female musicians and dancers who used to perform at her parties. Occasionally famous male musicians would be engaged, but they would be separated from the ladies by screens. Sometimes the guests themselves also took part in the musical performances. By way of more serious entertainment during the three holy months, notably in Ramazan, some eminent theologian would be asked to expound a chapter of the Qur'an or to preach a sermon. There were also literary competitions. The ladies wrote verses on a given theme and received prizes for the best poems. During the long winter evenings they amused themselves in a less brilliant but more restful manner. Braziers and all necessary ingredients for making sweetmeats were brought into the hall, where each guest prepared the dish at which she excelled. In summer there were moonlight parties on the Bosphorus. Veiled in white yashmaks and wrapped in silk *feraces* (cloaks), the ladies would be rowed in long kayiks manned by several pairs of oarsmen. Attached to the stern of the kayik, squares of cloth or satin, embroidered in gold or silver and edged with little silver fishes, floated on the waves. Musicians, both players and singers, preceded them in a separate boat, and as the oars dipped rhythmically into the moonlit waters, strains of music were wafted towards the following kayiks. These occasions were festive events in the sleepy little villages on the Bosphorus. Young and old thronged to the waterside and the windows of the yalis were crowded with onlookers. It was an accepted custom for many other boats and kayiks to accompany the party on the sea, forming a long procession, the bobbing lanterns attached to the craft shining dim and yellow under the brilliant moonlight.

These parties on the water took place when Princess Zeyneb lived in her yali at Bebek on the Bosphorus. Possibly one of the largest residences made entirely of timber ever known, it was designed and almost certainly built by the French architect Charles Garnier, of Paris Opera House fame. Both from an architectural point of view, and because of its garden and large park studded with pavilions, it was one of the most remarkable buildings on the shores of the Bosphorus. [...]

My Grandmother, Neşedil Kadinefendi, and my Aunt, Princess Emina Aziza

Neşedil, 'joy of the soul', was a name admirably suited to my grandmother's saintly, unselfish nature. [...] A great beauty in her youth, she retained her charm, erect carriage, and light, graceful walk throughout life. [...]

I used to question her about her youth, and was one of the very few in whom she confided. Neşedil Kadinefendi was a Circassian of the Caucasus, whose early childhood had been spent in the mountains. [...] Disaster overtook the clan when my grandmother was aged seven. [...] and the two youngest children were sold to a slave-dealer. He took them to Istanbul, where they were separated, and my grandmother never again saw or heard of her brother. She herself was bought by the wife of a pasha, who educated her according to the custom of the time. The child was kindly treated, received careful religious instruction, and was taught to read but not to write, as the latter accomplishment might have been an inducement to her to pen love-letters. She also became an accomplished needle-woman and learnt to make the finest lace, *oya*, and embroidery. [...]

At fifteen she was sold to the Khedive Ismail and went to Egypt. Together with other young Circassians she spent a year at the Guezireh Palace, being trained for a life at court, and was named Neşedil. She was about sixteen when my grandfather gave her a separate establishment at Zaaferan Palace, with fifty Circassian and thirty Abyssinian slaves of her own. Her clothes, lingerie, and house linen were ordered from Paris. After she had settled in her new surroundings, the Khedive said that it was time for her to go and visit his senior wives at the Abdin Palace. Trembling inwardly, she went dressed in the finest Brussels lace over pale blue satin, with a necklace and earrings of rubies and diamonds. Outwardly she maintained her composure. An old kalfa who saw her that day has told me that her radiant beauty caused a sensation. On her *ortaks*,[*] the senior wives, she must have had the effect of a bomb. Neither of them had expected so much grace and loveliness. My grandfather's unflagging devotion to her raised such a storm of jealousy that after the birth of her second child, during one of her visits to Abdin, she was served with poisoned coffee. Feeling desperately ill, my grandmother hurried home, nearly dying on the way. The efforts to save her were successful. She slowly came back to life, but never to her former health. After giving premature birth to a stillborn son, she was debarred from having other children. Neşedil Kadinefendi never mentioned names and disliked to talk about the incident, although she must have known who bore the guilt. My grandfather was so enraged that he made over to her name the title deeds of the Insha and Small Ismailieh Palaces, a gift such as he had never made to any of his former wives, and offered her a set of diamonds, comprising a tiara, with matching earrings, necklace, brooch, belt, bracelets, and rings. He also advised her never

---

[*]   *Ortak*, meaning associate, is a word used both in business and to designate a man's various wives. They were associated in the same husband.

again to take food or drink outside her own house. Contrary to his expectations, on receiving his gift my grandmother burst into tears, fell on her knees, and implored him not to give her anything that might cause further jealousy. She firmly refused the jewels, and only when threatened with the Khedive's displeasure reluctantly accepted the palaces. In Zaaferan Palace two daughters had been born to her, Emina Aziza, in 1874, and Nimetullah, in 1875, both in September.

[…]

When Hoshyar Kadinefendi died in 1885, my grandmother and her daughters went to Naples to rejoin the Khedive Ismail. Four years later, in 1889, the whole family sailed to Emirgan, on the Bosphorus near Istanbul. At Emirgan my grandmother, Aunt Emine, and my mother occupied the yali on the Tokmakburnu promontory, one of the seven buildings on my grandfather's estate. He himself lived in the largest of the four yalis, the other houses being at the disposal of his married sons and daughters, who came to visit him during the warm season.

The Khedive's death in 1895 caused my grandmother, whose health had deteriorated after months of sick-nursing, to fall seriously ill. She eventually recovered, but remained an invalid for the rest of her life. Henceforth she dedicated herself entirely to her daughters and, later, to her grandchildren. After both daughters were married and settled in their own homes, she used to live with either one or the other, but chiefly with the elder, who needed her companionship more. She travelled a great deal on the European continent, with one or both of her daughters, to various spas or towns famous for their doctors, notably in Switzerland. As far as I remember, my grandmother and Aunt Emine were always under doctor's orders, seeking the health which eluded them. My grandmother's kind and serene nature had won my father's affection, and we were all delighted when it was our turn to be visited. She certainly spoilt us, but such was her natural dignity that we never attempted any familiarity towards her. Going to her room was always a treat. In the early morning we would find her in bed, reading the Qur'an, and would wait quietly until she had finished her devotions. Having kissed her hand and been embraced by her, we were each given a sweet, to sweeten the day, she said. Our half-hour of freedom before lunch was also spent with her. Being on a strict diet, she always had her meals separately and often, when bored with the monotony of her food, allowed us to share it with her. Later in the day she would tell her maid to bring us small cups of coffee, another prohibited pleasure. Our love was sadly tinged with greed, I fear!

Neşedil Kadinefendi had perfect taste. Everything she owned was not only pretty, but of the best quality. The lace on the ruffles of her undergarments were of finest Valenciennes, and the materials of her clothes soft and pleasant to the touch. Neat in all her ways, she taught me that a woman, whatever her age, should invariably be tidy and of a pleasing appearance. She approved of my youthful interest in clothes, saying that I had inherited it from her.

In January 1922 my grandmother invited my husband and myself to spend a fortnight with her in Nice, where she and Aunt Emine had rented a villa. During our visit I noticed that she never left the grounds, although her doctor had recommended an hour's drive every day. When my aunt urged her to go out, she gently but firmly refused. Finally she confided to me that as she had not been well enough to do any shopping for the last two years, her hats were too old-fashioned to be worn in town. As soon as I had given a hint of the situation to my aunt, she ordered a number of hats to be sent up on approval. Next day Neşedil Kadinefendi went out for a drive.

It was on this visit that I asked my grandmother a question which I had not dared to formulate until my own marriage. Walking with her on the terrace of the garden, I said: 'Granny darling, were you never jealous of your ortaks [co-wives]?' She smiled. 'They were jealous of me.' 'But was there no one who gave you the slightest twinge?' She thought this over before replying. 'Yes, Cemalnur [Prince Ali Cemal's mother]. It is all so long ago. She was very pretty, though her legs were short. [My grandmother had beautiful long legs.] Cemalnur was very frivolous, always laughing and joking, and when we walked in the garden could never resist taking off her shoes and stockings to paddle in the basins of the fountains. She even lifted up her skirts so high that one could see the frills of her pantalettes. May God rest her soul.' Greatly daring, I went on: 'Dearest Granny, were you never pained by the favours which my grandfather would confer on others?' She ceased smiling; instead the expression of intense veneration which I had noticed in all women who had been close to him appeared on her features. 'Efendimiz', she said, 'was the kindest and most considerate of men. He was far too courteous to hurt anyone's feelings, and I never heard him utter an unkind word.'

[…]

Miss Machray, Aunt Emina's lady-in-waiting, told me the following details of her own experiences. At eighteen she had been companion to the daughters of Prince Halim Pasha, and had lived in his yali at Baltaliman on the European shore. When accompanying the princesses she often went in a kayik to the Sweet Waters of Asia, and said that during these diversions silent flirtations were not uncommon. Encouraged by the princesses, who found it amusing to watch, she herself had mastered the art of flirting by signs. Attracted by a pretty face, becomingly shrouded in a transparent white yashmak, a man would gaze at it. The lady either lowered her parasol, marking her displeasure, or else smiled without looking at him. The swain then boldly twirled his moustache, whereas the lady ventured a swift glance in his direction. Emboldened by her notice, he smiled and placed a hand upon his heart. If the lady repeated the gesture, he took the flower from his buttonhole and raised it to his lips. This was the cue for a virtuous woman, however belatedly, to lower her parasol. Miss Machray said that only the most abandoned would absent-mindedly lift a finger to their own lips, whereupon the flower was promptly thrown into their lap. Miss Machray herself, her pink-and-white complexion, blue eyes, and good looks enhanced by the flattering yashmak, received much attention but, as in most cases, this never went beyond the limit imposed by the kayik.

[…]

Our education began at an early age. Turkish was our own language, and came first, but we learnt German almost simultaneously from our Austrian nurse. I was three years old when a pretty English girl, a Miss Lafontaine, came to teach me to speak English. She was of Huguenot descent, and belonged to the English colony which was then settled in Moda. She continued to come as long as we lived in Istanbul. At the age of four I began to attend a class for athletic exercises and calisthenics which was being conducted by two English sisters at Moda. The pupils were all children of English and Turkish families who lived in the neighbourhood. Dressed in red silk blouses and navy blue skirts, we bent our knees, touched our toes, and swung wooden clubs. One of the sisters showed us the movements, while the other played polkas and waltzes. I was five when I began to read and write English, and learnt the Arab script in which Turkish was then written. It still astonishes me that nowadays six should be considered the earliest age for children to learn to read and write. Neither I nor my brothers ever felt any ill effects from having started our lessons earlier.

ജ INDEX ര